ISBN 978-0-259-48275-8
PIBN 10126450

1 MONTH OF
FREE
READING

at

www.ForgottenBooks.com

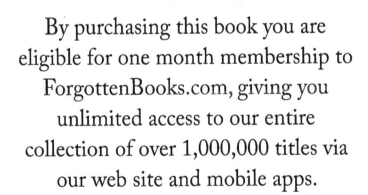

By purchasing this book you are
eligible for one month membership to
ForgottenBooks.com, giving you
unlimited access to our entire
collection of over 1,000,000 titles via
our web site and mobile apps.

To claim your free month visit:

www.forgottenbooks.com/free126450

English
Français
Deutsche
Italiano
Español
Português

www.forgottenbooks.com

Mythology Photography **Fiction**
Fishing Christianity **Art** Cooking
Essays Buddhism Freemasonry
Medicine **Biology** Music **Ancient
Egypt** Evolution Carpentry Physics
Dance Geology **Mathematics** Fitness
Shakespeare **Folklore** Yoga Marketing
Confidence Immortality Biographies
Poetry **Psychology** Witchcraft
Electronics Chemistry History **Law**
Accounting **Philosophy** Anthropology
Alchemy Drama Quantum Mechanics
Atheism Sexual Health **Ancient History**
Entrepreneurship Languages Sport
Paleontology Needlework Islam
Metaphysics Investment Archaeology
Parenting Statistics Criminology
Motivational

A QUEEN OF NAPOLEON'S COURT

THE LIFE-STORY OF DÉSIRÉE BERNADOTTE

By

Catherine Bearne

Author of " A Leader of Society at Napoleon's Court," etc.

ILLUSTRATED FROM CONTEMPORARY PORTRAITS
AND FROM DRAWINGS BY E. H. BEARNE

A VIKING SHIP

PREFACE

THE very kind reception given by the public and by most of the critics to my last book, "A Leader of Society at Napoleon's Court," and the interest shown in any anecdotes or information about Napoleon and his family, lead me to hope that the story of another woman whose lot was cast in those wonderful days and in that fascinating country may not be without attraction for the "general reader," to whom this book, like the last, is respectfully offered.

My present heroine, Désirée Clary, did not possess the striking talents and character of Laura Permon, the subject of my last volume. The interest attached to her life arises chiefly from the exciting times in which she lived, the terrors, triumphs, celebrated persons, and strange adventures surrounding her, and the exalted position she occupied during the latter half of her life.

Unlike as Désirée was to the brilliant, energetic, improvident Laura, whom in appearance she is said to have strongly resembled, the contrast was even greater between Bernadotte and Junot, both of whom were the sons of small provincial lawyers, enlisted in the republican army, were raised by their gallant deeds from the ranks, became at an early age distinguished generals, married women intimately connected with the Buonaparte family, and before both of whom seemed to lie a splendid career.

But one was a melancholy failure, the other a magnificent success.

Junot, by the reckless folly and dissipation of the life he led, ran through an enormous fortune, forfeited the favour of the Emperor, ruined his health, lost his reason, and committed suicide at forty-one, leaving his wife and children overwhelmed with debt and difficulties. Laura, far superior to him both in character and intellect, but equally devoid of common sense in managing her affairs, learnt nothing from experience, squandered the pension allowed her by the King and the money she earned by her literary talents, and died in poverty at fifty-three.

Bernadotte, on the contrary, a born leader, strong in character and intellect, ambitious, far-seeing, caring little for pleasure, rose higher and higher through the storms of the Revolution, the glories of the Empire, and the ruins of its fall, to one of the most ancient thrones in Europe, where he and Désirée spent the rest of their days in prosperity, ruling over two nations, and leaving to their descendants an honourable name and a splendid inheritance.

The history of the house of Bernadotte is just now all the more interesting to the English public, an English princess having so recently married its heir, and the present King of Sweden and Norway is the favourite grandson of Désirée and of the hero whose great qualities and wise rule brought the two countries from the brink of ruin to prosperity and peace.

It is only after his marriage with Désirée that this book treats of Bernadotte, for it is not and does not profess to be anything at all but the story of Désirée Clary, Queen of Sweden, with such descriptions and anecdotes of the remarkable people and events connected with her childhood in the Revolution, her youth at the court of Napoleon, and her later life at Paris during the Restoration, and at her own court in Sweden, as may interest and amuse the general reader. And I do not believe he would agree with the opinion expressed by one of the critics on my last book—that instead of all the stories of Napoleon's private life and court it would have been much better to have described the important historical events of his reign, about which of course most people who read at all have read over and over again in the histories and biographies of Napoleon to which these descriptions properly belong.

It seems incomprehensible that any one wishing to read accounts of battles, treaties, or political and commercial transactions, should expect to find them in the Life of a " Leader of Society " in any court, or should suggest that in writing the biography of a woman who was a conspicuous figure in a society especially celebrated for its splendour, extravagance, scandals and intrigues, the characteristic incidents and circumstances of that life and society should be left out. It recalls to one's mind a conversation in Miss Austen's famous novel, " Pride and Prejudice," in which, when a proposed ball is being discussed, Miss Bingley observes—

" I should like balls infinitely better if they were carried on in a different manner ; but there is something insufferably tedious in the usual process of such a meeting. It would surely be much more rational if conversation instead of dancing were made the order of the day."

" Much more rational, my dear Caroline, I daresay, but it would not be near so much like a ball."

Before beginning this book I was warned by a high literary authority that, in consulting some of the French writers on Bernadotte, I must allow for that intense, overpowering worship of Napoleon which makes them apparently consider it criminal to have opposed him ; and who call the good faith and devotion of Charles XIV. to his own kingdom and subjects " treason " and " disloyalty " ; as if Sweden had been a province of France and Bernadotte the born subject of Napoleon.

Guided by this caution I have consulted many excellent works, amongst which are those of Sarrans, Pingaud, Christian Schefer, Touchard-Lafosse, &c.

For other details I am indebted to the valuable writings of such distinguished modern authors as MM. Masson and Turquan, Baron Hochschild and Comtesse Armaillé, and to innumerable Memoirs of the last century, those amongst others of Thiébault,

MM. de Méneval, de Marbot, de Bausset, Bourrienne, Lucien Buonaparte, Mesdames de Rémusat, d'Abrantès, Campan, de Chastenay, d'Ancelot, Mesdemoiselles Avrillon, Cochelet, and others.

To the kindness and courtesy of M. Joseph Turquan I am also indebted for the portrait of the Duchesse d'Abrantès, from a miniature by Quaglia, which appears in his interesting book, "La Générale Junot"; and to that of Mrs. Hartcup for the curious miniature taken in a French garden which belongs to her family.

CONTENTS

CHAPTER XI.

1802—1803.

CHAPTER XII.

1803.

CHAPTER XIII.

1803—1804.

CHAPTER XIV.

1804.

1*

CHAPTER XVIII.

1808.

CHAPTER XIX.

1809—1810.

CHAPTER XX.

1809—1810.

CHAPTER XXI.

1810.

LIST OF ILLUSTRATIONS

xxi

A QUEEN
OF NAPOLEON'S COURT

CHAPTER I

1781—1793

The coming of the Revolution—The Clary family—The Terror in Marseille- The *Marseillaise*—Death of Robespierre—Story of Madame de Custine—Death of M. Clary—Arrest of his son.

BERNARDINE EUGÉNIE DÉSIRÉE CLARY was born at Marseille in those troubled times immediately preceding the great Revolution.

The early years of her childhood, like the hours before the breaking out of a fearful thunderstorm, were filled with gloom and uneasiness. There was a restless, unsettled feeling in the air : for all over France it seemed evident to most people that something extraordinary and terrible was going to happen; they were on the eve of some great change.

The country was divided into two parties : one,

composed principally of those who had everything
to gain, looked forward with ardent hope and
rejoicing to the coming events which were casting
their shadows before ; the other, to which belonged
those who had everything to lose, beheld with
indignation and terror the rising of the tide which
was so soon to overwhelm them.   The laws, manners,
and customs of the old *régime* were still in full
force, large families were usual in all classes in
France, the law of primogeniture enforced amongst
the nobles and country gentlemen with much more
severity than would be tolerated in England.   For
in many a French family it meant not only the
château, the estates, and the whole of the inheritance
for the eldest son, but also all the educational advantages ; for the younger ones often, especially amongst
the provincial *noblesse*, no education at all except
for those who took holy orders.   No profession was
available for them but the Church or the army, they
could not marry without fortune, so they spent their
lives as hangers-on in the château of their eldest
brother, hunting and shooting to supply the household with game, drinking at the houses of the *curés*
and doctors, playing cards in the evenings.   For some
of the daughters, for whom a *dot* could be saved and
scraped together, or who might have inherited money
from their mother or some other relation, marriages
were arranged by their parents ; for the others there
was the cloister.   All were educated in convents
until they were old enough to be married or take
the veil ; and the age supposed to be proper was
a much earlier one than we should now consider
allowable.   It was not at all uncommon for girls

to be married at thirteen or fourteen, and they had no choice in the matter.

The same kind of ideas prevailed among the *bourgeoisie*, that is to say, the middle class. The authority of the parents, even after the children were grown up, was absolute, and, failing them, the eldest son succeeded to his father's business and to his authority as head of the family.

Upon these lines was conducted the household of François Clary, the father of Désirée, a rich silk merchant of Marseille, who, with his wife and children, inhabited a large old-fashioned house in the *rue des Phocéens*. The daily life of the Clary family was arranged with all that mingling of comfort, hospitality, and order customary amongst the prosperous French *bourgeoisie*, and anything that interfered with it was particularly displeasing to M. Clary. He especially disliked the presence of the soldiers who from time to time were quartered in his house, to the disturbance and inconvenience of the household.

One day, in the year 1786, the regiment of Royal Marines landed at Marseille, having just returned from Corsica, which had recently become a province of France. A young soldier, a good-looking lad of seventeen, presented himself in the *rue des Phocéens* with a billet upon M. Clary, who persuaded him to go away, giving him a note for his colonel, requesting that an officer might be sent him instead. It is worth recording, as characteristic of those days of changing fortunes and strange vicissitudes, that the name of the young soldier M. Clary was so anxious to get rid of was Jean

Bernadotte, who was some years afterwards the husband of his youngest daughter and King of Sweden.

François Clary had married in 1751 Thérèse Gabrielle Flichon, daughter of a merchant at Marseille, who died in 1758, leaving him with three children; after which he married in 1759 Rose Somis, by whom he had nine more, seven of whom lived to grow up. He had in all thirteen children, there being more than thirty years' difference in age between the eldest and youngest; the two daughters of his first wife were married, the eldest to Louis Le Jean, deputy, of Marseille,[1] and the second to Guillaume Le Jean, senator, before the youngest child of his second marriage was born. The son of his first wife was named Etienne François. He had a wife and seven children. His sons appear as distinguished soldiers under the empire, one of his daughters married Henri, Comte Tascher de la Pagerie, the other the Baron Lejeune, one of Napoleon's officers.

The eldest son of François and his second wife was named Nicolas. The next brother, Justinien, committed suicide about the year 1793.

The eldest daughter, Marie Anne Rose Marseille, was married in 1786 to Antoine Ignace Anthoine, son of a lawyer of the *Parlement de Grenoble*. He had become a merchant, had travelled much, and lived abroad for many years, was a man of high

---

[1] He received *lettres de noblesse* from Louis XVI., 1786. The Clarys were one of those rich mercantile families just rising. They associated with and married their children to the small impoverished *noblesse* in the towns.

character, great capacity, and very rich. He was in later life Mayor of Marseille, for the benefit and improvement of which town he spent large sums of money. Being a man of religious principles, with a horror of the excesses and crimes of the Revolution, he left France when it broke out and retired with his wife and children to Genoa, only returning to Marseille when the reign of blood was at an end. Napoleon made him Baron de St. Joseph in 1808. He was also officer of the Legion of Honour, member of the Academy of Marseille, and Commander of the Order of the *Etoile de Suède*.

The second daughter, Catherine Honorine, was not so fortunate. In 1786 she became the wife of a captain in the Royal Engineers, who appears to have been a man of good family, his name being Henri Joseph Gabriel Blait de Villeneuve, de la Ciotat, chevalier de Saint Louis. In order to save his head when dragged before the revolutionary tribunal he vehemently denied that he was noble, crying out in the *patois* of the country, "I am not noble, you must not kill me, I am only Blait, nothing else." He was released, and immediately fled from Marseille, leaving his wife and children to take care of themselves. This worthy individual obtained some place at Paris, where he spent the rest of his life.

Catherine got a divorce from him in 1794, and spent her life in travelling or residing in other countries. She lived in Italy, Belgium, and Sweden, and ended her days with her sister Julie at Florence.

Her only son was killed in Spain (1808); her daughter married her cousin, Count Clary.

The third daughter, Julie, was several years younger, for there was a considerable difference in the ages even of the brothers and sisters of the second family of François Clary.

The youngest child, Désirée, was born on the 8th of November, 1781. While they were still very young she and Julie were, according to the general custom, sent to be educated at a convent, where they remained until the advance of the Revolution forced all the religious houses to be closed. They then returned to the house of their parents in the *rue des Phocéens.* Intolerably dull and tedious was the life of a French girl in those days ; and just then, added to the monotony and restrictions which must have deprived them of what we should now consider the natural amusements and pleasures of youth, there were constantly hanging over Désirée and her sisters the dangers and horrors of the Revolution.

The situation of the great southern port was most fortunate for those of its inhabitants who had enough prudence to foresee the awful state of things likely to arise, take precautions to remove and preserve as much as possible of their possessions, and escape by sea to some other country while there was yet time ; sacrificing the rest and thankful to save, at any rate, their own lives and those dear to them.

M. Antoine de Saint Joseph was one of these ; he removed his family to Genoa before there was much difficulty in doing so ; ere long those who got away at all fled for their lives, often at a moment's notice and with nothing but the clothes they wore.

The flight of so many of the richest citizens excited the fury of the revolutionists ; but, far from offering any encouragement to those who had remained, trusting to their tender mercies, they gave them cause bitterly to repent of their rash confidence.   ˙

Numbers of the principal merchants and other inhabitants were seized, and besides all those fined and imprisoned, 409 were guillotined between August 20, 1793, and April 25, 1794.

Many of them were relations or friends of the Clary family, who lived in a state of continual terror.[1]

One of the sons, Justinien François, a nervous, excitable lad of about nineteen, was so preyed upon by the horrors constantly going on around him that he lost control of his senses and committed suicide.

The disappearance of her brother and the finding of his body after three days (November, 1793) in a well in the garden adjoining their own, was a terrible recollection of Désirée's childhood.

The Clarys were, although they had also friends amongst the terrorists, in a dangerous position, for they were rich and the brother of Madame Clary, an officer in the Engineers, had emigrated.

With the exception of Nantes and Lyons there were few places where the Revolution raged with greater fury than in the great southern city whose fierce, turbulent populace supplied that ferocious horde which in June, 1792, marched to Paris drunk with wine, excitement, and thirst for blood, welcomed and feasted at the towns and villages through which they passed under triumphal arches; the sound of drums, the clash of arms, and the measured tread of the host mingling with the fearful chorus of the *Marseillaise.*

[1] " Napoléon et sa famille," t. i, pp. 92–98 (Masson).

This celebrated song, so grand in itself, so horrible in the associations from which one can never separate it, was not, in spite of its name, composed by a native of Marseille. It was written by Rouget de Lisle, a young officer in the Engineers, a native of Lons-le-Saunier, in the Jura. Deeply imbued with the poetry and romance of the wild, beautiful land where his childhood and youth had been spent, with a great natural talent for music and composition, a passionate love for a soldier's life, and an enthusiastic admiration for the ideas and principles of the Revolution, as it at first appeared to him, Rouget de Lisle was a great favourite with his brother-officers at Strasbourg, where he was quartered ; and was also, as a poet and musician, much sought after in the society of the place. Amongst his most intimate friends were the Baron de Dietrich and his family, whose château was near Strasbourg, and who shared his political opinions. In the winter of 1791-2 there was great distress from scarcity of food at Strasbourg. The Dietrich family, who had been very well off, were so nearly ruined by the Revolution, that one evening when de Lisle was dining there, as he constantly did, there was nothing upon the table but bread and some slices of smoked ham. Dietrich, looking at him with resignation, remarked, " What does it matter if abundance is wanting to our feasts, so long as enthusiasm is not wanting to our civic *fêtes* and courage to the hearts of our soldiers ? I have still one last bottle of Rhine wine in my cellar ; let them bring it, and we will drink to our country and liberty. There is going to be a patriotic function at Strasbourg ; de Lisle must draw from the wine the inspiration for one of those hymns which will carry enthusiasm into the hearts of the people."

The wine having been drunk amid general applause, de Lisle retired to his room, for it was late. There was a piano, or spinnet, and he seated himself before it. The night was cold, and he shivered, but with excited brain and heart stirred with emotion, he began, as in a dream, to improvise, words and music flowing alternately from his highly-wrought imagination, and blending into that immortal strain which has thrilled through the souls of multitudes, inciting them to bloodshed and crimes so horrible as to tarnish for ever the heroic memories it was intended to call forth. He would not stop to write, he sang on inspired and overpowered by the magnificence of the music and the fierce enthusiasm of the words, until, overcome by exhaustion, he fell asleep with his head upon the key-board.

He awoke at daybreak, the impressions of the night floating in his brain like a dream. Hastening to write down his recollection, he went out to look for Dietrich, whom he found at work in his garden, and who at once went in search of his wife and several of the friends who were in the habit of joining in their musical meetings and were accustomed to play and sing de Lisle's compositions.

Accompanied by one of them, a young girl, he began to sing : there was a moment's silence, then an outburst of applause, enthusiasm, and tears. The patriotic hymn, the immortal song of the Revolution, was found. It was sung a few days afterwards at Strasbourg ; received with the wildest acclamations, it spread from town to town ; it was adopted by

Marseille to be sung at the opening and close of the meeting of those assemblies of murderers, the revolutionary clubs, and was proclaimed throughout France on their terrible march to Paris, after which it was known as the *Marseillaise*.

The mother of de Lisle, a woman of fervent religious and royalist principles, horrified to hear the name of her son attached to the new song which was proclaiming and inciting to murder, treason, and sacrilege all over the country, wrote to him, " What is this revolutionary hymn which a horde of brigands are singing as they traverse France, and with which our name is being mixed up?" Her forebodings were soon fulfilled, for the *Marseillaise* brought no good to those by or amongst whom it originated. To the sound of its words and music Dietrich, a few months afterwards, walked to the scaffold, and de Lisle, as he fled for his life along the wild paths of the Jura, shuddered when he heard its distant echo, and turning to his guide asked, " What do they call that hymn?" And the peasant answered, " The *Marseillaise*."

Désirée was just beginning to grow out of childhood while the Reign of Terror was at its height. Her life and those of her family were at that time passed in continual alarm. It is true that the plebeian origin of the Clarys rendered their position less dangerous ; although any one belonging, either by relationship, friendship, or service, to any family of the *ancien régime*, or to any religious house or profession was in danger, and nobody in France could be said to be safe at all under the rule of the apostles of Liberty, Equality, and Fraternity. Even those individuals themselves were not safe from the jealousy and suspicion of their companions, whose accusations might, and often did, consign them to the prison and scaffold to which they had sent their innocent victims.

As to people in private life, any one who had an enemy, or even a person who owed him a grudge, or who could in any way profit by his removal, was at all times liable to be arrested for no reason whatever, but some secret accusation ; a careless remark repeated or misrepresented, the crime of being seen to say a prayer or to show sympathy with some victim, were enough to send any one to his death, and perhaps his whole family with him. It was dangerous to have a pack of cards in the house, because there were kings and queens among them, to be well dressed, to have too much clean linen or too large a store of food, candles, and other household necessaries, for children to play at any royalist games, for servants to use any respectful way of addressing their masters, for tradespeople to sell any article cheaper for silver or gold than for the *assignats* of the Republic ; in fact, everything was dangerous,[1] and the sudden sound of their door-bell would send a thrill of terror through the hearts of the whole family.

The fierce, bloodthirsty Maignet sat on the tribunal of the Convention at Marseille, and sent his victims by hundreds to be shot at Orange. All the townspeople, especially the richest and the most respectable

---

[1] "The Demoiselles de Saint-Leger, two girls of sixteen and seventeen, were guillotined at Paris for having played on the piano on the day of the taking of Valenciennes ; which they had not even heard of.—*Salons de Paris, Abrantès.*

families, trembled for their lives. The only chance of escape was to take care to give no offence to any one, keep as quiet as possible, and do nothing to attract attention in any way.

By these means, and by different friendships amongst the revolutionary authorities, the Clary family were fortunate enough to succeed in passing safely through the perils with which they were surrounded until in January, 1794, M. Clary died. He left large fortunes to his younger children, and the business by which he had made them to his eldest son, who, now become the head of the family, assumed a paternal authority over his brothers and sisters, all of whom, with their mother, continued after the custom of those days, to live in their old home with their brother and his wife.

All seemed to be going on as well and harmoniously in the family as was possible in those terrible times, when a sudden blow fell upon them which threw some, if not all, into the most imminent danger.

It appeared that their father, the late M. Clary, had, some years before his death, when there had been no danger in such a step, foolishly applied for *lettres de noblesse*, which request, fortunately for himself and his family, had been refused. But the remembrance of it had unluckily been recalled to the bloodthirsty monsters who were now terrorising Marseille, and who, as François Clary was dead, brought it as a crime against his son!

CHAPTER II

1793—1794

ACCORDINGLY Etienne Clary was arrested, thrown into prison, and would certainly have been murdered by the champions of liberty had he not fortunately been a friend of the younger Robespierre, a less atrocious character than his notorious brother, and at that time *commissaire* at Marseille.

To him the family of Clary appealed for protection, and young Robespierre, whose position was then a powerful one, interfered and delivered his friend out of the clutches of Maignet.

But the time was rapidly approaching when the name of Robespierre, instead of being a safeguard, would be dangerous to any one with whom it was associated. The spring of 1793 witnessed the height of the Jacobin fury, and beheld Robespierre with practically unlimited power, which, with his barbarous associates, Couthon and St. Just, he exercised in the perpetration of increasing enormities.

It is really not possible amongst the multitude of wicked and bloodthirsty monsters, by whom the great French Revolution was conducted and carried out, to say which was the worst.   It seems impossible that a greater fiend could have existed in human form than Carrier, who ordered hundreds of people to be drowned in the Loire, young girls and men to be tied together and thrown into the river, and five hundred little children to be collected together and mown down with grape-shot; and who found plenty of his countrymen to carry out his commands!   Some say that Foulquier-Tinville, Collot d'Herbois, Billaud-Varennes, and Barrère were even worse than Robespierre, while many others give the pre-eminence in infamy to Marat.

Jung, in his " Memoirs of Lucien Buonaparte," declares that Robespierre was the most cruel, the most cowardly, and the most hypocritical of all the revolutionists, and that it is quite untrue that his fall was owing to his being suspected by his colleagues of any leaning towards mercy ; the tribunal of the Revolution having been more ferocious and remorseless than ever during the last months of his power.   At any rate, there was a cry of relief and thankfulness throughout France at his death, and at once the bloodshed and cruelties relaxed ; every one breathed more freely.

The people were tired of carnage, and the mob began to murmur as the tumbrils passed, and to say that there had been slaughter enough.   The worst was over.

One of the victims saved when the prisons were opened was the young Marquise de Custine, whose

CONVENT OF THE JACOBINS, AFTERWARDS A NOTORIOUS CLUB OF THE
REVOLUTION.

adventures, like those of many others **at that time**, read like a romance.

She was not two-and-twenty : her husband **and her** father-in-law, General Custine, were **seized and** imprisoned, one in La Force, **the other in the** Conciergerie. All the time of **the trial of General** Custine she waited for him every morning **at six** o'clock, embraced and conversed with him, sat on **a** bench during the proceedings in court, **met him as he** came out, and when the prison doors closed upon him went to La Force, where she was allowed to see her husband. General Custine died like a hero and a Christian ; his son soon followed his example. There was no more for her to do but to save her child ; and she was preparing to emigrate, as her mother, brother, and uncle had done, when she too was arrested. She was busily occupied in burning or putting away papers, when she heard steps and voices in the ante-room, and had just time to push under a sofa-cushion a bundle of letters which would have condemned her to the scaffold for the crime of sending money to her mother, who was in poverty and exile, when the republican officials entered.

She was imprisoned in the Carmes, where for three months she was in daily peril of death. Her child was fortunately left with his nurse, a woman from their own estates in Lorraine, named Nanette, one of those numbers of faithful, noble characters who stand out in heroic contrast to the wretches around them, and who now prepared, regardless of her own safety, to protect by all means in her power her mistress and the child she loved. She had no money, and the child, about three or four years old, was ill of a fever. She sold her gold cross, her ornaments, and her clothes, managed to bring the little one through, and went to what she called *les pays* to see what could be done to save their mistress, *les pays* being a number of workmen who had been employed by General Custine at a china manufactory he had set up on his estate, and who, when his death put a stop to it, had come to Paris. They all signed a petition to Legendre that the "*citoyenne* Custine" imprisoned at the Carmes might be set free. Nanette took this petition to Legendre, but it was thrown aside, and nothing was heard of it.

One evening the clerks of Legendre took advantage of the absence of their master to indulge in a festive dinner, and after it to play games in the office, jumping over chairs and tables, throwing books and boxes about. In the turmoil some papers fell from a shelf, and a young man, picking up one of them, held it up, saw it was a petition, and, without reading it, proposed to his companions that they should all swear that the prisoner whom it concerned should be free next morning, "were it the Prince de Condé himself!" All agreed, waited till two o'clock in the morning, and, when Legendre returned, made him sign the *mandat de liberté*, which they carried triumphantly to the Carmes at three o'clock, waking up Madame de Custine with the news that she was free.

When they took her home she found everything, except the kitchen, sequestrated and sealed up; house and child under the charge of a cobbler whom the revolutionists had placed there. But Nanette had saved her life and that of the little

Astolphe, her son, who, pale and weak from fever, was so overjoyed to see his mother that he had a relapse, but after a time recovered.[1]

At one time all the nuns from one convent were guillotined together.

Another day a tumbril passed through the streets of Paris full of young girls, of whom the eldest was not eighteen, all dressed in white, looking, as some of the people said, like a basket of lilies, all of whom were put to death. When one reads of deeds like these it is impossible to help a feeling of intense thankfulness that no such spectacles have been seen in the streets of London, no such record stains the annals of our history.

For, deeply as the death of Charles I. upon the scaffold was, and still is, deplored and execrated, still the worst of the regicides of England did not torture or murder women or children. There was no brutality in the treatment of those children of the King who fell into the hands of the rebels. They were neither separated, tormented, nor insulted ; but were kept strictly guarded though treated with proper respect, in one of the royal castles or palaces ; a lady of rank was appointed to take care of the young Princess Elizabeth, and suitable guardians to be responsible for the Dukes of York and Gloucester.

Not the most fanatical republicans and revolutionists of the Parliament, or the roughest of Cromwell's Ironsides, not the most excited mob that ever filled the streets of London, would have suffered a woman and a child to be tortured as were the

[1] Mémoires, t. I, pp. 268–271 (Duchesse d'Abrantès).

unfortunate Queen and Dauphin of France, or done otherwise than shrink with horror from the September massacres and the *Noyades de Nantes*.

But though Robespierre was dead, all danger was by no means at an end. There were still ruffians enough on the tribunals who grudged the escape of any prey upon whom they had once laid their clutches, and furious that Clary had been snatched from them, when they found his friend could no longer protect him, they at once ordered his re-arrest.

His relations were now in despair, for the danger was not only great but immediate. The thirst for blood which animated the wretches who presided in the revolutionary courts caused them to hurry their victims through the mock trial to the place of execution.

Clary's wife knew that if anything were to be done to save him there was not a moment to lose, and she had heard that a certain *représentant du peuple*, named Albitte, with whom she or her family had some sort of acquaintance, happened to be just then passing through Marseille. She resolved, therefore, to go to the *Maison Commune*, where he would probably be found, and manage to see him on the chance of his being able and willing to help them.

She set off, therefore, without delay, and not liking to go alone she asked her young sister-in-law, Désirée, then between thirteen and fourteen years old, to go with her.

When they arrived at the *Maison Commune* they were shown into a large hall, in which a crowd of people were anxiously and sorrowfully waiting. They sat down in a corner until their turn should arrive to pass through the door to which all eyes were uneasily directed, but a considerable time elapsed, the afternoon drew to its close, and still they were not admitted. At last Désirée, overpowered by fatigue, excitement, and the heat of the place, fell asleep, and while she slept came the summons they had been so long expecting.

Madame Clary, thinking it would be useless to awake the child, and supposing that she would return the same way and could then call for her, left her sleeping and went in to the audience, upon the result of which the fate of her husband depended. She had the good fortune to obtain the order for his release for the second time, but finding that to return to the outer hall where she had left her little sister-in-law would cause delay, and being naturally eager to get to the prison and set her husband free, she hurried away, trusting to her young companion returning home when it became too late to stay there any longer.

As to Désirée, she slept on for a long time until she was awakened by the banging of a door, and sitting up with sleepy eyes perceived that it was night, and that she was alone in the hall, which was dark except for the dim light of a lantern just outside the entrance. Surprised and startled, she looked about her, and at that moment the door of the audience-room opened and a young man came out, who, seeing her there, approached and asked what she was doing in such a place and at such an hour.

Rejoiced to see a sympathetic face, Désirée explained her position to the new-comer, who at once assured her that her brother was now in safety, adding, " A young girl like you cannot walk about the streets alone at night, I will go with you as far as your home."

Désirée was glad enough to accept this proposal, for it was a long way to the *rue des Phocéens*, and the idea of going all that distance by herself, especially at that late hour, frightened her considerably. They set off, therefore, together, and by the time they reached the door of her house they had become excellent friends. Désirée wished her unknown companion good-night, thanked him for his kindness, and saying that her mother would certainly wish to express her thanks also, asked if he would not come and see them another day.

" Then one of these days you will introduce me to your family ? " he said.

" With pleasure," replied she. " But meanwhile I should like to be able to tell them the name of the one who took care of me this evening."

" Of course. Well, you can tell them that my name is Joseph Buonaparte."

" And that," Désirée used to say in after-life, " is the way the Clary and Buonaparte families made acquaintance."

Joseph Buonaparte then took his leave, while Désirée, going into the house, related to her mother and the rest what had taken place, none of them dreaming of the extraordinary change in the fortunes of the family which were to arise from this night's adventure.

Etienne Clary and his household were from this time left unmolested, and Joseph Buonaparte, who called the next day and made their acquaintance,

was received with gratitude, and soon became an
intimate friend and a frequent and welcome guest at
the *Hôtel Clary*, a large, old-fashioned house of which
the pervading atmosphere of wealth, order, and un-
pretentious hospitality formed a singular contrast to
that of his present home.

For the Buonaparte were at that time ruined
Corsican exiles, who had lately fled from their native
country and landed at Toulon. It was not many
years since the Italian island of Corsica had been
made a province of France, to whom it had been
ceded by the Genoese, and the Buonaparte were not
French at all, but a Corsican family of Italian origin.
They did not speak French, but Italian, and the
Corsican *patois*, and Napoleon, whose claim to be
French was simply that he was born the year after
the cession of the island, was a Frenchman just as the
child of Dutch parents in the Orange State, born a
year after the late war, is an Englishman.[1] Joseph
Buonaparte had not even this claim, as he was born
while Corsica was still Italian.

When Letizia Ramolino married Carlo Buonaparte
she was fifteen and he eighteen years old. They had
thirteen children, of whom five sons and three
daughters lived to grow up. Buonaparte had been
secretary to the governor of the island, the patriot
Paoli, during whose exile he died before he was forty
years old. Carlo Buonaparte was a pleasant, dis-

---

[1] Napoleon hated to be called a Corsican when he rose to power.
When on one occasion the Mayor of Lyons, wishing to compliment
him, observed "It is astonishing, sire, that, not being a Frenchman, you should love France so well and do so much for her": he
turned on his heel, saying, "It was like a blow with a stick to him."

JOSEPH BUONAPARTE, KING OF NAPLES, KING OF SPAIN, COMTE DE SURVILLIERS.

sipated man, fond of society and with cultivated tastes, but extravagant and volatile. After his death, his wife, who in no way resembled him, being badly educated, rather stern, and so economical that she was always accused of avarice, was left very badly off, and when Paoli returned to Corsica in 1790 Joseph Buonaparte was one of the deputation sent to meet the old general, and Napoleon was chosen to read him the address of his compatriots.

Paoli gave Joseph a post in the municipal administration, assisted Napoleon and Louis in many ways when they wished to leave the island, and took Lucien for his secretary at Rostino, where he was living in an old monastery formerly belonging to the Jesuits, high up amongst mountains and surrounded by great forests of chestnuts.

The surpassing beauty of the place and the enthusiastic admiration he felt for Paoli captivated Lucien, a romantic, impressionable lad, with much more talent than any of his brothers except Napoleon, filled with the traditions of Greece and Rome, and visions of a Republic like those of ancient Greece, which in his youthful inexperience he imagined possible under the changed conditions of modern life.

The venerable figure of Paoli, the picturesque surroundings, the wild figures of the mountain chiefs who gathered round the Corsican leader, the patriotism and purity of his constant endeavours to prevent the de-nationalisation of Corsica, and to resist all abuses and oppression, appealed strongly to Lucien, and added to his personal affection for his hero, the friend of his father, and the benefactor of his family, and for some time his loyalty to Paoli was shared by Joseph and Napoleon. The first period of the Revolution strengthened Paoli's loyalty to France, the abolition of the *corvée*, the *dîme*, the *droits seigneuraux*, and all the oppressive privileges of the nobles, had his entire approval, but what he really wished for was a constitutional government like that of England, a country where he spent years of exile, and which had ever since been his ideal, as it had been of many of the early and moderate members of the new *régime*.

But the excesses and crimes of the French Revolution alienated his sympathy, filled him with abhorrence of its bloodstained leaders, and caused him to direct all his energies towards the project of transferring his native island from their rule to that of England.

For what reason this attempt should be characterised as a crime and treason by French writers, or why it should be right and praiseworthy for an Italian island to belong to France but criminal and treasonable for it to belong to England, seems difficult to be understood by any one who is not French. Such, however, was the opinion of all the French party at that time, and amongst them of the Buonaparte family—Joseph and Napoleon (the latter of whom was constantly to and fro between France and Corsica) detached themselves from Paoli and his party, and in May, 1793, Lucien, who had remained with his chief, was sent by him to Ajaccio to see his brothers, find out what was the cause of their absence, and tell them that their presence was immediately required. " Tell your brothers I am expecting them, matters are more urgent than they think, and you come back with them," said Paoli to Lucien, to whom he also gave letters to take to Ajaccio. Here is Lucien's account of what followed :—

" The hopes I entertained of the political union of my brothers with Paoli were not dissipated until I arrived at the gates of Ajaccio, which I found shut. It was mid-day, the drum was beating, and I heard a *fusillade*, which a man on guard told me was the firing of the national guard, who were exercising. Before I was admitted I had not only to give my name, but to wait until the citizen Giuseppe (Joseph) and the captain Napoleone had been told. Joseph came to the gate at once, caused it to be opened, took my arm, and told me to be silent as we walked . . . we entered our own house. I found mamma, as usual, surrounded by my young brothers and sisters. Napoleon was sitting in a window-seat where I had caught sight of him as we came in, watching for Joseph and me. They both wore the uniform of the National Guard. . . . This picture of our family, so different from what it is to-day, in the midst of the phantasmagoric agitations in which it has been placed by the glory and the fortune of my brother Napoleon, and where, in spite of the prestige by which it is everywhere surrounded, I always see the abyss yawning under its steps ; this picture, at once graceful and touching on my return, after a long absence under such circumstances, has remained engraven on my memory.

" Napoleon, in his handsome uniform of command-ant of the National Guard, held on his knees our youngest sister, Annunciata, now the wife of Murat, who was playing with the charms on his watch-chain.

Louis was scribbling alone in a corner of the room. Paulette and Jérôme were playing together and Marianne-Elisa, the grown-up young lady of the house, sat working busily by the side of our mother.

" ' Here he is at last ! ' exclaimed mamma as she saw me come in. ' I was afraid that magician Paoli would not let him come back to us.'

" ' On the contrary, mamma, it was the general who sent me.'

" ' Ah ! ah ! ' cried Napoleon, getting up from his seat.

" Joseph made a sign to me to wait and then said, ' Mamma, wouldn't it be better for the children to go out ? '

" Marianne, very curious to know what it was about, sat still and said, ' Must I go too ? '

" ' Yes, little girl, you too,' said Joseph, ' although you are a *grande demoiselle de Saint-Cyr* '; and mamma added, ' Yes, Marianne, go, and take the others with you.'

" Marianne looked annoyed, but rose, made a fine French curtsey to mamma, then to Joseph, and then to Napoleon. As to me, in whom the *droit d'aînesse* was not yet sufficiently important in her eyes, she gave me a caressing pat on the hand as she passed, whispering, ' You will tell me all about it, won't you ? '

" I intended to do so, for ever since this sister had come home we had been the best friends in the world.

" ' Well, now, sit down,' said Joseph, ' and tell us what brings you back.'

" I told everything without any interruption from my brothers ; only from time to time mamma

exclaimed, 'It is folly! He will not succeed!' or,
'It was all very well before, when the towns were on
his side. Now the *bourgeois* care nothing about the
national independence.' When I had told them all
I knew of Paoli's plans and preparations for a *levée
en masse*, and of the enthusiasm I had witnessed, I
came to what I most disliked to say, because I knew
that it would be like setting powder on fire amongst
those whose opinions were opposed to my hero and
to the principles I still held. Directly I had finished
the sentence, 'I will spare nobody, not even the
sons of Charles,' it was as if they had all been stung
by a tarantula. They started up, walking up and
down, exclaiming, 'He said that? *Parbleu !* that's
a little too much! What! he said that?'

"'Yes,' said Napoleon ; 'that is going too far. Yes,
parbleu ! we shall see! Friend Pasquale has not got
me yet! Ah! he declares war upon us? For my
part I don't detest the idea of war. I've never made
it ; I will willingly begin with him.'

"Joseph, who, like all quick-tempered men, calms
down when he meets some one more angry than
himself, recovered his composure, shrugged his
shoulders, and replied to Napoleon—

"'War! that's easily said! I daresay you may
like war, but with whom or what are you going to
make it?'

"Our mother, who had till now been walking up
and down the room with as much irritation as her
two sons, now supported Joseph, shrugging her
shoulders. 'Yes, what are you going to make war
with? Tell me that, Napoleon. You know very
well that even with equal numbers, which we have

not, one of our mountaineers is worth four of the others. Oh! if they were with us I should feel as ready as Napoleon to fight in my own person. But it is very different. Without wishing to discourage you, I tell you frankly that unless the fleet with the troops come quickly—very quickly—we can't resist. The least we should risk would be to be made prisoners.'"

The discussion was a long one, Napoleon still persisting that he and Joseph would fight, their mother and the younger children being put for safety on board the boat of a coral-fisher they knew ; his mother declaring that she would not embark except in the last extremity.

"More than an hour and a half had passed," continues Lucien. "It was dinner-time. Mamma observed that the traveller must be hungry. I said that I was more tired than hungry. Napoleon took leave of us, saying that he had no time for dinner, as he had to attend a review of the National Guard, which he had fixed for three o'clock ; he would be satisfied with supper. Mamma begged me to go and lie down and rest till supper-time.

"I was just leaving the room when Joseph said, ' It's a pity you can't go to the *Société populaire* to-night, but you must certainly go there to-morrow.'

"' What do you say? To-morrow!' I exclaimed. ' But, my dear brother, I must go back to Paoli to-morrow.'

"' Are you mad?' said mamma. ' This time he would not let you come back. Now that he must know what has passed here he would keep you as a hostage. Did you promise to go back?'

"'He could not keep him as a hostage if he returned in good faith on his parole,' observed Joseph. 'But I hope he has not given it.'

"'But, *mon Dieu!*' I replied, 'there was no occasion for me to promise to go back. Neither Paoli nor I had any doubt of it.'

"'Ah, well, so much the better!' exclaimed mamma and Joseph together.

"'But, dear mamma, dear Joseph, the reason I had not to promise was that he trusted to it. So that it is the same——'

"'Not at all,' said mamma; 'it is quite different.'

"'Yes,' said Joseph, 'it's different; if you had absolutely promised, I should say——'

"'Well,' said mamma, 'if he had promised, promised, promised, he had not the right to do so. I affirm that he could not and ought not to have promised, because—since—well—anyhow he is a minor, and cannot engage himself without my consent.'

"'That is legally true,' answered Joseph; 'but we have not come to that. Happily he has not promised. Therefore you can and ought to stay with us, my dear Lucien.'

"'But what you say is dreadful, *mon frère*. It will be said that I have betrayed Paoli, and I don't want to be called *vitello* all over the island.'

"'What folly!' cried mamma.

"'And I am over seventeen, which is more than the age of reason, I hope; and it will always be said that I betrayed the great Paoli, knowing quite well what I was doing.'

"'They will say the same of us all, *mon cher*, and one will be as true as the other.'

"When the family were assembled at supper the discussion was resumed, and the remarks on Paoli's preference for England above all other nations led the conversation to the preponderance of that power in India. I remember that Napoleon prophesied that she would increase in strength every day for various reasons, which he gave, but which I forget ; but I have never forgotten that he said that was the country to make a fortune in, and if he did not get the promotion he expected he would have no objection to seek for service there. That made me doubt whether then he was so attached to France as Joseph was or as he afterwards showed himself. I have several times heard him say about this time that the English valued a good artillery officer much more than the French, and that in India they were rare. ' In fact,' he said, ' they are scarce everywhere ; and if I ever take that step I hope you will hear me spoken of. I shall come back in a few years a rich Nabob and bring large fortunes for my three sisters.' His mother exclaimed against the idea, saying how she disliked Napoleon's interest in India, as she knew he was quite capable of taking service there if he did not get the promotion he wished for, and that the Indian climate was fatal to Europeans. Joseph consoled her by saying that there was no fear of Napoleon's not being advanced, and that if he were not satisfied with being captain at his age he must be difficult to please.

"'Ah ! you are very good,' said Napoleon, shrugging his shoulders, ' if you think my promotion, which I confess to be rapid, is due to any merit I may or may not have. You know as well as I do that the reason I am captain is because all the superior officers of the *régiment de la Fère* are at Coblentz.[1]   Now you will see how long they will leave me a captain. I begin almost to fear that Admiral Truguet, on whom I reckon, has received, or will receive, some counter-order for the fleet.'

"' It would be much worse for us,' remarked Joseph. ' As for Napoleon's promotion, I trust much more to his personal merit than to the protection of Truguet or anybody else.'

"' Then you make a great mistake, *mon frère,*' answered Napoleon. ' I have seen quite enough into things at Paris to know that without protection one will never get on.   Women, above all, they are the best protection machines.   And I, as you know, am not what they like.   One cannot please them unless one knows how to make love, and that is what I never did know, and probably never shall. I am not like Joseph ; now he knows how to make love to ladies.   He has already turned many heads at Florence, where they call him "*le beau cavalier Corse.*" '

"' Be quiet, *mauvais plaisant,*' " returned Joseph ; and the conversation went back to Paoli, Lucien protesting with tears and sobs against being forced to abandon the leader for whom he entertained a strong affection, while his mother and brothers assured him that at his age his duty was clearly to submit to the authority of the heads of his family. At last he yielded reluctantly to their representations, and a letter was composed, respectful and full of regret and affection from Lucien to Paoli, explaining

[1] Having emigrated.

the reasons of his obedience to his mother and elder brothers.

The letter was given to the brave mountaineer who had accompanied Lucien and whom Napoleon wanted to detain as a hostage, to which Joseph would not consent, much to the relief of their younger brother. Napoleon was already very arbitrary amongst his brothers and sisters, and

AJACCIO.

would take offence at the slightest opposition or reproof. They all yielded to him, even Joseph seldom answered him again when he became angry.

Some time after the circumstances just recorded the insurrection had spread through Corsica, and Madame Buonaparte and her children were obliged to escape, their house burnt down, their property confiscated, and themselves reduced to destitution.

Joseph was then twenty-six, and Jérôme, the youngest of the family, eleven years old.[1]

[1] It has been alleged by one or two modern writers that Napoleon was really the eldest and Joseph the second son, an assertion which Bourrienne expressly declares to be untrue, and which the friends and family of Napoleon repeatedly deny. In 1784, their father, in applying for presentations to military schools for the two boys, declares Joseph to be his eldest son. Lucien remarks that the wonderful fortunes of the family were owing to the power and favour of the second brother ; Jérôme claimed that his American marriage was legal, as he had the consent of his mother and eldest brother, Joseph. Madame Junot, in her memoirs, says that Napoleon, after he was in power, was irritated because his brothers and sisters persisted in considering Joseph as head of the family whenever it suited them to do so, and, in fact, there seems no reason whatever for so unusual a supposition.

CHAPTER III

1794

UPON their arrival Joseph applied to the *Comité de Salut Public* at Marseille for the assistance allowed to patriotic refugees by the Convention. He obtained a sufficient sum to keep his mother, sisters, and youngest brother from starvation, and a post under the revolutionary government for himself. Lucien, who, in spite of the accusations of callousness brought against him by one or two writers, was horror-stricken at the executions going on, and managed to escape from amongst those who tried to induce him to be present at one of those terrible spectacles, and to hide himself in a *café* till it was over, refused to go to Paris with the Marseillais club, and got employment at a mill at Saint-Maximin, a village in the neighbourhood. Napoleon returned to his regiment at Nice, taking Louis with him, having contrived to get the boy appointed his *aide-de-camp*.

35

For Napoleon was already beginning to have some influence. He was able to help Lucien out of a dangerous scrape into which he had got himself, and had been offered a post of importance in Paris, which he refused, saying that it was much easier to keep one's head on one's shoulders at Saint-Maximin[1] than there; besides that, he would not support the Montagne, and at present the only honourable place for him was in the army.

At the time the acquaintance began between the Buonaparte and Clarys, Madame Buonaparte and her younger children were living at Marseille with Joseph. They were very poor, and the friendship of the rich Clary family was considered a very advantageous one, especially when Joseph, after having devoted his chief attentions to his little friend Désirée, who was not quite fourteen, proposed to marry her as soon as she should have completed her sixteenth year.

Nobody could foresee the extraordinary career of Napoleon. His family were without any connections of the slightest use, and "ruined for many years at least," as Madame Buonaparte informed Lucien on his arrival at Marseille, their house, and everything in it, having been burnt and their crops destroyed, so that all they had left were the bare lands and the clothes they were wearing. Joseph had no money and no talent, while Désirée was a mere child, and had a large fortune, therefore her family might reasonably have objected to such a marriage for her, but they do not seem to have done so; on the contrary, with one exception, they all appeared

[1] Referring to Lucien's escape.

to be quite satisfied with the proposed arrangement.

That exception was Désirée's favourite sister, Julie, who had always been her constant and dearest companion, and was the person she loved best in the world. Through all their childhood, youth, and later life Julie and Désirée clung together with that deep, unchanging confidence and affection which sometimes exists between sisters who are nearly the same age, and whose dispositions suit, although they do not necessarily resemble each other.

It was so in this case. Désirée was a pretty, merry brunette with dark eyes, all the grace and vivacity of the south, and that light-hearted, easy-going, superficial temperament which is, perhaps, the most likely to carry its owner safely and happily through life, untouched by the sorrows and dangers, if deprived of the greater and more fervent joys which fall to the lot of those whose feelings are stronger and their natures higher and deeper.

Julie was a year or two older than Désirée, plain, gentle, shy, and very religious. She had hitherto played rather the part of Cinderella in the family; of Cinderella, that is to say, before the arrival of the prince. But now, in the mind of Julie, the prince had appeared in the shape of Joseph Buonaparte, who was just the sort of man likely to please an inexperienced young girl, being good-looking, good-natured, pleasant, courteous, and extremely fond of society, especially that of women. Of a weak, amiable disposition, regarded with much affection in his own family, but with no capacity for making

his way in the world, a rich marriage was not a
chance to be neglected by him ; but as his choice
had fallen upon Désirée, and he paid no attention
to Julie, she took care that neither he nor any one
else should perceive the secret love she could not
help feeling for the *fiancé* of her little sister.
Always quiet, retiring, and *dévote*, a little more
melancholy and resignation on her part attracted
no attention in the large domestic circle of brothers
and sisters, aunts, uncles, and cousins with whom she
was surrounded.

As to Désirée, she had no sort of love for Joseph
Buonaparte, though she liked him, and was quite
willing to marry him when she was sixteen, which,
as it would not be for two years, seemed a long way
off to a girl of her age. Meanwhile, it was amusing
enough to have him constantly in and out of the
house, and one day he brought with him his brother
Napoleon, of whom he had often spoken to Désirée,
and her relations, to whom he was anxious to
introduce him.

Napoleon was then at home on leave, and was
soon on intimate terms with the Clarys, who appear
to have been homely, hospitable people, and who
called him " the General," and made him welcome
at their house. He, as well as Joseph, wanted a rich
wife, for he was desperately in need of money. He
had already made an offer to a French girl, who had
refused him, and he had then fallen passionately in
love with an Italian, whom he could not marry as she
was without fortune. He was much pleased with his
brother's prudence and good luck in his betrothal to
one of the daughters of the wealthy mercantile house,

but he soon perceived the state of affairs between Joseph and the two sisters.

One day, in the presence both of Joseph and Désirée, he accordingly assured them that they had made a mistake in their arrangements, as they were really not at all suited to each other.

"In a well-conducted household," he observed, "one must yield to the other. You, Joseph, are of a most undecided character, and Désirée is just the same; whereas Julie and I know what we want, therefore you had much better marry Julie. As to Désirée," he added, pulling her on to his knee, "she shall be my wife."

Joseph was now and always, in spite of his being the eldest brother, as completely under the influence of Napoleon as all the rest of his family except Lucien, so he made no objection to this alteration of his matrimonial plans. Désirée was certainly much prettier than Julie, but, after all, a rich wife was the essential matter to him, and Julie being older than Désirée, his marriage with her could take place much sooner. Désirée had taken a fancy to Napoleon, and liked him much better than Joseph, therefore she was delighted at the proposed change, and Julie joyfully accepted her part of this not very flattering arrangement. Therefore the next day Madame Buonaparte called on Madame Clary with these proposals, and the marriages were arranged, that of Joseph and Julie to take place immediately, while Désirée was to wait till she was sixteen, and then become the wife of Napoleon.

Madame Clary was much blamed by her friends for her imprudence in consenting to any such marriages for her daughters. With their fortunes, she was told, they ought to do much better than that ; and it was especially foolish in the case of Désirée, as she was a mere child, and Napoleon, while just as poor as Joseph, instead of being good-looking and pleasant like him, was miserably thin and sallow, disagreeable, and badly dressed.

" He wears threadbare clothes and shabby, dirty boots," remarked one, " and he is brusque, sulky, and subject to fits of absence, out of which he only wakes up to express his opinion in an abrupt, dictatorial manner upon some subject that interests nobody but himself and those of his profession. His having become general so young does not prove that he will rise any further. He is born for mediocrity."

Madame Clary, however, paid no attention to all this chorus of disapproval of her two proposed sons-in-law, one of whom was in a few years a king, the other an emperor. The preparations for Julie's wedding went on, and the friendship between the families of Buonaparte and Clary became more and more intimate.

Madame Buonaparte's affection for the wife of her eldest son continued unchanged through all the extraordinary vicissitudes of their lives, and so also did her fondness for Désirée, in spite of later events, which might well have estranged them from each other.

It was, indeed, a time of strange and romantic changes ; the most unlikely things were constantly happening. Who that frequented the sober and decorous evenings of that worthy *bourgeoise* family could have imagined that amongst the simple, in no way distinguished, young daughters were two queens ;

that two of the younger brothers of that very Joseph, for whom the silk merchant's daughter was considered such an excellent *parti*, would marry the daughters of the Emperor of Austria and King of Wurtemberg, and that of all the badly-dressed, ordinary-looking, young Buonaparte, the lowest in rank, would be a prince and a grand-duchess before many years had passed !

For the Buonaparte family was then by no means an interesting or distinguished one. At that time the colossal genius of Napoleon was not recognised ; few persons supposed he would ever be anything greater than a distinguished officer of the republican army ; whilst of the others only two possessed any particular gift or attraction. Lucien was exceedingly clever, but at this period of his life so crotchety and extravagant in his ideas that his talents and good qualities were neutralised by his folly. Pauline, the second daughter now about fourteen, was and always remained extraordinarily beautiful and also incredibly silly.

In a prettily-written book called " Une Fiancée de Napoléon," the Comtesse d'Armaillé quotes from the Baron de Larrey a high-flown description of the daily routine of the Buonaparte family at this time ; giving the picture of a life decorous, and severe as that of a convent, occupied entirely in prayers and domestic duties. No one, however, who knew anything about the sisters of Napoleon would believe that any of them would ever have led such a life as is thus described ; even if it were not absolutely disproved by existing love-letters and anecdotes which depict a very different state of things.

The fact was that Madame Buonaparte, or, as after the Corsican custom she was called, Signora Letizia, herself a strong, simple, serious woman, devoted to domestic duties, with an upright, courageous character, a narrow mind, no ambition and no education, either could not or would not control her children when they had passed out of early childhood. She would express her opinion strongly enough, as in the case of Lucien and Paoli, and in many other instances recorded in the lives of her sons and daughters. She was not in the least afraid to say what she thought, and would oppose and reproach any of them in their most powerful days, even Napoleon himself, if she thought them in the wrong ; but for some reason or other, although most of them were very fond of her, she does not seem to have had any real influence over them, most probably in consequence of her above-mentioned narrowness, want of education, and ignorance of the world.

While they lived at Marseille, Jérôme,[1] entirely without instruction of any kind, ran about the streets all day as he chose, until Napoleon sent for him to Paris, and placed him at school ; while the conduct of his sisters gave rise to continual scandal.

They lived at first in a miserable apartment on the fourth floor of a house which had been entirely depopulated during the Terror, in the *rue Pavillon*, near the Cannebière. As Joseph and Napoleon were able to give them more money, and their friends among the revolutionary powers took more interest in them, they gradually moved from one house to another, and were rather more comfortably established.

[1] " Les Sœurs de Napoléon " (Joseph Turquan).

Their house was frequented by the friends of their brothers and other young Marseillais, and it was with the society of these dissipated, unscrupulous young men, with intrigues, flirtations, and endeavours to make advantageous marriages, not with evening prayers and household work, that the daughters of the Signora Letizia occupied themselves during their residence at Marseille, where their reputation became so bad, and the stories about them so numerous, that Napoleon is said to have owed a grudge ever afterwards to the town where so much more was known about his family than was agreeable to him. Amongst the most conspicuous of the admirers of the sisters of Napoleon were two young members of the Convention whom he had himself introduced to them. Barras and Fréron were amongst the most corrupt of the revolutionary gang, and their intimacy with her daughters so displeased and alarmed the Signora Letizia that, before the engagement of Joseph and Julie Clary, she had left Marseille with the three girls, the eldest of whom was not more than eighteen, and gone to live near Antibes, where Napoleon, who was then at Nice, found them a charming house, and introduced his sisters to the gaieties of that delightful place, with the view of finding husbands for them amongst his brother-officers. However, after five months they returned to Marseille, where matters went on as before ; but the marriage of Joseph to one of the *demoiselles* Clary, the engagement of Napoleon to another, and the intimacy that arose between the two families, was a considerable advantage to their position in the town, where the reputation of the Clarys was as good as that of the daughters of the Signora Letizia was deplorable.

A gentleman from Dauphiné, a certain **M. de Lasalcette**, of good fortune and position, made their acquaintance at Marseille, and was struck with the beauty of Pauline, to whom he paid a good deal of attention. The Signora Letizia was most anxious for this marriage, and did all she could to promote it, but the outrageous flirtations of Pauline with various people, and particularly with Fréron, and the general want of education and propriety of the family, so disgusted him that he withdrew. Junot, *aide-de-camp* to Napoleon, was also in love with her, and would not have been so fastidious, but he had neither money nor position, and Napoleon, who was bent upon rich marriages for his family as well as himself, would not hear of him as a brother-in-law, though he was then his greatest friend.

It was only for her fortune that Napoleon wished to marry Désirée, who in every other respect was a most unsuitable wife for him, as he very soon began to realise. For he believed firmly in his future and was resolved to rise in the world ; he felt that a great career lay before him, and as time brought reflection could scarcely have seen, in a half-educated provincial child of fourteen, the woman he should choose to share it with him. Countless were the intrigues and *liaisons* with which he amused his leisure moments, but through all his life he never permitted a love-affair to stand in the way of his interests. Both his marriages were arranged for reasons of expediency, and although he repeatedly declared that his first wife was the woman he had loved above all others, he sacrificed her remorselessly to his ambition.

Désirée Clary's fortune would just at that moment have been very useful to him, but they had not been engaged many months before he began to see that the sort of wife he required was an attractive, well-connected woman of the world with influential friends and connections, who knew how to *tenir salon* and surround herself with friends that would be useful to him.

In fact, soon after breaking off his engagement with Désirée he proposed to Madame Permon, whom he had known all his life, who had no fortune, was the widow of an official of finance, had three children, and was old enough to be his mother as she told him when she refused his offer. But she was, as he remarked more than once in later life, perhaps the most beautiful woman he ever saw, was descended from Greek Emperors, her brothers, the Princes Comnenus, were acknowledged as royal at the court of France, and her *salon* was filled with her intimate friends of the *faubourg Saint-Germain*.[1]

Napoleon's reply to her objections was that he did not care about her age, since with her grace and beauty she did not look thirty; that he wanted to marry a woman who should possess those attractions, should know how to *tenir salon*, and should belong to the *faubourg Saint-Germain*. And not long after this episode he did marry a woman possessing these

[1] "Mémoires de la Duchesse d'Abrantès," written by the daughter of Madame Permon; also "A Leader of Society at Napoleon's Court" (Catherine Bearne).

qualificatious, namely, Joséphine Tascher de la Pagerie, widow of the Vicomte de Beauharnais.

Joseph Buonaparte and Julie Clary were married August 1, 1794. As they wished the wedding to be a quiet one, the civil ceremony was performed at a small village called Cuges, a few miles from Marseille; but as Julie's principles were, of course, against a mere republican marriage, and there was still some risk in a religious one, this was celebrated secretly in a private chapel by the Abbé Raymonet, a friend of the family.

There was as yet no idea of Désirée's engagement being broken off. Napoleon was still quite satisfied with it, and Désirée appeared to be very much in love with him, and pleased with the growing importance of his position.

The disapprobation with which most of her friends regarded her proposed marriage made no impression on Désirée. She assured the young girls who were her confidants that no one could be more affectionate, merry, and cordial than the young Corsican officer, that he was the good providence of his own family, and that his poverty did not signify as he was certain to make his way.

But not more than a week after the wedding of Joseph and Julie, Napoleon was suddenly arrested, and by the machinations of his enemies Salicetti and Albitte was thrown into prison, all his papers being seized. For a few days his family and friends were in the greatest alarm, but the official to whom the examination of his papers was committed being fortunately an honest man, and discovering nothing in them that could be objected to, declared that a

mistake had been made ; and the vehement indignation of his comrades of the Army of Italy forced his
persecutors to set him free after a week's imprisonment.

But a few days later a new complaint was brought
against him; that he had refused to join the army
sent to reduce La Vendée, where the frightful
cruelties exercised by the republican soldiers upon
the helpless peasantry have perhaps seldom been
surpassed even by savages.   One of their generals
boasted, "We have massacred the women and
trampled the children under our horses' feet." [1]   For
refusing to take part in this campaign Napoleon was
now deprived of his military rank.

Depressed and discouraged by this check to his
career and the enforced inactivity it brought about,
Napoleon passed the winter at Marseille, spending
his time at the *Hôtel Clary* or at the house of his
brother Joseph, now the most flourishing member
of the family.   To marry Désirée seemed under the
present circumstances the best way out of the poverty
and difficulties which beset him, and it was decided
that their wedding should take place in the spring.
Meanwhile he found it amusing enough to make love
to Désirée, or Eugénie, as he preferred to call her,
accompanying her and her family in their walks and
excursions into the country, and arranging plans for
their future life, the nature of which seems to show
the extreme depression and discouragement from
which he was then suffering.   For his project was
to buy a small estate in the neighbourhood of
Marseille, settle there with Désirée, and occupy himself with the cultivation of it.

[1] General Westermann (see " The Real French Revolutionist ").

It was not possible that the idea of such a preposterous career for Napoleon should last very long ;
but Désirée seeing the prosperous household of her
sister and Joseph Buonaparte, and being from her
age and character without any ambition, was quite
contented with the obscure and peaceful lot prepared
for her, and delighted to stay in her own province
and near her family instead of going to Paris, the
very thought of which filled her with terror.   However, these projects were not destined to be fulfilled :
a far different future lay before both the young
people in question.

CHAPTER IV

1794—1796

THE Revolution, which had upset and altered all existing arrangements, had considerably relaxed the severe seclusion in which young girls were formerly kept; in consequence of which Désirée, instead of being introduced to her future husband at the *parloir* of a convent and shortly afterwards being called upon to sign the contract, was continually in Napoleon's society during the summer, autumn, and the first part of the winter that followed their engagement, and became more and more in love with him, trying to believe in his promises and professions, respecting which, young as she was, she could not help now and then feeling some disquieting doubts.

For Napoleon's heart was evidently with the army; the stir and excitement, the hopes and fears, the dreams of victory, and the soaring ambition of the career that had been cut short filled his soul; not

5

the farm near Marseille, nor the little school-girl who was to share it with him. Ever restless, ever watching for a chance of recovering the position of which he had been deprived by the malice of his enemies, he took an opportunity which offered itself of going to Toulon, where he was engaged in suppressing a revolt which had broken out there ; and where he succeeded in saving the lives of some unfortunate *émigrés* who had been captured in a Spanish ship, and whom the ferocious mob wanted to murder. This was in February, and having, in spite of his services, failed to regain his military rank, he returned to Marseille and announced his intention of going to Paris to obtain justice.

As it was impossible to know how long he might be absent, this, of course, necessitated his wedding being put off ; but he assured Désirée and his family that he would come back and be married at the end of the year, and that arrangements should be made for the purchase of an estate in the neighbourhood, presumably with his wife's fortune, as he had no money of his own. And in the month of April he set off to Paris, accompanied by his brother Louis and his friend Junot.

To Désirée the unexpected postponement of her marriage and departure of her *fiancé* were a bitter disappointment and trial ; in addition to which were her fears for his personal safety in Paris, and the suspicions she felt of the constancy of his affection for her when they were separated.

As a slight consolation to her on the day of his leaving Marseille, she, with her mother and her brother Nicolas, removed from Etienne's house in

the *rue des Phocéens* and went to live with Julie and
Joseph.   To be again in the constant society of her
favourite sister was a happiness to Désirée, but the
departure of Napoleon was the beginning of the end
of their engagement.

Just at first he wrote often to her, giving accounts
of his journeys and proceedings.   He had been to
look at an estate near Montélimart which he thought
might suit them; he had been in Lyons during a riot
which had, as usual, ended in a massacre, after which
he had gone to Châtillon, where he stayed some time
with the father of Marmont, but he does not appear
to have dwelt upon the friendship he made there
with the daughter of the Comte de Chastenay, then
about four-and-twenty years old, a clever, handsome
woman, whose literary and social talents were afterwards well known in Parisian circles.   The Marmonts
brought Napoleon to the Comte de Chastenay's house
in Châtillon, and his daughter,[1] in her " Mémoires "
thus writes of her acquaintance with him :—

" General Buonaparte was accompanied by his
brother Louis, then sixteen years old, whom he was
educating himself, and who seemed a good sort of
lad, with nothing remarkable about him.   I only
remember that his brother having ordered him to
calculate the *logarithme de 44*, mamma had to intercede to get him leave to go for a walk, as his

---

[1] Madame la Comtesse Marie Victorine de Chastenay, Chanoinesse : born 1771 of a distinguished Burgundian family.   Her
father, the Count de Chastenay, though of liberal opinions, was
imprisoned under the Terror, but released after the death of
Robespierre.   She was associated with many of the most remarkable personages of all parties, and spent her life in protecting
and helping those in danger or trouble.   She died 1855.

severe mentor would not forgive him for not having finished his task.

"Every one has known Buonaparte. He was then pale and thin, which made his face all the more characteristic. Madame de Marmont brought him to see us the day after his arrival. The good lady did not know what to do with her guest, whose constant and absolute taciturnity threw her into despair. The recent recollections of the Terror had left more aversion than attraction for all who bore the republican exterior. The reactionary spirit of the day almost permitted one to show the dislike one felt for the *officiers bleus*, as they were called, and if we had not been above the prejudices of small towns we should not have received the little general, whom those who had met him did not scruple to treat as a fool.

"At his first visit, to pass away the time, I was asked to play on the piano ; the general seemed pleased ; but his compliments were short. They asked me for songs, and I sang an Italian one which I had set to music. I asked him if I pronounced well ; and he simply replied, 'No.' . . .

"The next day we dined at the Châtelot. . . . It was then the custom at Châtillon to dine at two ; we were a long time at dinner, and when we left the dining-room I was asked to talk to the general, whose monosyllables had not made the same impression upon me as upon the rest of the company. I went up and asked him a question about Corsica, and our conversation began. I believe it lasted more than four hours. . . . It was only when mamma gave the signal for departure that our conversation came to an end. I am sorry not to have written it down, it interested and amused me extremely. . . . I soon discovered that the republican general had no republican maxims or belief. . . . He spoke of the resistance experienced by the revolutionary progress, and showed me that it was too incomplete for success to have been possible. He could not conceive a civil war without a nobility, a *haute noblesse* powerful through public opinion, through the support of a numerous following of gentlemen, and by the authority which a *grand seigneur* in past ages exercised over an army of vassals. According to our modern customs, the inheritor of the greatest name in France was more or less a party man, and his talents alone gave any importance to his concurrence. What had lately happened in La Vendée confirmed this opinion. Should not one study the late events in Lyon, at Toulon? No plan, no foresight in the *Lyonnaise* resistance. The courage and energy of the finest characters there had lost their influence for want of clear conception and through uncertainty of aim. At Toulon the merchants had begun by placing a great part of their property on board ship, ready to sail themselves if fortune went against them. That was not the way to conduct a civil war. . . . The substance of his opinions, then new to me, were certainly shown me during this conversation. . . . I believe, and Buonaparte very little objected to its being believed, that he would have emigrated if emigration had had any chance of success. Toulon might possibly have had him for a defender if the commercial interest had not put defeat into the elements of his calculations. The young soldier had then his fortune

to make: still an adventurer, he must never advance
without success. . . .

"The general told me—and it was true—that the
mass of the army had nothing to do with the
sanguinary events of which unhappy France had
been the theatre: it knew scarcely anything about
them. . . . He found me naturally deeply hostile to
the terrorists and full of enthusiasm for the *thermi-
doriens*: he had seen some of them in their proceedings before the thermidor, and thought less
favourably of them: at the same time, he said, one
might do much harm and cause infinite mischief
without being really very bad (*méchant*): a signature
given without reflection might cost the lives of
numbers of victims which the pen would have refused
to sign had the result been realised. A picture
showing the actions, scenes, and misfortunes arising
from a determination made without thought, ought
to be often presented to men's eyes, and would be
a safeguard to threatened humanity. Buonaparte
talked to me of the poems of Ossian, which inspired
him with enthusiasm . . . novels had their place in
the conversation . . . the tragic end of *Paul et
Virginie* was the chief cause of the interest of the
story. . . . He could not bear his melancholy impressions to be disturbed by lively ones; after a
tragedy he would hurry away from the theatre,
wrapped in his cloak, to indulge his emotions. . . .
He spoke of happiness, and he remarked that for
man it ought to consist in the highest possible
development of the faculties.

"Buonaparte never forgot our conversation. . . . We
saw each other every day either at the Châtelot or at

my parents'. I can see him now, helping me to make
a bouquet of cornflowers. . . . We played games in
the *salon*, and, in consequence of a forfeit, I saw
before me on his knees him who shortly saw all
Europe kneeling before him. . . .

"One day the post brought unexpected news . . .
his immediate departure was decided . . . Buonaparte
came to say goodbye. I was out. He only had an
interview with mamma, and went away without being
able to wait for me. It would be difficult for me to
say how surprised and grieved I was." [1]

The letters of Napoleon to Désirée have not been
preserved, but from some of hers still in existence it
appears that she fretted at his absence, begged him
to keep his promise to love her always as she loved
him, complained that she was *triste* and anxious,
that she could not take an interest in anything
around her, but found everything insupportable since
he left her; and a great deal more to the same effect.
She entreated him not to forget his little Eugénie,
and already, when he had only arrived at Aix, began
slightly to reproach him for not having sent her
a letter and his address when she thought he might
have done so. Shortly afterwards Joseph Buonaparte
was sent to Genoa on a mission of the Government,
and with him went his wife, Désirée, and their mother,
where, after their long separation, they met again
their sister, Madame Antoine, her husband and family,
who were living there. From France to Italy, from
the great commercial port of Marseille to the stately
streets and marble palaces of Genoa, was a new and
interesting experience for Julie and Désirée, and

[1] "Mémoires de Madame de Chastenay," t. i. pp. 283 7.

although the members of the French diplomatic
corps under the government of the Republic were
rough and unpolished to a degree which astonished
and disgusted those of the other legations, there
were plenty of Italians and diplomats belonging to
different countries, amongst whom Désirée and her
sister were introduced to a society very different from
that of the *rue des Phocéens.*

But the enjoyment she would naturally under
other circumstances have felt in her new position was
spoilt for Désirée by her constant uneasiness and
fretting about Napoleon, to whom she continued to
write in the same strain ; his letters growing fewer,
shorter, and more indifferent. In fact, after his
arrival in Paris at the end of May, Napoleon found
himself at once surrounded with interests and pre-
occupations which soon put out of his mind all the
projects of the last six months. The idea of settling
in a country place near Marseille was no longer to be
entertained, and after some time he wrote rather a
peremptory letter to Madame Clary with a request,
which looked more like a command, that she should
buy a house in Paris and bring her daughter there.

Both Désirée and her mother were thrown into
the greatest consternation by this proposal, and, not
knowing what to do, they appealed to Joseph, who
was not of the slightest use. He could neither help
nor advise them, and if they decided to go to Paris
he certainly could not go with them, as he was
obliged to stay at Genoa.

But Désirée did not want to go to Paris. She
clung with all her heart to her own sunny south, and
she hated and dreaded the idea of living in Paris as

vehemently as in later years she hated and dreaded the idea of living anywhere else.

Besides, things were not going smoothly between Napoleon and herself. It was the old, oft-repeated story ; he was careless, negligent, and indifferent ; she was susceptible, jealous, perpetually taking offence, and writing letters filled with complaints and reproaches which irritated Napoleon and made him desire more and more to put an end to the engagement.

He was living in a scrambling, poverty-stricken way in a small hotel with the help of various friends. Joseph sent him what money he could ; Junot, whose father was a country lawyer tolerably well off, shared all his family gave him with his friend. Barras, of whom Napoleon said many years afterwards that he was worse than Robespierre, was then the most powerful man in Paris ; and Napoleon approached him, at first in the hope of saving Lucien, who was just then in prison at Aix and in great danger.

Afterwards, taking part in the dissolute society of which Barras [1] was the leader, he entered freely into the wild orgies of that set of which the beautiful and notorious Madame Tallien was a conspicuous member. She seems to have excited the especial jealousy of Désirée, not altogether without reason, for Napoleon fell in love with her, and it was only her absolute indifference that limited their relations to friendship alone.

[1] Barras was a man of noble family, Barras being one of the twelve noblest names in Provence. He was polished and well educated ; but one of the most cruel and blood-stained of the revolutionists.

Madame Tallien,[1] " Notre Dame de Thermidor," as she was called by the revolutionary mob, had then all Paris at her feet. Her striking beauty was increased by the Greek costume she habitually wore. Her influence with Tallien and Barras was unbounded, and was always exercised on the side of mercy. Many a royalist victim had she saved from the tigers over whom she reigned by her beauty and charm ; her *salon* in *Cours la-reine* was the scene of the maddest revels of the lawless, disorganised society of this capital and the resort of the most notorious men and the most beautiful women of Paris. Madame de Châteaurenault,[2] Madame de Cambys, and other well-known beauties, formed part of her intimate circle, and Madame de Stael was often to be found there. The advances of the moody, obscure, poverty-stricken young Corsican were not likely to meet with anything but a peremptory refusal from her. She showed him much friendship, however, used her influence with Barras and Tallien in his favour, and even procured cloth from the *magasins de l'État* to make him a new uniform, owing to the shabby and deplorable condition of what he was wearing.

It may be remarked that after he became First Consul Napoleon refused to allow Joséphine, in spite of her tears and entreaties, to receive Madame Tallien, Madame Hamelin, and many others of her present friends, remarking that none but respectable women

---

[1] Madame Tallien afterwards married the Prince de Chimay. She was a Spaniard, a native of Cadiz ; her maiden name was Cabarrus.

[2] Or Château-Regnault.

must be received in the *salon* of the first magistrate of the Republic. The suspicions of Désirée were soon transferred to the *ci-devant* Vicomtesse de Beauharnais, also an *habituée* of the *salon* of Madame Tallien, who, although not so regularly beautiful as some of the others, was so graceful, seductive, and charming as to compare well with them in attraction.

Joséphine Tascher de la Pagerie was a Creole, who had passed her childhood in Martinique, from whence she had been taken to France, and married when scarcely more than a child to the Vicomte de Beauharnais, a *mauvais sujet* with whom she had led a stormy life for a time, then separated from and become reconciled to not long before the Vicomte had been imprisoned and guillotined, leaving her with two children and nobody to take care either of her or them.

Having escaped the guillotine, Joséphine fell into the dissipated, licentious society of Barras, Tallien and their set, through which she was not likely to pass unscathed.

Her acquaintance with Napoleon began by her son, Eugène de Beauharnais, going to ask if he might be allowed to have his father's sword. Napoleon was pleased with the boy, called upon the mother and thus began an acquaintance of which Désirée soon heard reports, probably exaggerated, for at that time there was no question either of marriage or love-making between them. But all kinds of gossip were repeated to Désirée by people who came or wrote from Paris; she decidedly refused to go and live there, and either wrote complaining, offended letters to Napoleon or became sulky and would not write at all,

Under these circumstances the proper and dignified course would certainly have been to put an end to the engagement, which was evidently becoming an annoyance to her *fiancé;* but Désirée was too young and inexperienced to know what to do herself, and does not appear to have had any one with enough decision of character or knowledge of the world to direct her. Consequently this unsatisfactory state of things was allowed to go on until it was put a stop to by Napoleon himself in the following September.

During the month of June a member of the War Office named Pontécoulant wished for certain information respecting the Army of Italy, and was advised by Boissy d'Anglas to send for "a little, pale, thin, sickly-looking Italian" whom he had met the day before, who had singularly bold, energetic views, who knew all about the Army of Italy, and who would give the information required.

The next day Napoleon was sent for to the Tuileries, went up to the office of Pontécoulant on the sixth floor, and made such an impression that almost immediately afterwards his rank as general was restored to him ; he was attached to the *Comité de la guerre,* and became at once an influential personage. His advice was listened to, his plans were adopted : his fortunes were rising : he left the miserable little hotel for a suitable house of his own; he was poor and obscure no longer.

Under these altered conditions his marriage with Désirée was not now desirable. Her fortune was not necessary, for he had plenty of money, and to his present life and surroundings what sort of wife could be more unsuitable than a jealous, touchy, half-educated child not fifteen, brought up in a provincial town, afraid to come to Paris, whose great wish was to spend her life in a dull country place, and for whom the fancy he had for a short time entertained no longer existed?

Early in September, therefore, he wrote to Joseph and to Julie explaining the change in his feelings for Désirée, and announcing that "the affair must be at an end."

Désirée behaved like a foolish child: she cried, refused to give back Napoleon's promise, and was with difficulty persuaded by the representations of her mother, Joseph, and Julie, to leave off resisting what she could not possibly prevent and behave with common sense.

It was certainly hard upon her. Her second engagement, which had been publicly announced for more than a year, and of which she was not a little proud, was broken off by her *fiancé* in a manner which showed he could not have had any real affection for her, and she cried and fretted and poured out her sorrows to the young girls who were her friends; indulging in the childish hope that perhaps after all Napoleon would change his mind and marry her.

But such an idea never entered his mind. He was now deeply in love with the Vicomtesse de Beauharnais, and saw, moreover, that in a marriage with her he would combine inclination and interest. She was older than himself, but, as he had told Madame Permon, to whom he appears to have proposed after breaking his engagement with Désirée and before his proposal to Joséphine, that was not an insuperable objection. Joséphine had beauty, grace, and charm ; she belonged to the *faubourg Saint-Germain*, and although her position had not been so distinguished as in his ignorance of social matters he supposed, still it was undoubtedly very superior to his own, and besides her friends of the *ancien régime* and her knowledge of society, taste, and refinement, she had a little property of her own.

Upon business connected with this she sent for her notary, M. Raguideau, when, some time after the late events, her marriage with Napoleon was decided. Her friends disapproved of it quite as much as Désirée's betrothal to him had displeased those of the Clary family.

M. Raguideau agreed with them. He was shown into Joséphine's room, where she was in bed, but where he found several of her friends, all of whom retired except a young man,[1] who remained standing in the window, and whose presence he did not observe. After talking over the business matters referring to the marriage, the Vicomtesse asked M. Raguideau what he thought of the affair?

He replied that he regretted it exceedingly, and that all her friends highly disapproved ; that she had 25,000 fr. *de rente* and might do very much better ; and he proceeded to point out that Napoleon, besides being younger than herself, was only a penniless soldier, whom she would have to support, and who might any day be killed in battle, leaving her and her children unprovided for. " He may be a very good officer," continued M. Raguideau, " but he has nothing but his sword and cloak. As a confiden-

---

[1] Baron de Méneval.

JOSÉPHINE TASCHER DE LA PAGERIE, VICOMTESSE DE BEAUHARNAIS
EMPRESS OF FRANCE.

tial friend who has your interest at heart, I feel in duty bound to tell you all this ; my conscience would not permit me to do otherwise."

Joséphine laughed, thanked him for his friendship, and calling the young man standing hidden in the window, presented him as General Buonaparte, saying—

"General, did you hear what M. Raguideau said?"

"Yes, I did," answered Napoleon. "He spoke like an honest man, and I esteem him for what he said to you. I hope he will continue to look after our affairs, for he inspires me with confidence."

Napoleon did not forget this episode, but when he was in power he made M. Raguideau *notaire de la liste civile,* and always treated him with kindness.

In March, 1796, was announced the marriage of Napoleon with Joséphine, late Vicomtesse de Beauharnais, and this news stirred up again all Désirée's anger and regret.

She wrote Napoleon a long, foolish, useless letter, full of reproaches and lamentations, assuring him that he had ruined her life, that she would always be constant to him, that life was now nothing but suffering to her, that she wished to die, and a great deal more,[1] equally wanting in pride, self-control, and common sense, a letter, in fact, which her friends had much better have persuaded her to put into the fire. Considering the surveillance exercised over French girls, it is surprising that she should have been permitted to send it at all.

Fortunately the troubles and resolutions of fifteen are not very enduring, but just at first Désirée

[1] "Désirée Clary" (Comtesse d'Armaillé).

seemed inconsolable. Every one was very kind and very sorry for her ; the Buonaparte family, who hated Joséphine and always behaved shamefully to her, were very angry, sympathised with and tried to comfort Désirée, and the broken engagement, which would have done harm to the prospects of a French girl in an ordinary case, did not affect her chances of making a good marriage. For besides her large fortune the fact of her sister being the wife of Napoleon's brother was now considered so great an advantage that it would be easy enough to find her a suitable establishment.

CHAPTER V

1796—1798

Pauline Buonaparte and Fréron — General Duphot — Désirée refuses him—The Embassy at Rome—Fight and death of Duphot—Désirée goes to Paris—Napoleon and Joséphine.

THE mother and sisters of Napoleon were meanwhile still at Marseille, where in their improved fortunes they contrived to amuse themselves very well. They entertained continually; dancing, recitations, acting, and all kinds of diversions filled their thoughts and time and added to the scandalous stories circulated about them. Fréron had, after an absence of some time, returned to Marseille, and pursued his love-affair with Pauline more ardently than ever. Whether, as was supposed by many persons and has been asserted by writers of memoirs well acquainted with the family, there was really a *liaison* between them or not, their letters to each other and the terms upon which they were appeared most unusual, especially among young Frenchmen and girls of respectable families, whose matrimonial arrangements were always conducted by their parents, and whose intercourse was restricted to the most

ceremonious and distant politeness, and by whom un-
chaperoned interviews and private correspondence
were not to be thought of. But Fréron and Pauline
paid no attention to the *convenances*. They took
every opportunity of being together, they kissed
each other, made use not only of their Christian
names, but of the still more familiar " *tu*," which in
Corsica a girl did not even say to her brother, and
the letters Pauline wrote to "Stanislas" were filled
with passionate protestations of love.

"Je n'ai pas répondu à ta lettre d'hier, vu que
j'aimais mieux t'en parler. Mon amour t'est garant
de ma réponse. Oui, je te jure, cher Stanislas, de
n'aimer jamais que toi seul; mon cœur n'est point
partagé, il est donné tout entier. Qui pourrait
s'opposer à l'union de deux âmes qui ne cherchent
que le bonheur et le trouvent en s'aimant? Non, ·
mon ami, ni maman ni personne ne peuvent te
refuser ma main.

"Nonat m'a dit que tu ne devais pas sortir de
toute la semaine; eh bien, il faut prendre patience,
nous nous écrirons et cela nous d'edommagera de la
privation de ne pas nous voir. Je te remercie de ton
attention à m'envoyer de tes cheveux; je t'envoie
également des miens, non pas ceux de Laure, car Laure
et Pétrarque, que tu cites, souvent, n'étaient pas aussi
heureux que nous. Pétrarque était constant, mais
Laure. . . . Non, mon cher ami, Paulette t'aimera
autant que Pétrarque aimait Laure. Adieu, Stanislas,
mon tendre ami, je t' embrasse comme je t'aime."

In another of these effusions she says :—

"Tu connais ma sensibilité et tu n'ignores pas
qui je t'idolâtre. Non! il n'est pas possible à

Paulette di vivre éloignée de son tendre ami Stanislas.

"Ti amo sempre, e passionatissimamente, per sempre amo, bell 'idolo mio, sei cuore mio, tenero amico, ti amo, amo, amo, amo, si amatissimo amanti."

These letters, for a girl of fifteen or sixteen, seem certainly precocious, and one wonders what Madame Buonaparte, who did not like Fréron or the marriage, could have been about to allow all this to go on under her very eyes.

Elisa was the chief confidant of Pauline, and Lucien approved of the marriage. Fréron was a friend of his, a dandy, whose carefully - arranged dress and dissipated habits contrasted with his fanatical craze about the republics of antiquity and the blood-stained methods with which he tried to establish one in France.

He would have been a very good *parti* for Pauline when first they became acquainted, but now he had lost his influential position and become poor, whereas Pauline, the sister of the rising General Buonaparte, was now a most desirable wife, by whom, besides his love for her, he hoped to raise his declining fortunes. He wrote a pressing letter to Napoleon, speaking of his marriage as a settled affair, and begging Napoleon to persuade his mother, who was still unfavourable to it, to allow it to take place in a few days. Napoleon, however, was much annoyed by this letter, for he no longer considered Fréron a suitable husband for Pauline, and had made up his mind to put a stop to the affair. So he wrote to his mother that this marriage was out of the question, and to Joseph and

Lucien that he did not intend Fréron to marry
Pauline, and they were to tell him so.[1]

Pauline was obliged to submit, and though she
first declared she would marry Fréron in spite of her
family, and then became inconsolable and said she
should die, the marriage of her sister Elisa with
M. Bacciocchi, the departure of her mother, Caroline,
and herself to join Napoleon in Italy, and the
distractions and diversions she found there, soon
turned her thoughts into another channel.

Désirée, meanwhile, was still at Genoa, where she
spent the winter of 1797.

Madame Faitpoul, wife of the French minister
there, took a great fancy to her, and was anxious to
arrange her marriage with one of the officers of the
French army now occupying that city.[2]

There was a certain General Duphot, a great friend
of M. and Madame Faitpoul, who was considered to
be a very rising man, and in spite of his general's
rank, was only six-and-twenty. Attracted by the
prospect of an alliance with the family of Napoleon,
and perhaps also by Désirée herself, who was much
admired, he pressed his suit vehemently, and finding
that she declined his advances, he had recourse to the
Faitpouls, who promised to help him, and did all they
could to influence their young friend in his favour.
They assured her that he was a brilliant officer with
excellent prospects, that he was also deeply in love
with her, and was a "constant loyal man," whose
happiness depended entirely upon her decision.

Désirée replied that she did not care about him,

[1] "Les Sœurs de Napoleon," p. 128 (Joseph Turquan).
[2] "Desirée Clary" (Comtesse d'Armaillé).

and never should, and it soon transpired that the
"constant loyal man" had a mistress to whom he
was also much attached, and a son of three years old,
to both of whom Désirée and her mother decidedly
objected.

The Faitpouls tried to explain them away, but
without success, and Duphot, who was obliged to
rejoin the army, could not induce Désirée before his
departure to give him the slightest hope. But after
he was gone M. and Madame Faitpoul resumed their
efforts, having set their hearts upon making up the
marriage. M. Faitpoul especially, who seems to
have been a busy, fussy, meddlesome little man,
some of whose absurd letters on the subject still
exist, so tormented Désirée about General Duphot
that when, soon afterwards, Joseph Buonaparte was
appointed Ambassador to Rome, and was preparing
to move there with his family, Désirée allowed him
to wring from her the admission that if General
Duphot were to succeed in getting himself attached
to the embassy at Rome she would be glad to see
him.

M. Faitpoul set off for Milan, where Duphot then
was, carrying this as a message, by which he was
so encouraged that he went at once to get leave
of absence from Napoleon, and Faitpoul wrote a
bombastic, ridiculous letter to Désirée, who must
have bitterly repented the incautious words she had
been over-persuaded to speak ; for she still disliked
the idea of marrying Duphot, and now he arrived in
Rome bringing with him a letter from Napoleon to
Joseph, saying :—" General Duphot will give you
this letter. He will speak to you of the marriage he

wishes to make with your sister-in-law. I think it would be a good one for her ; he is a distinguished officer." [1]

Another silly, pompous letter came from M. Fait-poul, and, what was worse, Joseph and Julie, finding that Napoleon wished this marriage to take place, tried all they could to persuade Désirée to consent to it. In fact, although in later life she always declared that she had never liked Duphot, and never would have married him, it does not appear at all impossible that she might have been badgered into doing so had not unforeseen circumstances prevented it in the following tragic manner.

Napoleon gave General Duphot a month's leave, and he took up his abode with Joseph Buonaparte and his family at the French Embassy, then in the Palazzo Corsini, and resumed his attentions to Désirée, whom he accompanied in all the excursions, sight-seeing, and other amusements and gaieties going on.

Their enjoyment was, however, considerably interfered with by the disturbed state of the city owing to the hatred between the two parties into which it was divided ; the red Republicans, who sympathised with the French, and the Papal, which was the patriotic party, infuriated by the invasion of the country by the troops of Napoleon, who had robbed the Romans of several provinces, a large sum of money, and many precious works of art. The insolence and blasphemies

---

[1] "Le Général Duphot te remettra cette lettre. Il te parlera du mariage qu'il désire contracter avec ta belle sœur. Je crois cette alliance avantageuse pour elle ; c'est un officier distingué."— "Désireé, Reine de Suède et de Norvège" (Baron Hochschild).

of the revolutionary invaders were continually provoking quarrels, fights, and riots with the excitable,
hot-blooded Italians, and one night in December a
great tumult suddenly arose in the narrow streets
around the French Embassy which caused those who
heard it to start up in alarm.

Joseph Buonaparte and Duphot, by whose emissaries it had been provoked, seized their swords and
ran out. Désirée, Julie, and their mother went on to
the great staircase of the palace, where they waited
in anxiety and terror listening to the shouts and cries
and firing outside.

Presently a group appeared, two of whom were
carrying a third. It was Duphot, covered with blood
and almost insensible. They laid him down, for he
was too seriously wounded to be carried upstairs, and
died in a few minutes.

Although, having lived at Marseille during the
Terror, the Clary family must have been accustomed
to be in the midst of danger and bloodshed, this
horrible scene was too much for Désirée and her
mother. They were obliged to stay where they were
during the Revolution which followed these disturb-
ances, but they had now a horror of Rome, and
were eager to get away as soon as possible. Therefore they received with delight the news that Joseph
had been recalled to Paris, and Désirée, notwithstanding her former dread of going there, was glad to
accept her sister's invitation to accompany them.

As to Madame Clary, she declared she had had
enough of travelling, and went back to Marseille.

Three years had passed since Napoleon and
Désirée had taken leave of each other at Marseille,

years full of momentous changes for them both. The young girl, scarcely more than a child, who fretted and cried after Napoleon, and was afraid to leave the neighbourhood of her native town, had developed into a pretty woman, quite aware of her own attractions, with plenty of suitors in a much better position than Buonaparte had been when she was so eager to be his wife. She had seen other countries, mixed in other society, gone through many experiences, and, as the sister-in-law of the French Ambassador, found her life much more amusing and herself of much more importance than in the old days of the *rue des Phocéens;* and her childish love for Napoleon had changed into a secret, not at all surprising, resentment against him, accompanied by a jealous spite against Joséphine, who was really not at all to blame in the matter, as Napoleon had asked Madame Permon to marry him before his proposals to her.

The rising fortunes of the man who had deserted her, and the ardent devotion to Joséphine, which contrasted so vividly with his lukewarm affection for herself, were evident and irritating enough to Désirée, and her great wish was now to marry a man who could place her in a position in which she should not be obliged to look upon Napoleon as her superior. That she should have succeeded in realising so improbable an aspiration is one of the strangest events of that extraordinary time; and yet twenty years later Napoleon was a ruined prisoner upon a lonely, distant island, while Désirée, sheltered, honoured, and beloved, sat on one of the most ancient thrones in Europe.

In the passionate love-letters of Napoleon to
Joséphine it would be difficult indeed to recognise
the calculating prudence and patronising affection of
his intercourse with Désirée.   Here are some speci-
mens.   These letters are, of course, written in the
second person singular.

> " MILAN, MARMIROLO,
> " *Le* 29 *Messidor*, 9 *heures du soir.*
> " (17 *July*), 1796.

" I have received your letter, *mon adorable amie ;*
it has filled my heart with joy.   I am obliged to you
for the trouble you have taken to give me news of
you ; your health must be better to-day ; I am sure
you are cured.   I strongly advise you to ride, it
cannot fail to do you good.   Since I left you I have
always been sad.   My happiness is to be near you.
Without ceasing I recall to my memory your kisses,
your tears, your amiable jealousy ; and the charms
of the incomparable Joséphine kindle incessantly an
ardent, burning flame in my heart and senses.   When,
free from anxieties and affairs, shall I be able to
pass every moment with you, having nothing to do
but to love you, and nothing to think of but the
happiness of telling you so and proving it ?   I will
send you your horse, but I hope you will soon be
able to join me.   I thought I loved you a few days
ago, but since I saw you I feel that I love you a
thousand times more.   Ever since I knew you I adore
you more every day, which proves that La Bruyère's
saying, ' L'amour vient tout d'un coup,' is false.
Everything in Nature has its own course and its
different degrees of increase.   Ah ! I implore you,

let me see some of your faults ; be less beautiful, less graceful, less tender, less good ; above all, do not be jealous, never cry ; your tears deprive me of reason, burn my blood. Believe that it is no longer in my power to have a thought which is not yours, or an idea which is not in submission to you.

"Rest yourself. Re-establish your health. Come to me ; and at least before we die let us be able to say, for so many days we were happy.

"Millions of kisses, and even to ' Fortune,' [1] in spite of his *méchanceté*.

" BUONAPARTE."

" BRESCIA,
" *Le* 13 *Fructidor, an IV*.
" (10 *August*), 1796.

"I have arrived, *mon adorable amie ;* my first thought is to write to you. Your health and your image have not been out of my thoughts during the whole journey. I shall not be at rest until I receive letters from you. I expect them with impatience. You cannot possibly picture to yourself my anxiety. I left you melancholy, unhappy, and unwell. If the deepest and tenderest love can make you happy you ought to be so. I am overwhelmed with business. Adieu, my sweet Joséphine ; love me, keep well, and think of me often and often.

" BUONAPARTE."

" BRESCIA,
" *Le* 14 *Fructidor, an IV*.
" (31 *August*).

"I am just starting for Verona. I had hoped to receive a letter from you ; it makes me frightfully

---

[1] Joséphine's little dog.

anxious. You were not very well when I left; pray do not leave me in such anxiety. You promised me to be more exact; your tongue and your heart were then in accordance. You to whom Nature has given such sweetness, gentleness, and everything that pleases, how can you forget him who loves you with such fervour? Three days without letters from you; and I have written several times. This absence is horrible; the nights are long, dull, and wearisome; the days monotonous.

"To-day, alone with the thoughts, works, and writings of men and their ostentatious projects, I have not even a note from you that I can press to my heart.

"The *quartier-général* is gone; I start in an hour. I received an express from Paris to-night; there was only the enclosed letter for you; it will give you pleasure.

"Think of me, live for me, be often with your loved one, and believe that for him there is only one calamity he dreads, which would be not to be loved by his Joséphine. A thousand kisses most tender, sweet, and exclusive.

"Send M. Monclas at once to Verona; I will place him. He must arrive before the 18th.

"BUONAPARTE."

CHAPTER VI

1798

IT was in the spring of 1798 that Joseph Buonaparte and his family arrived at Paris.

They took a house in the *rue du Rocher*, where
they were at once surrounded by a large circle of
acquaintances, whom they entertained with lavish
hospitality.

Paris was changed indeed since the stately, polished,
exquisitely-dressed *beau monde* had disappeared, to
make way for the motley throng by whom they were
succeeded. The strangest figures jostled each other
upon the stairs of the new society, the most uncouth
accents and extraordinary manners were to be met
with in their *salons*. In some houses where a rich
republican had married a wife belonging to or connected with the old order, a sprinkling of well-
educated, well-bred, well-dressed people might be
seen, whose presence made the loud, rough voices,
awkward manners, ungrammatical speech, and absurd
dress of the other guests appear still more appalling.

77

Such was the case in the little *hôtel* in the *rue
Chantereine*, where Joséphine and her young son and
daughter, Eugène and Hortense de Beauharnais, preserved the usages of civilised society, and collected
round them as many of their former friends as could
be persuaded to meet the clumsy, unmannerly republican officers, and to endure their barrack-room
familiarity, their perpetual cursing and swearing, and
the manners and customs of their wives.

In the *salon* of Joseph Buonaparte there was at first
no such contrast or mitigation ; but Julie and Désirée
found their surroundings quite good enough, and
entered heart and soul into the pleasures and amusements of their new life. Joseph delighted in entertainments of all kinds ; he gave balls, picnics, and
dinners on an extravagant scale, squandering, like the
rest of the Buonaparte family, the enormous sums of
money with which they were so lavishly supplied by
the generosity of Napoleon. Julie, though her own
tastes were quiet and domestic, was devoted to her
husband, and happy in the life she shared with him,
and Désirée, now a bright, pretty girl of eighteen, had
only to choose from amongst the many rising officers
who were eager to connect themselves with the family
of Napoleon.

The Buonaparte, with whom Désirée was now so
intimately connected, were all united in their malicious
hatred and envy of their sister-in-law ; although
nothing at this time could have been more advantageous to their brother than his marriage with
her.

But she was better born, better bred, and better
dressed than they were ; her friends and habits were

of a different class ; and all this was unendurable to
the greedy Corsican family, whose rapacity and pretensions were increasing day by day.

Everything that could be devised by petty spite to
injure Joséphine they did. They raked up every
indiscretion of her former life, they repeated every
story they could lay hold of to her disadvantage,
whether true or false ; they exaggerated or invented
foolish flirtations to excite the jealous, tyrannical
anger of Napoleon, while all the kindness and
friendly advances of Joséphine were of no avail to
win either friendship or gratitude. And their
behaviour was all the more outrageous because of
its hypocrisy, there being no son or daughter of
Madame Buonaparte, whose conduct did not cause
open scandal.

Désireé was a favourite of theirs and much under
their influence ; she listened eagerly to all the slanders
and abuse of Joséphine, whose position at this time
excited her jealousy ; and watched with irritation the
rising power of Napoleon, whose genius exalted him
so far above every one around him.

One of the offers of marriage she received shortly
after her arrival at Paris was from Junot, *aide-de-
camp* to Napoleon, who afterwards married Laure
Permon and became Duc d'Abrantès.

He sent Marmont to Désireé with his proposals,
which she refused, saying afterwards that Junot was
awkward and shy, which latter defect he appears to
have lost before very long. She also observed that
she did not care for Junot, but liked Marmont much
better, and that if he had spoken for himself perhaps
she would have accepted him. For Désireé was no

longer controlled and directed in these matters by her
family: the Revolution had broken down the barriers
of old ideas in domestic as well as political matters,
and she intended to choose for herself the husband
she preferred. On hearing that Joseph had made a
pathetic incident out of the death of Duphot, calling
him her betrothed husband, she observed—

"Joseph must have wanted to make fine phrases,
then. I never liked Léonard Duphot, and I should
never have married him.'

Another objection to Junot in her eyes was that he
was blindly and absolutely devoted to Napoleon,
whereas her great wish was to find a husband who
might be a rival, not a slave, to the man by whom she
had been deserted, and whose glory and prosperity
were a continual provocation to her.

Napoleon was now triumphant with the victories
of the Italian campaign and preparing to seek fresh
laurels in Egypt; he was the idol not only of the
army, but of most of the new society and the people;
while by many of his generals and other officers he
was regarded with a blind infatuation which grew
and strengthened with the success of his marvellous
career.

There was, however, one especially amongst the
generals who looked upon him with very different
eyes. Jean Baptiste Bernadotte, in talent, courage,
and capacity one of the foremost in the republican
army, was by many people, and by himself amongst
the number, considered a rival to Napoleon. To him
the brilliant Corsican was neither hero, demi-god, nor
master; but simply a comrade inferior to himself in
years, length of service, and fidelity to the Republic;

whose advancement he rather envied, and with whom he frequently disagreed.[1]

Bernadotte, like most of his comrades, had risen from the ranks. His father was *avocat du parlement* at Pau ; his mother had been Mademoiselle Saint-Jean de Boeïl, so she was of gentle birth. Jean Baptiste was her second son, and her unjust partiality for his elder brother made his childhood unhappy, and gave him a dislike to his home, from which he ran away as a boy and enlisted as a common soldier in the *regiment royal de la marine*, with which he was sent to Corsica, and with which also he landed at Marseille when M. Clary objected to receive him into his house.

He had a narrow escape from the clutches of the *Comité du Salut Public*, who had for some caprice ordered his arrest. Fortunately for him it was the eve of the battle of Landrecies, and the tyrants thought it better to defer their proceedings until it was over. But young Bernadotte so distinguished himself in the battle that it was impossible for his persecutors to put their plan into execution, and for the order of arrest was substituted the brevet of *général de division*.[2]

In appearance and manners, as well as in character, Bernadotte was far superior to most of Napoleon's officers. He was tall, dark, and very handsome, the Comte de Rochechouart, in his memoirs, speaks of his fascinating manners, saying that his appearance

---

[1] Bernadotte remarked to his *aide-de-camp* after first seeing Napoleon, " I have seen a young man of six or seven and twenty who wishes to give himself the air of being fifty, and seems to me to be dangerous to the Republic " *(et cela ne me dit rien de bon pour la république).*

[2] Sarrans, " Histoire de Bernadotte."

recalled the great Condé. He was honourable. straightforward, and exceedingly kind-hearted ; his talents and capacity were remarkable, and it was evident that a brilliant career lay before him.

He was thirty-five years old when he first saw Desireé as he rode at the head of some troops entering Paris. She was standing with some friends on a balcony to see them go by, and just as he passed the house he happened to look up and their eyes met. Very shortly afterwards they were introduced to each other, and it was apparent that the attentions he paid her were by no means unwelcome. He was attracted by the pretty, lively girl ; her fortune would, of course, be useful, and her connections still more so to his rising career. She liked and admired him, her family were very much in favour of the marriage, and, what she considered most important of all, every one said that Bernadotte was quite capable of holding his own against Napoleon. When she heard that, she at once accepted him, as she remarked many years afterwards -

"In 1798, General Bernadotte, already very intimate with Joseph Buonaparte, asked me in marriage. He was in a high position and justly enjoyed the esteem of every party. As Minister of War, he had refused his support to the *coup d'état* which some of his companions meditated to destroy the Directory. . . . I scarcely knew him. But this was quite a different thing from what I had refused ; and I consented to marry him when they told me he was a man who could resist Napoleon."[1]

The consent and approval of Buonaparte were

[1] Hochschild.

JEAN BAPTISTE BERNADOTTE, MARSHAL OF FRANCE, CHARLES XIV., KING OF SWEDEN AND NORWAY, OF THE GOTHS AND VANDALS.

written from Cairo, and immediate preparations were made for the wedding, which took place in August, 1798, at Sceaux, where Bernadotte possessed property.

The marriage was only celebrated in a secular form, for Désirée, unlike Julie, was careless and indifferent about religious matters, and Bernadotte, whose family were partly Calvinists, and his comrades mostly without any religion at all, was not likely to be more particular.

Désirée was, as Napoleon had realised, not the sort of woman to be of any use to her husband's career. She was neither clever nor ambitious enough to share the interests and aspirations of a great soldier or statesman, and she had not what Napoleon desired, the good connections, cultivation, and knowledge of the world which would have been invaluable in the wife of a rising man. But to Bernadotte her alliance with the Buonaparte family was then and afterwards of the greatest use, for, notwithstanding the dislike and jealousy that Napoleon always felt for him, when once Bernadotte became the brother-in-law of Joseph his interests were identified with those of the Buonaparte family, and he was certain to receive his share of the place and power soon to fall into their hands.

Désirée's friend, Pauline Buonaparte, was also married. Napoleon, after putting an end to her romance with Fréron, had looked about for another *parti* for her. He had offered her hand to Albert Permon, promising to give him a good post and push him on if he would marry her. For he liked Albert Permon, whose want of fortune was his only drawback and was now easy to remedy. They were old friends and schoolfellows, and Albert was well bred, cultivated, and of high character. But he declined, probably from these very reasons, to become the husband of Pauline, and preferred a less prosperous career without her.

Then Napoleon tried Marmont, who was also of a different class and education from most of his officers, and would have been a good marriage for her ; but Marmont did not approve of Pauline any more than Permon had done. He said that he wished for a wife with whom he could be happy, and he declined the offer that Joseph made him by Napoleon's order. And he says in his memoirs that he had never repented, but had always congratulated himself that he had done so.

General Leclerc, however, was not so particular. He was the son of a rich mill-owner, who had given him a good education, but he had neither talent nor attraction, being a quiet, insignificant-looking young man with no strength either of mind or body. He was deeply in love with Pauline, and eager to marry the sister of his *général-en-chef*. Pauline was quite contented, and the wedding was celebrated in Italy. During all the years of their marriage she treated Leclerc as her slave, showing him no consideration whatever. He was a man of no weight, and was generally looked upon as a harmless, well-meaning individual. Thiébault, indeed, brings a heavy accusation against him in his celebrated memoirs, in which he states that on one occasion, in time of war, Leclerc, who had some ill-feeling towards him owing to his having, in two cases, prevented the unjust condemnation of certain soldiers whose conviction he was trying to force, revenged himself by arresting

a soldier of Thiébault's brigade for some trifling
offence and causing him to be shot; but it is possible that Thiébault, who was not a man whose
impartiality could always be relied upon, may have
put his own interpretation upon the matter, and that
the conduct and motives of Leclerc in this affair may
not have been as guilty as he represents.

CHAPTER VII

1798–1799

AFTER spending a few weeks at Sceaux, Bernadotte, who was then Minister of War, returned with his wife to Paris, where it had been arranged that they should live with Joseph and Julie. In the same house in the *rue du Rocher* were also living Madame Buonaparte, mother of Napoleon, Lucien, and his wife. But it soon appeared that this plan did not answer at all.

That a girl so young and thoughtless as Désirée should have passed so many years in the constant, intimate companionship of such a family as the Buonaparte without any injury to her reputation is a sufficient proof that she possessed none of their vicious tendencies ; but her want of education, reflection, and self-control involved both herself and her

husband in difficulties at the very outset of their
married life.

Although her chief desire had been that Bernadotte should be the rival of Napoleon, Désirée,
incapable of following any serious, consistent line of
conduct, now fell completely under the influence of
the Buonaparte, and allowed herself to be made the
tool of Joseph, by whose directions she spied upon
her husband, repeating to her brother-in-law all she
could find out about his political affairs.

Besides this annoyance, she was perpetually complaining that he could not be always with her, and,
as Madame Junot relates in her memoirs, she cried
when he was obliged to go out, and when he came
home she cried because he would have to go away
again, even if it were not for another week.

One may well wonder what would have happened
if she had had her wish and been the wife of Napoleon ; it is at any rate certain that she would have
experienced very different treatment at his hands.
But Bernadotte was patient and good-tempered ; it
was, of course, not possible that he could make a
companion and confidant of a wife so childish as
this, but he treated her with the indulgence usually
shown to a spoilt child, and since his affairs obliged
him to be often absent, congratulated himself that
Désirée was in the care of her sister, who would look
after her.

But it became evident, before long, that they could
not go on living in Joseph's house. The situation
was intolerable : there was no peace with the constant intrigues of Joseph, Lucien, and their friends.
Bernadotte therefore took a small house called the

Maison Cisalpine, near the *barrière de Monceau*, to which, in spite of her tears and lamentations, Désirée was obliged to accompany him.

He also bought an estate called Lagrange, where he was anxious that she should spend at any rate part of her time, in order that she might be removed from the Buonaparte influence ; but she would do nothing of the kind.   She now liked to be nowhere but in Paris, and as the *Maison Cisalpine* was very near the *rue du Rocher*, she still spent most of her time at her sister's house, mixing herself up in a most inexpedient manner with all the gossip and intrigues that went on there.   She continued her reprehensible practice of prying into her husband's affairs and repeating to Joseph Buonaparte whatever she discovered, or thought she discovered ; and as he was the favourite brother of Napoleon, and Bernadotte was at this time carrying on a secret correspondence with Barras, who was opposed to him, her conduct was not only irritating, but dangerous.

At the same time she had no wish to injure her husband ; on the contrary, she was by this time very much in love with him ; it was merely the inconsiderate mischief-making of an idle, capricious girl, delighted to think herself of importance, and without knowledge or sense enough to see the harm she was doing.

Bernadotte continued to treat her with astonishing forbearance ; he took care to prevent her knowing much of his affairs, only laughing at her and calling her a little spy, until in July, 1799, she was provided with a more harmless and rational interest by the birth of a son in the *Maison Cisalpine*.   Désirée was

greatly delighted with this child, the only one she
ever had, and, according to the teaching of Rousseau,
which she had lately been studying, she decided to
nurse him herself.

Julie was, of course, his godmother, and his godfather was Napoleon, by whose wish he was named
Oscar, after one of the heroes of Ossian, whose poems
were just then very much the fashion.

In October, 1799, Napoleon returned from Egypt,
and Bernadotte ceased to be Minister of War.
Amongst all the generals now regarded by Buonaparte with suspicion as possible rivals, the two most
important were Bernadotte and Moreau ; and of
Moreau he was not afraid, as he once remarked to
Bourrienne, " I believe I shall have Moreau and
Bernadotte against me ; but I am not afraid of
Moreau ; he is weak, without energy, and cares more
for military than political power ; he could be won
over by promising him the command of an army.
But Bernadotte ! he has Moorish blood in his veins ;
he is enterprising and daring ; he is the ally of my
brothers, and does not like me. I am nearly certain
he will be against me, and if he became ambitious
there is nothing he would not venture. The devil of
a fellow can't be gained over ; he is disinterested, and
has brains."

To Napoleon, Bernadotte was, as he called him,
l'homme obstacle.

He saw clearly enough that Buonaparte was
aiming at supreme power, whereas he himself, while
regarding with horror the crimes and cruelties of
the Revolution, believed that, the struggle being
over, the Republic, already powerful and victorious,

would rise out of the crimes and terrors amongst which she was born into a strong, free, well-governed State, able to protect herself from external and internal foes ; as he remarked to Napoleon at an evening party in the *rue Chantereine*, which he had been persuaded by Joseph to attend.

These words, and the significant look by which they were accompanied, so irritated Napoleon that only the ready tact with which Joséphine interposed and changed the conversation averted a quarrel.

A few days later Napoleon, meeting Bernadotte as he came out of the *Théâtre Français*, walked with him to the door of the *Maison Cisalpine* and asked if he would give him a cup of coffee. They went in together, and before separating it was settled that Napoleon and Joséphine should call on the following day and take Bernadotte and Désirée to a *déjeûner* to be given by Joseph at a country place he had just bought, called Mortefontaine.

Accordingly they drove there together, and Joséphine walked about with Julie and Désirée, making herself as charming as she well knew how to do, while they visited cascades, grottoes, conservatories, gardens, &c. ; but Désirée could never forgive her for being Napoleon's wife, and was, perhaps, too much under the influence of the Buonaparte to do justice to the woman who was an object of the envy and spite of that family. It was not a successful day, for Napoleon, who had spent most of the time in walking about in earnest conversation with Bernadotte, endeavouring to bring him round to his own views, had failed in doing so, although supported by his brothers and by Regnault de Saint-Jean d'Angely, and left Mortefontaine with sombre looks, his dislike and distrust increased.

In spite of the idolatry of the army and the mass of the people, Napoleon had dangerous enemies. Besides the royalists, there was the determined republican party, of which Bernadotte was a conspicuous member, and so also was Lucien, although in the day of what was then called the " 18 *Brumaire* " he allowed his affection for his brother to overpower his political opinions.

For during the dangerous and stormy meeting of the Assembly at Saint-Cloud, amidst the clamour and strife, Lucien, who was " President of the Council," undoubtedly saved Napoleon not only from failure and from arrest by the republican party, but from the daggers of the violent minority whose aim was to bring back the Terror.

The following letter, written in 1804 by Bernadotte to Lucien, is interesting as concerning this matter—

" I know very well that you were only *bourgeoise-ment, bon frère* when, as President of the Council, you ought to have heroically voted for the *mise hors la loi* of that brother who violated by armed force the seat of the national representatives. . . . But have I a right to reproach you . . . when I myself yielded to the entreaties of Joseph ? And why ? I ask. Because he is the husband of Julie, the sister of my wife, Désirée. And it is thus that are decided the destinies of a great empire."[1]

Madame Junot, speaking of this event, says—

" On the 19 *Brumaire*, an. VII., my mother, who was much attached to the Buonaparte family, and

[1] " Mémoires de Lucien Buonaparte," t. i. p. 362 (Jung).

at whose house they all constantly were, seeing the
uneasiness of her friend Letizia, invited her and
Madame Leclerc to dine and go to the Faydeau to see
a new piece. . . . We had no news till seven o'clock;
my mother ordered the carriage and we set off for the
theatre, with Madame Letizia, Madame Leclerc, and
my brother Albert. . . . As we were waiting for the
second piece the curtain rose and the principal actor,
coming forward, announced : ' Citizens, a revolution
has just taken place at Saint-Cloud ; General Buonaparte has fortunately escaped the daggers of the
répresentant Arena and his accomplices. The assassins are arrested.' "[1]   (At these words Pauline gave a
shriek and fell into a hysterical fit of sobbing and
crying.) " Madame Letizia became as pale as marble,
and, bending towards her, said in a severe tone,
' Paulette, what is all this noise for? Hold your
tongue. Did not you hear that nothing has happened to your brother? Silence! Get up—we
must go and make inquiries. . . ."

"'Where will you go?' said my mother to
Madame Letizia when the servant asked for orders.
' To the *rue du Rocher* or the *rue Chantereine ?* '

"' *Rue Chantereine*,' said she, after a moment's
thought. 'Joseph will not be at home, and Julie will
not know anything.'

"' If we went to the *rue Verte ?* '[2] said I to Madame
Letizia.

"' It would be useless. Christine will not know
anything, and we might frighten her; no, no, *rue
Chantereine.*'

" We arrived in the *rue Chantereine ;* but at first

---

[1] " Salons de Paris," t. v. p. 25.   [2] Lucien's.

it was impossible to get near the house. The confusion was deafening : coachmen shouting and swearing, men on horseback galloping up, knocking aside
every one before them, people on foot asking for
news or calling out that they could give it. . . . And
all this tumult and commotion on a cold, dark,
November night. . . . Hippolyte de Rastignac, one
of the most intimate *habitués* of my mother's *salon*,
recognising our carriage and not seeing who were with
us, exclaimed, '*Eh bien! voilà de la belle besogne!*
Your friend Lucien, Mademoiselle Laure, . . . has
just made a king of his brother the corporal!'

"As M. de Rastignac was close to the carriage
door, I was obliged to tell him hastily to be quiet,
and to touch his hand, for he did not understand.
Then he recognised Madame Letizia and Madame
Leclerc, whom he saw every day at my mother's,
and ran away. . . . Madame Letizia sent Albert to
ask if General Buonaparte had returned from Saint-
Cloud. At that moment an officer galloped into the
courtyard, . . . and by the lights from the hall we
recognised my brother-in-law, M. de Geouffre.

" ' It's all right,' he cried. . . . ' All is over ; there is
to be a Consulate, of which two are members of the
Directory, the third is General Buonaparte.'

" 'That is a pike who will eat up the other two !'
said my mother.

" '*Oh, Panoria!*' cried Madame Letizia, reproach-
fully ; for she still believed in the pure republicanism
of her son."

Unable to do anything openly against Bernadotte,
Napoleon sought an occasion to get him out of the
way, and gave him the painful and difficult task of

pacifying Bretagne and La Vendée, the strongholds
of the royalists ; an enterprise wherein he could gain
no glory, as he would be fighting against his own
countrymen.

Bernadotte accordingly went to Rennes, then the
headquarters of the Army of the West, accompanied
by his wife, who amused herself very well there,
being greatly admired and receiving considerable
attention from the officers, who were ready enough
to entertain the pretty young wife of their favourite
general.

But in the autumn (1800) came the news that
Portugal, supported by England, had declared war
upon Spain, and that, France having allied herself
with the latter power, troops were to be sent at once
to Bordeaux and Bayonne. All the grenadiers now
in Bretagne and La Vendée were ordered to Tours
to form the reserve of what was now to be called the
Army of Portugal, of which the command was to be
given to Bernadotte.

Désirée was obliged, therefore, to set out at once
for Tours with her husband, and she would probably
have found life there still pleasanter than at Rennes,
for the ancient capital of Touraine, the garden of
France, with its broad river, ancient walls and towers,
bright sun and profusion of flowers and fruit, besides
the gay shops and amusements, was especially in
those days a most delightful place.

But her stay there was short ; for Bernadotte, who
did not at all desire the command of the Army of
Portugal, decided to return to Paris on the pretence
of escorting his wife and child, but really to see the
First Consul and induce him to alter his plan.

Having succeeded in doing so, the command of the
Army of Portugal was given to Leclerc, the husband
of the beautiful and senseless Pauline Buonaparte,
and Bernadotte went back to Rennes, leaving his
wife and child in Paris.

Although Désirée was now and always fond of her
husband and on perfectly good terms with him, the
days when she could not bear him to be out of her
sight were at an end. She was quite happy with her
baby, her sister, and the numerous friends with whom
she was surrounded, and she entered with natural
enjoyment into the gaieties of Paris, where every one
was eager to throw off the gloom and depression of
the Terror and plunge into the feverish pursuit of
pleasure and luxury.

The *émigrés* were returning, as fast as they could
get their names *rayés* (struck off the proscribed list),
to the scene of their former prosperity, now so
changed as to be almost unrecognisable. In consequence of the inconvenient habit, which the French
still retain, of changing the names of the streets to
suit their political opinions, it was nearly impossible
to find the way about. The Terrorists having forbidden the words "*palais*" or "*hôtel*," the inscriptions
"*maison ci-devant* Bourbon," "*maison ci-devant Conti*,"
"*propriété nationale*," &c., were still to be seen upon
the walls of those ancient edifices, with here and
there inscriptions about "liberty and fraternity or
death." Figures of saints were thrown down, and
those of philosophers put in their places; the *hôtels*
of the *noblesse* were occupied by the rich *parvenus*
who had bought them, and by whom they had been
filled with a confusion of costly and tasteless furni-

ture which looked as if it had been put there by mistake. Ancient halls and *salons* where harmony and grace had formerly reigned supreme had now the appearance of showrooms in upholsterers' shops, and were inhabited by people who, having no idea how to behave in civilised society, presented the most ridiculous appearance, and frequently thought to give themselves consequence by excessive impoliteness. Others, in spite of the hatred they professed to entertain for whatever was connected with the old society, tried to imitate the *grands seigneurs* of the ancient court, the models they especially chose being MM. de Talleyrand, de Valence, de Narbonne,[1] and de Vaudreuil, of whom they made the most absurd caricatures.

The *chaises à porteurs*, or sedan chairs, had disappeared, giving place to *cabriolets de places*, or cabs, in which many a returned *émigré*, as they passed him in the streets, recognised the confiscated carriages of his family or friends.

In the shops along the quays and streets they constantly saw their own things—books, furniture, portraits of their ancestors or of those they loved who had perished in the Terror.

Madame de Genlis, writing of her experiences on her return from exile, says—

" I stopped on the *quais*, before little shops in which I saw books whose bindings bore the arms of

---

[1] Comte Louis de Narbonne. It was told of him that once while fighting a duel he kept between his lips a rosebud which had been given him, and when it accidentally dropped he stooped without discontinuing his stroke, and having picked it up, went on without interruption to disarm his opponent. (" Salons de Paris," t. iv. p. 89, Duchesse d'Abrantès.)

a great number of people of my acquaintance, and in other shops I saw their portraits exposed for sale. One day I went into the shop of a dealer who had at least twenty or thirty of them; I recognised them all, and my eyes filled with tears as I thought that three-quarters of these unfortunate people had been guillotined, and the rest, ruined and exiled, were wandering in foreign lands.

" Leaving this shop, I walked along the boulevard ; in a few minutes a man passed me carrying some pretty osier baskets. . . . I chose half a dozen, and as I had no money with me, and could not have carried them . . . I went into the open door of a wine-shop . . . asked for ink and paper, and rapidly wrote my address, which I read aloud to the basket-maker, upon which the lad at the counter exclaimed—

" ' Well ! you are at home !'

" ' What !'

" ' Yes, *pardi !* you are in the *ci-devant hôtel de Genlis !'*

" In fact, it was the house in which my brother-in-law, the Marquis de Genlis, had lived for fifteen years. It was impossible to recognise it ; the ground floor was turned into a row of shops. . . ."

Suppers were no longer in fashion—"the hours were so changed as not to admit of them ; plays did not finish till eleven in the evening ; after dinner people paid visits or went to the theatre. . . . Formerly supper was the end of the day . . . the suppers in Paris were celebrated for their gaiety ; people talked and amused themselves without interruption, because they sat where they chose, next those they liked best. Perfect politeness prevailed . . .

ANCIENT HÔTEL DE NOAILLES.

one treated all one's guests with the same respect
and consideration. . . . When one went to the dining-
room, the master of the house did not rush to the
woman of highest rank, lead her to the other end of
the room, passing triumphantly before all the rest of
the women to place her with pomp by his side at the
table. The other men did not precipitate themselves
towards the ladies to give them their arms. The
ladies went out of the drawing-room first, those who
were nearest the door taking the lead with some
slight excuse or compliment . . . the gentlemen
followed ; every one sat down to the table as they
liked, and the host and hostess always contrived
without ceremony to get the four most distinguished
women of the party near them." [1]

[1] " Mémoires de Madame de Genlis," t. v. pp. 82-3.

CHAPTER VIII

1800

Napoleon at the Tuileries--Désirée and her friends—Lucien Buonaparte — Elisa — Pauline — Caroline—Murat — Letters of Bernadotte.

NAPOLEON was now First Consul, the second was Cambacérès, the third Lebrun ; but, as Madame Permon had foretold, the two latter were mere shadows to their chief, whose power was increasing day by day.

The little *hôtel* in the *rue Chantereine* was no suitable residence for the head of the French nation, and the palace of the Luxembourg did not satisfy him as the centre either of political or social affairs.

The Tuileries, the ancient palace of the Bourbons, as the Louvre, Vincennes, and, earlier still, the vanished *Palais de la Cité* had been of the Valois— the palace of the Tuileries alone was the home to which the secret thoughts of the great genius who was already in fact, though not in name, sovereign of France naturally turned.

The great majority of the people, far from objecting to the idea, received it with enthusiasm, and preparations were made for the move from the

Luxembourg to the Tuileries to be conducted with as much state as was practicable under the existing order of things.

It was not altogether easy. No kind of ceremony or display had been permitted by the Directory; nobody but the ministers had carriages or any sort of liveries; the members of the Council were obliged to go in cabs; the only splendour or striking effect possible in such a procession being the troops, especially Napoleon's favourite regiment, whose grey uniform he so often wore, the *guides*, or *chasseurs de la garde*, commanded by Bessières and Eugène de Beauharnais.

It was an important day for Napoleon, whose first exclamation when he awoke that morning was, "We shall sleep to-night in the Tuileries!" And he embraced Joséphine, joyfully repeating the words.

His carriage was perfectly plain and unadorned, but was drawn by six magnificent white horses, the gift of the Emperor of Austria. Cambacérès sat by his side, and Lebrun opposite; Joséphine, who as yet assumed no attributes of royalty or state, arrived first, accompanied by several ladies.

The crowds assembled in the streets were delirious with enthusiasm, but as the procession entered the court of the Tuileries, still encumbered with the *débris* of the Revolution, the eyes of the Consuls fell upon this inscription: "The 10th August, 1792, royalty is abolished in France, and will never be restored." [1]

As they read these words, indignant exclamations

---

[1] "Salons de Paris," t. v. p. 14.

and subdued curses broke from the lips of some, and a singular and significant smile was to be seen on the face of Napoleon, who overheard them as he triumphantly entered the palace.

Some of the young girls who were now becoming conspicuous members of the new society, such as Laure Permon, who had just married General Junot, had, owing to the closing of all religious houses, been brought up at home, where they were constantly associated with relations and friends of education and distinction, and acquired in the *salons* of their mothers a knowledge of the world which would have scandalised their convent-bred grandmothers, but which proved very useful to themselves ; especially if, as occasionally happened, their friends yielded to circumstances, and married them to the young officers of the new *régime* who were eager to ally themselves with the old one.

But although the closing of the convents had sent Désirée back to her father's house, there was no social instruction to be gathered in the respectable household in the *rue des Phocéens*, and her inexperience and ignorance of the world were an additional disadvantage to her now that she was left alone with plenty of money, beauty, very little education, no decided religious principles, and such people for her most intimate friends as the Buonaparte.

Three worse friends for a young woman thrown by herself into a mixed, extravagant, fast society than the three Buonaparte sisters cannot well be imagined, and it seems surprising that Désirée should have passed safely through dangers and difficulties which proved too great for many whose talents and advantages were far superior to hers. But her instincts were good, she had no bad tendencies, was kind-hearted and affectionate, though without the capability of any deep and passionate feeling ; which was probably a considerable safeguard to her. Her faults were trivial and childish, not such as to lead to any tragic or disastrous consequences, and her sunny, light-hearted nature, easily vexed, easily consoled, and easily pleased, made her a general favourite.

It was fortunate, indeed, for her that she had not a husband selfish and tyrannical like Napoleon, nor a dissipated spendthrift like Junot ; but that Bernadotte, besides his brilliant talents, possessed a strong character and common sense, by which and his other good qualities he guided himself and her to the safe and exalted position in which they remained securely established when the thrones and fortunes of their companions had crumbled away.

Lucien about this time lost his first wife, an excellent but perfectly uneducated woman, who left him with two little daughters. He had quarrelled with Napoleon, to whom he refused to bow down like the rest of his family, and had gone to Italy.

Elisa, wife of Bacciocchi, whose name her family had changed from Pasquale to Félix, was the only one of the sisters who possessed cultivated tastes. She had been educated at Saint-Cyr as *élèse de Saint-Louis*, and professed an enthusiastic love of literature and art. Her marriage had rather displeased Napoleon, as it was concluded without consulting him, and Bacciocchi, though a good-natured, harmless sort of man, was a nonentity, and cared for very little but playing the violin. Elisa soon got tired of him and turned her attention to somebody else.

Her favourite brother was Lucien, whose intellectual tastes she shared; her house, like his, was frequented by artists, poets, musicians, and authors of all kinds, but the absurd, pedantic airs she gave herself irritated Napoleon. She was the least good-looking of the sisters, being angular and awkward; people said she looked like a boy in petticoats, a type never admired in France. She was then about three-and-twenty and Lucien five- or six-and-twenty years old.

Pauline, who was three years younger than Elisa, was surpassingly beautiful, and her folly even exceeded her beauty, notwithstanding which she was Napoleon's favourite sister, and if she had any real affection for anybody it was for him. He was also the only person she was afraid of, or who had any influence over her. Never having been sent to school or given proper instruction, and having no capacity for learning, she was absolutely ignorant, her love-affairs were countless, and her vanity and selfishness almost incredible, but yet she had a certain friendliness and good temper which made her on the whole preferable to Annunziata, or, as she now chose to be called, Caroline, although perhaps when one considers the characters of the two sisters, it is difficult to see much to choose between them. Still, the vanity of Pauline was so transparent and her folly so outrageous as to be often really amusing.

But there was nothing amusing about Caroline's bad qualities, and she had not the charm of Pauline's grace and beauty to make them less insupportable to those who suffered from them.

She was nearly as ignorant as Pauline, and with less excuse, for being younger than the others at the time the Buonaparte family emerged from obscurity she had been placed at the school of the celebrated Madame Campan, where all the rich members of the new society were eager to send their daughters ; for Madame Campan had been one of the bedchamber women of Marie Antoinette, and knew how it was usual for girls of good position to speak and look and behave.

Caroline was eighteen years old, and had recently been married to Joachim Murat, one of the most brilliant officers of Napoleon, who had given his consent rather unwillingly, as he was beginning to wish his family to connect themselves with more distinguished people. Since the *faubourg Saint-Germain* held aloof, and foreign princes were not yet to be thought of, he would have preferred to give Caroline to Moreau ; Lannes also wanted to marry her, but she had fallen violently in love with Murat. Joséphine, to whom she never showed the least gratitude, took her side in the affair, and it was agreed in one of those family councils so useful and so frequent in France, that the marriage should be allowed.

Napoleon remarked that if he had given his sister to any one of noble blood the Jacobins would at once have made an outcry and declared that he wanted to destroy the Republic, but at any rate they could not object to Murat, who was one of the bravest of his officers, and had risen from the ranks.

Joachim Murat was the son of an innkeeper in the south. His parents intended him to be a priest, and got him a nomination for the college at Cahors, where he studied for some years, wearing the *soutane* like his companions. But at the end of this time, being on his way to spend a holiday with his parents, he had to pass through Toulouse, and was so delighted with that town and the diversions it offered that he stayed there until he had spent every sou of the money given him for his journey. What was to be done? A cavalry regiment (*chasseurs*) was passing through Toulouse; he threw off his *soutane* and enlisted.

For two years he went on well, and rose to be quartermaster, when some act of insubordination led to his dismissal. Then a relation of his, a draper, took him into his shop; but this sort of life did not suit him at all. The Revolution was approaching rapidly; three cavalry soldiers were ordered to be sent up from each department to form the *garde constitutionelle* of the unfortunate Louis XVI., and Murat, by the protection of the deputy Cavaignac, succeeded in getting himself appointed one of them. Of the two others one was Bessières.

From that time his promotion was rapid, and he attracted the attention of Napoleon, who made him his *aide-de-camp*. It was while he was at Milan that he fell in love with Caroline Buonaparte. He was then thirty-six years of age.

To the greater number of Napoleon's generals the acquisition of political power was not the object of their wishes or endeavours, for the majority of them were gallant, reckless young soldiers, who cared for nothing but battles and plunder. Their whole delight was to be either fighting for the glory of France and of themselves, or else spending in the revels and dissipations of Paris the enormous sums of money which they had seized or with which their services had been rewarded by Napoleon.

Bernadotte differed from them in his ambition as well as in many other respects ; but even the absorbing interests with which at this time his mind was engrossed did not prevent his giving careful consideration to the proceedings of the young wife he had left at Paris, in the constant companionship and influence which he did not like but could not prevent. For it was the Buonaparte connection which had been the chief advantage gained by his marriage, and the more his wife identified herself with that family, the better for his career. On the other hand, the outrageous conduct of Elisa, Pauline, and Caroline was known to every one except Napoleon ; and Bernadotte, who gave no cause for scandal himself, and had no taste for the folly and dissipation in which so many of his comrades delighted, was resolved that Désirée should not be led into them either.

He wrote to her often, took care to know what she was doing and who were her associates, persuaded her to take lessons in order to improve her imperfect education, and gave directions on various matters, to which and to the advice and opinions of her sister

Julie she seems to have attended, being neither obstinate nor self-willed.

The following letters, written to her at Paris during his absence in Bretagne, show the terms they were upon and the rather paternal tone of Bernadotte, natural enough when one recollects that there were seventeen years between him and his wife, and that their marriage may certainly be considered a *mariage de raison* :—

"RENNES, 16 *Floréal, an IX.*

" I send you, *ma bonne petite*, a copy of the letter I am writing to Joseph, relating to Ernouf. His *aide-de-camp* is taking it. I beg you to attend to it, so that you may be able to help Ernouf by making Joseph understand all the claims he has to his esteem and my friendship.

" As I employ you in this matter, you can judge of the degree of interest I attach to the success of the affair. . . . I know your shyness and your invincible objection to asking favours ; but, *ma bonne petite*, the position of Ernouf is such that if he lets this opportunity slip it will be very difficult to find another.

" I trust to your friendship that as soon as you get this letter you will go to Mortefontaine, unless Joseph is at Paris, and that you will induce him to speak to his brother, or at any rate to write to him. It would be best if he could see him, he will no doubt decide so.

" I have not had a line from you since my departure. I shall become jealous if you go on being so idle. You know that I do not like extremes ; in everything there should be a happy medium.

"My affection for you will last as long as the existence of

"J. BERNADOTTE."

"PS.—I am curious to know what masters you are having. Love to the family."

"PONTIVEY, *le* 24 *Floréal, an IX.*

"I reply, *ma bonne Désirée,* to your letter of the 16 *Floréal,* and begin by thanking you for your kind exertions in favour of General Ernouf. . . . Whatever may be the issue, I am not any the less grateful for the trouble and interest you have taken.

"I have too much esteem for you to be jealous, but I love you enough to desire you to be happy, which one cannot be if one is restrained or followed. Your docility charms me, and I am delighted that you have decided to go on taking dancing lessons.[1] You would be very good if you would go on also with your music. Then you would be divine.

"Chiappe goes to see you too early, but his friendship for me, his character, and your reserve tranquillise me.

"*Adieu, ma bonne amie;* I embrace you as I love you, that is to say very tenderly.

"J. BERNADOTTE."

---

[1] To dance well was then essential in good French society. M. de Trénis was said to be the best dancer ever known. Some one once said to him, "Je vous ai vu danser hier"; to which he gravely replied, "Etiez vous bien placé?" He was a general favourite, but his fate was melancholy; he died mad at Bicêtre; poor and forgotten except by one or two friends who used to go and see him and take him clothes.

" PONTIVEY, *le* 6 *Priarial, an IX.*

"MON AMIE,—I am anxious to know, *ma bonne amie,* if you have at last decided to wean Oscar. He seems to me to be old enough to bear that privation. Anyhow, you are, of course, free to act as your experience and affection for him seem best to you. The desire to preserve his beauty ought to make you incline to vaccination, but in this, as in the other matter, do just as you like. . . .

" I shall not buy any horses unless I get very good ones ; but it does not seem to me that yours will do much longer.

" It is folly to torment yourself. You are young, and should amuse yourself, and my affection and advice ought to make you reasonable. The spring-time of life passes like a shadow, and winter, with its icicles, overtakes us only too quickly.

" If, at the end of this month, Buonaparte does not send me to Flanders, I will write and remind him of his promise, and if there is nothing new you might come and spend a month with me if you liked. In spite of the wish I have to see you, I am very anxious that you should go on improving your education. Accomplishments such as dancing and music are very essential. Some lessons from M. Montel would be useful to you. I see that I am giving too much advice, so I will say no more. I kiss your lips.

" Ton ami,

"J. BERNADOTTE."

The next letter is written on official paper.

"Armée de l'Ouest"—République Française
—Liberté—Égalité.

"Au Quartier Général Pontivey,
"*Le 8 Priarial, an IX.*

*De la République Française, Une et Indivisible.
Bernadotte, Conseiller d'État, Général en Chef à sa
Petite.*

"During the last week, *ma bonne Désirée,* I have written you four or five letters; I do not imagine that they have not reached you.

"I am quite well. I wrote you a long letter by the last courier; let me have news of you, and let me know if you have received the letter in which I speak of what I am going to send you.

"You tell me nothing about your progress in dancing, music, and other things. When one is absent one likes to hear whether *sa petite* is profiting by the lessons she is taking. Adieu. I kiss your little eyes; do the same to Oscar.

"Ton ami,

"J. Bernadotte."

Désirée seems to have taken offence at something in her husband's letters, for in the next one he says—

"Pontivey, *le* 18 *Priarial, an IX.*

"I do not know, *ma bonne Désirée,* what strictness you can find in my letter of the 6th, of which you complain. I have had no wish, either in that or in any other, to speak in any way but as a true and sincere friend. I sincerely regret that you should have attached any other signification to them. I do not wish to treat you like a child, but as a friend and a reasonable woman ; all that I say should tend to convince you of this. Gérard must have written to you. His letter should prove to you that you are free to make your own arrangements. I think as you do about accomplishments ; whatever gifts one may have they are difficult to acquire, and plodding is tiresome. But still, with a little patience and resolution, one succeeds when one has not finished the fifth lustre.

"Give me news of your health, and tell me you love me. I embrace you tenderly.

"J. BERNADOTTE.

"PS.—Your little horse is quite well."

CHAPTER IX

1800

SOCIETY at Paris was still in a state of confusion. Rarely did any great dinner or evening party take place at the Tuileries without some absurd mistake or ludicrous story being circulated after it for the diversion of those who watched with curious eyes the development of the new order of things.

At Saint-Cloud and La Malmaison, especially at the latter, it was much pleasanter, more simple, and less formal. All through the Consulate and Empire those favourite abodes of Napoleon were the scenes of relaxations and amusements in which he took the greatest interest and pleasure. He liked the dinners out of doors, the dances, theatricals, and music which perpetually went on.

Every week Joséphine gave a concert at La Malmaison at which the best *artistes* in Paris appeared.

Nauderman, the harpist; Baillot, the violinist; and amongst others the celebrated singer, Garat, who had once, like Michau, the actor, also a frequenter of La Malmaison,[1] narrowly escaped from the claws of the revolutionists.

It was in the days of the Directory that on one occasion he was taking a walk outside Paris, and on his return found the *barrière* closed. He was not allowed to enter the city, but was arrested and conducted to the *corps-de-garde*, when it appeared that he had no passport or papers about him.

"*Citoyens,*" said he to the men who had arrested him, "let me go. I am Garat, the singer."

"You are Garat, the singer! That is very easy to say, but how are you going to prove it to us?"

"*Parbleu!* nothing is easier!" he replied. "By singing."

And he began to sing *La Gasconne* with a voice so enchanting that when he had finished his captors broke into an estasy of admiration, exclaiming—

"It is true! No one but Garat could sing like that." And he was at once released.

.During the first years of the Consulate the road from La Malmaison to Paris was by no means safe, owing to the bands of robbers infesting the country in consequence of the disorders and confusion that still prevailed; and there was also the danger of falling a victim to some attack upon the First Consul, against whom there were many conspiracies.

Junot had lately married Laure Permon, then a girl of sixteen, and they both took continual and lead-

[1] "A Leader of Society at Napoleon's Court," p. 182 (Catherine Bearne).

ing parts in the private theatricals at La Malmaison. One evening they were driving back to Paris after a rehearsal, and as it was getting dark and they were rather later than they had intended to be, they were going at a rapid pace; their carriage being a light one and preceded by a *piqueur*, who cleared out of the way any of the little carts belonging to the peasants, market-gardeners, &c., which might obstruct the road.

It was in winter, and Junot was driving; his liveries were almost exactly like those of the First Consul.

Suddenly a large faggot was flung before the horses, stopping them with a sudden jerk. Madame Junot uttered a cry and Junot an oath as a tall man, wrapped in a large cloak or coat, with his hat pulled down over his face, stood by the carriage, the forms of two or three others being dimly discernible a few yards off.

"Who are you?" cried Junot; but instead of answering, the tall man, after looking as closely at him as the darkness permitted, exclaimed—

"It is not the First Consul!"

"What do you want with him?" called out Junot, as the man turned rapidly away to rejoin his companions.

"To give him a petition," replied he, stopping and hesitating for a moment. He then disappeared with the rest.

Junot and his wife returned at once to La Malmaison to relate their adventure. Junot left Laure in the carriage while he went to Napoleon, who presently sent Duroc to bring her through the garden to his cabinet, where were also Cambacérès and Bourrienne. Duroc was about to withdraw, when the First Consul called him back.

"Madame Junot," said Napoleon, in a serious but friendly voice, "I have sent for you so that your version may throw a little more light upon Junot's, for I confess that what he tells me seems to me most astonishing."

Laure accordingly related what had happened, and the First Consul, turning to Cambacérès, said—

"That's it! And this man pretended he had a petition to give me?"

"He had, in fact, a folded paper in his hand. I saw it when he was near us."

"Could you distinguish his features?"

"The whole appearance of him, yes, General; but not his features at all; his hat covered not only his eyes, but all the upper part of his face."

"And what was his figure?"

"That of a very tall, thin man."

"Taller than Bourrienne?"

"Yes. But, after all, I may be mistaken: it was late, and I was badly placed to judge of the proportion of a figure."

The First Consul made her repeat the account three times, and was pleased that there was not the slightest variation in the statements. Taking her by the ear he led her to the other end of the room and said—

"Listen! Take care you don't repeat a word of all this to Joséphine and Mademoiselle Hortense. This is a *prohibition*, you understand, and you know how far it extends. Do you comprehend me, I say?"[1]

Laure looked at him in silence, and he went on impatiently—

" I allude to your mother, Lucien, Joseph. In fact, I require your silence for the house in the *rue Sainte-Croix* just the same as for all others; promise me."

" Well, I promise."

" On your word of honour?"

" My word of honour?" and she laughed.

"What are you laughing at? You ought not. Give me your word without laughing."

" General, the more you tell me not to laugh, the less I can keep serious. You laugh so little that you ought to be glad to see other people laugh."

He looked at her. " You are a singular person," he said. " Then you promise?"

" I promise."

" It is well! Let us go to dinner; you and Junot will stay."

" But, General, we are expecting people to dinner."

" Well! they will dine without you. . . . Go all of you into the dining-room, and do not mention anything. I will follow you."

Just as they were rising from the table after dinner Napoleon whispered to Laure, " You see that the rascals *(les méchants)* can do nothing to me. They have not even the power to make me fear."[2]

It was not until the spring of 1802 that Napoleon established himself at Saint-Cloud, and then it was without abandoning La Malmaison, of which he was

---

[1] The conspirators were never discovered.

[2] "Salons de Paris," t. v. p. 40 (Madame Junot).

NAPOLEON AT LA MALMAISON.

passionately fond. He had a short cut made from one to the other, so that it was easy to go whenever he fancied.

"The Tuileries," he observed, "are really a prison ; one can't go to a window to get a little air without becoming an object of attention to three thousand people."

Madame Junot, *née* Laure Permon, was a great favourite of Napoleon. He had known her from childhood. Her parents had received his father into their house when he was ill at Montpellier, and had nursed him until he died : they had shown him constant kindness when he was at college with their. son Albert, and, though the foolish quarrel made by Madame Permon after she refused to marry him had for some time broken off their intercourse, when Laure became the wife of Junot, Napoleon behaved with great kindness and generosity to them. Laure was not only extremely pretty, but brilliantly clever, amusing, and fascinating, and the fact of her being the daughter of those to whom he was under such obligations and the wife of one of his greatest friends would not apparently have protected her from his lawless love if, young as she was, she had not known very well how to take care of herself.[1]

Désirée strongly resembled her in appearance, though not in talent, nor yet, it may be remarked, in the headlong extravagance which in after years proved the ruin of Laure and her children.

Between Désirée and Napoleon there was now nothing but the friendship which her connection

[1] "A Leader of Society at Napoleon's Court," p. 165 (Catherine Bearne).

with his family made natural ; both her love and
her resentment had subsided, and she was from
henceforth always upon good terms with him,
rather flattered by his liking for her, which never
changed into any stronger feeling nor yet into
one of those capricious fancies so disastrous to
the women who inspired them. Even the growing
distrust between Bernadotte and the First Consul
scarcely affected her friendly relations with the latter,
whose displeasure she never incurred by extravagance, flirtations, or intrigues, and whose suspicions
were never directed to her as they were to those
women whose connection with the *faubourg Saint-
Germain* suggested connivance with his enemies.

Any influence she may have had was always used
by her to help those in danger or difficulty, and her
affection for her sister Julie, far from being interfered with by the distractions of society or the new
interests in her life, grew and strengthened as time
went on.

The opera balls were amongst the favourite diversions of the time, masks and disguises lending
themselves to many a simple mystification, malicious
trick, imprudent love intrigue, or absurd adventure.

Several of these latter befel M. de Rivière, one of
the most ardent followers of the follies and dissipations of the day, and who, married to a young and
attractive wife, tormented her life by the incorrigible
way in which he ran after other women.

On one occasion he was accosted by a masked
figure of graceful appearance to whom he attached
himself with admiration and curiosity, but whom all
his entreaties failed to induce to remove her mask, or

to grant him a rendezvous.[1]   Having amused herself
with him during many balls, extending over more
than one carnival, allowing, or rather encouraging,
him to make love to her and yet managing to keep
him at a distance, she at last fixed a time when
all this reserve and coldness should come to an
end.   It was at the last ball of the carnival, towards
the end of the evening ; Rivière had in his pocket
the key of the box he had secured, to which he
hastened to conduct his companion, overjoyed at
the success at length within his grasp.

Just as he was about to open the door of the
box his unknown companion stopped short, saying
as they stood under the lamp which shed its full
light upon her—

" Before we cross this threshold you had at least
better look at me and see if you recognise me."
And pulling off her mask, she disclosed the features
of the *parfumeuse* to whose shop he was in the habit
of going—who had been a well-known and rather
notorious beauty, at one time very much in vogue,
whose wit and mischievous pranks had been celebrated, who still retained her slight, graceful figure,
but who was on the eve of her sixtieth birthday,
as she informed him with shouts of laughter, amid
which he retired in a rage.

Another time, attracted by the beauty of a figure
which, though not tall, was exceedingly graceful
and well-proportioned, he approached and offered
his arm, which was accepted, and they proceeded
to the ball-room together.   They passed a considerable part of the evening first among the

[1] " Thiébault Mémoires," t. iii. p. 167.

dancers and then wandering about in dimly-lighted rooms and corridors, Rivière making violent love to his unknown companion, admiring the beauty of the hand and arm he was holding, and listening with sympathy to the confidences she poured into his ear.[1]

Domestic unhappiness, a careless, faithless husband, a life made miserable by jealousy—all her griefs met with ready sympathy from Rivière, who advised her to take her revenge, declared his adoration, and besought her to allow him to console her. As his entreaties became more and more vehement they came to the door of a box, to which he had purposely led her and of which he had the key. Suddenly opening the door, he drew her in, and throwing himself at her feet, implored her to unmask, which she immediately did. It was his wife, whose unexpected appearance had more effect than she had intended, for it made him not only ridiculous but ill, and caused her to regret the success of her plan.

A splendid *fête* was also given by Berthier, then minister of war, to celebrate the pacification of La Vendée.

This *fête* consisted of theatricals and a ball, and was, of course, attended by the First Consul, his family, and all the important personages in Paris. There was a perfect rush to get tickets for it, and so great was the crowd of those invited that many carriages leaving the Pont Royal at nine o'clock did not reach the War Office until four in the morning. Those who had arrived

[1] " Thiébault Mémoires," t. iii. p. 171.

found it impossible to get their carriages to go away again ; the *rue du Bac* was crammed with them, and people waited for hours before they could get into the line even at their own door. So long and frequent were the halts and so hungry was everybody in the carriages that all the pâtés, cold chickens, roast veal, bread, cakes, &c., in the shops of the *faubourg Saint-Germain* were eaten up by those who were waiting. One lady was found crying in one of the ante-rooms, having left her child to come for an hour to the ball, and waited for three hours without being able to get back to it.

That the manners and customs of the old society should prevail at what was rapidly becoming his court was the anxious wish of Napoleon ; and he welcomed with joy any man or woman whose knowledge and advice could be made use of, and whose presence would help to refine and instruct the motley assemblage of which it must necessarily be composed.

For all this there was no more suitable person than the Marquise de Montesson, widow of Philippe, Duc d'Orléans, at whose *hôtel* [1] in the *rue de Provence* and country house at Romainville it was now the ambition of all the members of the new society to be presented.

For here were to be found all the dignified politeness and charm of that *ancien régime* which Napoleon so greatly admired, but whose precepts he himself refrained from following.

[1] Afterwards belonged to the Austrian Embassy. Scene of the terrible fire at Prince Schwarzenberg's ball, 1809.

However, he paid the greatest attention to Madame de Montesson, and showed her the utmost consideration.[1] Although now more than sixty years old, she still preserved the remains of great beauty, had all the grace and stately courtesy of the former generation, with the *esprit* and knowledge of the world naturally resulting from the life she had led and the place she had filled.

When the Terror was over, the *émigrés* gradually returning, and the manners and customs of civilised life no longer dangerous but desirable, her *hôtel* was one of the earliest to reopen, and there, for the first time, were to be seen again the liveries, silk stockings, and powder which had so long disappeared from French houses. The First Consul, whose court had already begun to exist, seeing quite well that without somebody to advise and assist her Joséphine was not capable of organising it according to his intentions, which were that it should resemble that of Louis XV., applied to Madame de Montesson to help him. He even wished to create for her the post of *surintendante*, which she refused to accept,[2] but she was willing enough to give advice and instruction to Joséphine about all the details and usages of court life with which her connection and intimate

---

[1] Napoleon continued to Madame de Montesson the pension of 150,000 francs left her by the Duc d'Orléans and restored all her property.

[2] The Comte de Valence observing one day that the First Consul had told him how delighted he would be to see Madame de Montesson habitually in the most intimate society of Madame Buonaparte, Madame de Genlis exclaimed, "That is to say, her *dame de compagnie*—yes, indeed—that would please Buonaparte. The Duchess-Dowager of Orleans"! ("Salons de Paris," t. iv. p. 116 —Duchesse d'Abrantès).

association with the royal family had made her so well acquainted, and to give magnificent *fêtes* to please the First Consul, where everything was done with the stately magnificence he was so anxious to revive.

Madame de Montesson was small, slight, and upright, her eyes of so dark a blue as to be almost violet; her hair had been fair. She always wore in summer a white dress of some costly material, made in a fashion becoming to her age; in winter her dress was grey or dark. She was generally surrounded by young people, who were very fond of her, and to whom, if they were favourites of hers, she would give excellent advice.

" *Ma belle petite*," she once said to Madame Junot, " you are just married, you are young and pretty, you are now entering the world : recollect one important thing; that is, never to allow yourself the very slight pleasure of evil-speaking ; for not only does it ruin the tone of a woman, but it makes her ugly. It is like gambling. . . . And do not give way either to that mocking spirit which would give you the air of wishing to show your pretty teeth. Ridicule is a weapon which only frightens fools, and which would make you hated by everybody. Ridicule is at the same time school-girlish and stupid. Do not be *moqueuse*, for your own sake, my dear child."

The Marquise de Montesson was a widow, and a famous beauty, when, in 1773, she became the second wife of the Duke of Orléans. The marriage was a morganatic one, and never officially recognised at Court, though it was perfectly well known, and when, after Louis XVI. was practically confined to the

Tuileries, where she had formerly been presented only as Marquise de Montesson, she generously asked for and obtained permission to pay her court there, and was then always received by the King as his cousin.

Society at her *hôtel* was extremely interesting, the most brilliant and distinguished in Paris during the Consulate and early days of the Empire. There were to be found all the *émigrés* [1] who had returned or who were on the proscribed list without having quitted France; all the *corps diplomatique*, literary men and women, artists, musicians, women of almost puritanical severity of character, others of very little reputation at all, and of course all the *élite* of the new court, amongst whom was Madame Bernadotte, for Désirée was very fond of the old Marquise, or, as her friends considered her, the Duchess-Dowager of Orléans; and amongst the cultivated people with whom she was now thrown she began to take an interest and pleasure in intellectual pursuits and studies, and to form friendships with clever and distinguished persons which were greatly to her advantage. Madame de Montesson was passionately fond of painting flowers, and Napoleon would send them to her from the conservatories of La Malmaison. Madame Junot declares that he was more courteous to her than he ever was to any other woman, and seemed to look upon her as a princess of the blood-royal of France.

The old Marquise gave herself rather the airs of royalty in some respects; she had the royal liveries,

[1] "The *émigrés* were coming back in crowds : one heard names announced which seemed to have risen from the tomb."

the arms of Orléans on her carriage, never rose from
her chair for anybody, never, except on special
occasions, returned visits, and never accompanied
any one for a single step unless to show that she did
not wish to see her again. A lady who had called
upon her, and whose visit she considered to be a
liberty, said to the Abbé de Saint-Far, [1] not knowing
this " princely " custom of hers—

" It is extraordinary ; she was very cold at first,
and then, all on a sudden, when I was going, she
showed me a politeness she had not shown to
any one. *Elle m'a reconduite.*"

" *Comment?* " exclaimed Saint-Far ; " *elle vous a
reconduite ?* "

" Yes, certainly."

" Well, then, don't go there again ! "

During the lifetime of the Duke of Orléans, her
husband, she had been present with him at the
distribution of prizes at the military college, where
Napoleon was. The Duke being requested by the
Cardinal de Lourenie to give the crown to the
lauréats, begged Madame de Montesson to do so.
At the same time she said a few gracious words to
each pupil, and as she placed the crown or chapter
on the head of Napoleon, she remarked, " I wish
it may bring you good fortune, Monsieur." [2]

Politics were forbidden in the *salon* of Madame
de Montesson, and what she considered of the first
importance in those presented to her was *bon ton*.
On one occasion she refused to allow General Suchet

---

[1] Natural son of Philippe, Duc d'Orléans ("Salons de Paris."
t. ii. p. 322).

[2] "Salons de Paris," t. iv. p 7 (Duchesse d'Abrantès).

(afterwards Duke of Albufera and Marshal of France)
to be introduced to her.

"No, no, my dear child," she said to Madame
Junot. "I am very fond of you, but I don't like
all your *donneurs de coups de sabre ;* your general
does not suit me."

"But, Madame, I assure you that he does not
swear like Colonel Savary. . . . "

She looked at her and laughed.

"You are a malicious little person," she said. "Ah!
he does not swear! Well! God forgive me, I think I
should like it better if he did than those everlasting
bows and honeyed compliments. No, no, *il m'ennuie-
rait.*"

It was perfectly true that the manners of many,
in fact of most, of the officers of Napoleon, were
more fit for the barrack-room than the drawing-
room. Respect, courtesy, and distinction had been
swept away by the Revolution; the confused
mingling of ranks had brought about a rude
familiarity of speech which, when applied to himself,
greatly irritated Napoleon. Some of his generals,
Lannes especially, forgetting his present exalted
position, treated him not as the head of the government, but as an old comrade, using the familiar *tu* and
toi, which, as every one knows, is the greatest proof of
intimacy and familiarity. Such was the impropriety of
their behaviour and the want of due respect displayed
by them, that Napoleon found it necessary to leave
off taking part in the blind-man's buff and other
games ill suited to the dignity of a court, but much
in vogue at La Malmaison, in which he himself took
more pleasure than might have been expected.

One day some Arab horses, having been sent as a present to the First Consul, were brought into the courtyard, where Napoleon and Lannes went out to look at them. Lannes immediately proposed that they should play a game of billiards for one, to which Napoleon consented, and lost the game. Thereupon Lannes, without ceremony, went out again, and remarking, " I have won, so I have the right to choose," selected the best of the horses without waiting for permission, ordered it to be saddled, mounted, and rode away, calling out, " Adieu, Buonapate, I shan't dine here, I'm going ; for if I stayed you would be quite capable of taking your horse back again " (making use of the obnoxious *tu*), and rode off. Napoleon resolved to put a stop to this sort of thing, and shortly afterwards Lannes was sent to Portugal.

Savary, on the other hand, was such an absolute slave to Napoleon, that later on, when Emperor, the latter carried on an intrigue with his wife, who was very pretty, making no secret of the matter to the husband, but forbidding him to take any notice of it to his wife. Savary obeyed, and continued to live on excellent terms with her, making no objection whatever to the *liaison*.

But of all his generals, the only one Napoleon always spoke of with enthusiasm, and never ill-treated nor abused, was Desaix, who was killed at the battle of Marengo (June 14, 1800).

He was jealous of his marshals, especially of Bernadotte and Moreau, and grudged honour and glory to any one but himself. In his arbitrary nature neither truth nor justice had any part if they inter-

fered with his wishes; and the bulletins after a
victory were arranged without the slightest regard
to either. The events were described, not as they
really took place, but as he wished them to be.
He was heard to say that glory must be given to
those who knew how to wear it; and he awarded it,
not to those who had really earned it, but to those
who were in his confidence or did not excite his
jealousy. He would omit to mention a general who
had gained a victory if he disliked him, and would
praise a failure and proclaim it as a success if made
by one of his favourites. Now and then a general
saw with astonishment in a newspaper an account
of a victory attributed to him which he had not
gained, or a speech made by himself not one word
of which had he ever spoken; and of these omissions
and misrepresentations it was useless to complain.
The bulletins often caused the greatest surprise and
anger amongst the generals when they appeared,
and sometimes gave rise to violent scenes.[1]

[1] There was a violent quarrel between Napoleon and Lannes
after the battle of Eylau, because the Emperor insisted on giving
the credit to Murat, when it should have been shared by Lannes
and Augereau ("A Leader of Society at Napoleon's Court,"
pp. 272–3).

CHAPTER X

1801

THE peace of Lunéville, between France and Austria, securing to the former the possession of the Ionian Islands, Parma, and her other Italian conquests, making the Rhine from Holland to Switzerland the boundary of France, and confirming Austria in the possession of Venice, was signed in February, 1801, and was received with great jubilation in Paris. It was, however, followed in March by the battle of Alexandria, the capitulation of the French army, and the necessity of signing a treaty with England, which put an end to Napoleon's favourite project of ruining the latter country by making Egypt a stepping-stone to the conquest of India. The loss of Egypt was the first check to Napoleon's victorious career, and from the power he hated above all others; it caused him the deepest depression and disappointment. Désirée spent a great part of that summer with Joseph and Julie at Mortefontaine.[1] They had made it a most charming place; it was the scene of a constant succession of entertainments, and amongst the guests there besides the Buonaparte family and their connections were to be met with many names well known in the political and intellectual world. Madame de Stael, Stanislas Girardin, and other literary characters took part in the evening entertainments, which consisted chiefly of *petits jeux*, charades, and what was then very much the fashion, the reading aloud of plays and pieces, such as " Atala," " René," &c. The Austrian ambassador, Count Cobentzel, was the life and soul of it all, especially the acting. He was short, fat, remarkably ugly, and very amusing. They induced Palissot, one of the veteran *beaux esprits* of the court of Louis XV., to go and stay there for a few days, during which he was treated with the greatest deference and consideration; but the old man did not feel at home in a state of things so different from all the ideas and recollections of his vanished past, from which he could not dissociate himself, and with many expressions of gratitude for the attention he had received he gladly returned to the solitary life he had now chosen.

The three sisters of Napoleon were constantly at Mortefontaine, and Lucien, who was a widower with two daughters, afterwards Princess Gabrielli and Lady Dudley Stuart. Joséphine came occasionally, but the hostility of her husband's family prevented

[1] " Mémoires de Méneval."

any great intimacy, although Julie is said never to
have joined in the malice and spite of the others,
but always to have been on friendly, even affectionate, terms with her sister-in-law. The Signora
Letizia herself, notwithstanding her good qualities,
indulged in a jealousy which can only be called
contemptible of Joséphine and her children, to
whom she grudged all the favour showed them by
Napoleon. What he did for them now and for long
after was nothing in comparison of the riches and
honours he showered upon his brothers and sisters ;
but the Buonaparte and their mother also hated to
see anything worth having given to anybody else,
and between them and the Beauharnais there was
a continual feud. Désirée belonged to the Buonaparte faction, but being naturally of a good-natured,
kindly disposition, her attitude was more passive
than active in this and most matters of the sort.

When Napoleon took up his abode in the Tuileries,
Hortense de Beauharnais was taken from school to
live with her mother, who occupied the *entresol*, the
first floor being inhabited by Napoleon. Hortense
was rather a pretty, fair girl of about seventeen, one
of the favourite pupils of Madame Campan, who
wrote her long letters of advice on her entering the
Tuileries, reminding her of the grandeur of its past
associations, and urging her to try to fashion her own
life in accordance with the greatness of her surroundings. There was, however, nothing great about
Hortense : she was gentle, sweet-tempered, affectionate, yielding, and very fond of amusement, though
she is said to have at first cared only for the balls
where she met the members of the old *régime*, and

to have despised the Buonaparte and their friends, always excepting her step-father, who was fond of and indulgent to her, and for whom she seems to have also had a good deal of affection ; although she cried and lamented for days when she was first told that her mother was going to marry a little Corsican officer of the republican army.

Madame Campan was a clever, practical woman, whose prosperity was the result of her own good management. Reduced by the Revolution to such poverty that she had only 500 francs left, she resolved to set up a school at Saint-Germain-en-Laye, which, being pleasantly situated by the Seine, besides being conveniently near Paris and Versailles, seemed likely to be suitable and attractive. She then proceeded to write out circulars, not being able to afford to have them printed, and sent them to all the families of distinction with whom she had been acquainted in former days who had remained in France; and to various *nouveaux riches* who had daughters or nieces. The plan answered admirably, for a school of this kind was very much wanted. People did not know where to educate their daughters ; there were no convents to send them to, and many parents who had suddenly become possessed of large fortunes were most anxious to give their children the education and manners that would fit them to take a place in society, but which they certainly could not acquire at home. Madame Campan was exactly what they wanted ; she had lived at the court of Marie Antoinette. She at once got pupils from the old families of her acquaintance ; she had the Abbé Bertrand for her *aumônier*, or chaplain, and a nun to look after the religious instruction of the children; her two sisters helped her, and by the end of a year she had a hundred pupils. The first professors from Paris attended; dancing especially was admirably taught, and in a very short time the school was the height of fashion. Madame Campan not only made her own fortune, but that of her family. Of her three nieces who were amongst her pupils, one married Marshal Ney, another the Comte de Broc.[1]

After some time the number of Madame Campan's pupils increased to three hundred. All the most distinguished people came to see her, and every year she gave a brilliant *fête*, attended by a large assemblage of the relations and friends of the pupils, who took part in the dancing, recitations, acting, and other diversions.

Napoleon had placed his sister Caroline at this establishment, where were also Hortense and several nieces and cousins of Joséphine. He took great interest in the school, and recollecting the mortifications which in his boyhood had fallen to his lot owing to his poverty when amongst companions who had plenty of money, he insisted always upon all the girls being treated with absolute equality, and was much displeased when on one occasion he arrived at their dinner-time and found that some of the girls of higher rank were dining at a separate table, a distinction he at once put an end to.

He liked and respected Madame Campan, and often talked to her, especially about her pupils. When Caroline was about to leave school and marry Murat

[1] The third married M. Garnot, who had an appointment under Napoleon.

her to Lavalette, whom she afterwards so heroically saved.

As to Hortense, she was entirely sacrificed to the interests and tyranny of her mother and step-father, and it must be confessed that her miserable marriage was a blot upon Joséphine, kind-hearted and gentle as she generally showed herself.

But she was tormented and alarmed by the persistent hostility of her husband's family, whose one aim, in which she always feared they would succeed, was to persuade Napoleon to divorce her in order to have an heir ; and she had the idea that by marrying Hortense to one of the brothers she would secure an ally in her son-in-law. There were three available ; Lucien was a widower, and to him she first proposed the marriage, which he declined. She next thought of Jérôme, a mere boy, who at that time was apparently very fond of Hortense, with whom he used to run about in the Tuileries gardens. Perhaps he might not have objected, but his brothers influenced him against the marriage, and he might possibly have been no improvement upon the husband finally given her, for although he was less disagreeable, he had a worse character in other ways. He was an odious boy ; spoilt, selfish, brainless, ungrateful, extravagant, and dissipated to an extent that irritated Napoleon in spite of his blindness to the faults of his own family.[1]

He had placed Jérôme at school at the Collège Irlandais, which was not far from the school of Madame Campan. The boys used to go to the *fêtes*

---

[1] " Le Roi Jérôme " (Joseph Turquan). The marriage of Jérôme, however, proved happier than that of Louis ; he was more dissipated, but less tyrannical.

given by her, and there were always flirtations going on between them and the young girls in her establishment. One day Jérôme wanted money as usual, but dared not ask Napoleon, who refused to give him more than the ample sum he was allowed. Joseph, Lucien, and Louis were all away; he knew it would be useless to ask his mother, so he went to his uncle, Cardinal Fesch, asked him for 25 louis, and on his refusing, drew his sword, and declared he would cut to pieces a valuable picture hanging on the wall unless he got what he wanted. The Cardinal yielded to the threat, and could never succeed in having Jérôme punished, as Napoleon and the rest of the family only laughed.[1]

Another time Joseph wrote to Napoleon that he had been obliged, after advancing 40,000 francs to Jérôme, to let him have 60,000 more, or he could not leave Paris for Brest on account of his debts. As he was himself short of money, he begged Napoleon to pay him back at once 100,000 francs, to which Napoleon replied—

" I have cause to be very much surprised that you should have drawn upon my civil list. I will not give Jérôme anything beyond his allowance; it is more liberal and larger than that of any prince in Europe. My positive intention is to allow him to be imprisoned for debt if this allowance is not enough for him. What do I want with the follies they are doing for him at Brest? It is inconceivable what that young fellow costs me; whilst he gives me nothing but annoyance, and is no use at all to my system."

[1] " Le Roi Jérôme " (Joseph Turquan).

These incidents, of course, happened later on, but they are characteristic of Jérôme.

Failing him and Lucien, there only remained Louis as a possible husband for Hortense, and to him accordingly Joséphine turned her attention. The affair did not look promising, for not only did the young people rather dislike each other than otherwise,[1] but Louis had not got over his affection for Emilie de Beauharnais, and Hortense was in love with Duroc. The Buonaparte family opposed the marriage vehemently, and did all they could, then and afterwards, to poison the mind of Louis by scandalous assertions about Napoleon, whose affection for Hortense they declared to be not at all that of a step-father. Louis was, however, half persuaded, half forced into the marriage, and Hortense, after many tears and entreaties, yielded to the commands of Napoleon extorted by the representations and persuasions of her mother. The ill-starred marriage was celebrated with suitable splendour. Madame de Montesson gave a great ball in honour of it, at which everything was done with the stately magnificence of former days. Eight hundred guests were present, including the *Corps Diplomatique* and all the principal people. The great staircase of the *hôtel* in the *rue de Provence* was lined with a double row of *valets-de-pied* wearing powdered wigs and the blue liveries of Orléans, holding torches. Hortense, dressed in pink and silver, looked pale and sad, and was now and

---

[1] Lucien, in his memoirs, states that before his marriage Louis told him that he was in love with Hortense. In that case he may have been repelled by her aversion for him, but it is certain that his so-called love for her was of very short duration.

then unable to restrain her tears, while Louis presented an equally melancholy aspect.

The success of Joséphine's plan had ruined the happiness of three people—her daughter, her son-in-law, and Duroc—besides making Duroc her enemy for life, without having any of the favourable effects she hoped for as regarded her position in her husband's family.

In May, 1801, the Consular Court was for the first time visited by a king and queen, who, though only raised to the throne to serve the ambition of Napoleon, were yet Bourbons, she being a daughter of Charles IV., King of Spain, and he son of the Duke of Parma and elder sister of Marie Antoinette. The French had seized Parma and Napoleon had given Tuscany to the Duke and Duchess, creating them " King and Queen of Etruria."

The King was tall, good-looking, but so stupid and frivolous that he did not seem to feel the humiliation and embarrassment of his position as he drove through the streets of the capital which had been the scene of the murder of his relations ; but to the Queen, who was ugly, but had much more sense and brains, it was extremely painful.

It was the will of Napoleon that they should be received with great attention and consideration. He went himself into the drawing-room at La Malmaison to see that all was prepared for their reception, and came out exclaiming, " Bourrienne, just think of their stupidity : they had not taken down the picture representing me on the top of the Alps, pointing to Lombardy and demanding its conquest. I have ordered its removal. How mortifying it would have been if the prince had seen it ! "

The Queen was very gracious to Madame de Montesson whom, she received as her cousin, and who gave a splendid ball in honour of her and of the King. They were loaded with costly presents, and all the ministers gave *fêtes* for them, the most magnificent being that of Talleyrand, which included a concert by all the best *artistes*, a supper served amongst orange-trees, while the park was lit up by the illumination of the château which represented the façade of the *palazzo Pitti*, their future home, ending with a great show of fireworks.

The entertainment given by Berthier was a picnic, or bivouac, which was not altogether successful, for the King having bet Eugéne de Beauharnais that he would jump over one of the bivouac fires, fell into it and burnt his legs.

It was at this time that Madame de Stael, who began by having an unbounded admiration for Napoleon, was doing all she could to captivate him, but without success, for he only repelled her rudely, as he could not bear her. One morning she went to Madame de Montesson and asked her to speak to him in her favour, as she knew he did not like her but could not imagine why.

After a long discussion, in which M. de Valence,[1] who was present, also took part, Madame de Montesson observed—

" You see too often, *ma belle petite*, the men who are professedly his enemies ; I don't say in your *salon*, where you receive a hundred people, but intimately and perhaps . . . "

" If I could see the First Consul I am certain I

could convince him of my innocence. . . . Does not he come to your house sometimes?"

Madame de Montesson, much embarrassed, hesitated and murmured something or other, whereupon Madame de Stael, with a contemptuous smile, took up a flower and began picking it to pieces, while her attention seemed to wander to other people in the room. Presently she rose abruptly and went out.

"What a singular woman!" exclaimed M. de Valence as he returned from following her and sat down in an armchair.

"Why did you not ask her to *déjeûner* to-morrow? It would have been an excellent opportunity to let her speak to the First Consul."

"Are you mad? What! you who know me, you ask me why I do not invite to meet the first man in the kingdom a person who displeases him? I remember my *code de courtisan* well enough not to do that."

"Have you my mother-in-law?"

"No. Not that I think she is disagreeable to the First Consul, certainly not importunate like Madame de Stael, but it does not signify, your mother-in-law, my dear Valence, is a little *ennuyeuse*, between ourselves, and I want the First Consul to amuse himself *chez-moi*. He likes pretty women and simple, agreeable women: your mother-in-law and Madame de Stael are nothing of the kind."

Next day, at half-past twelve, the guests began to arrive for *déjeûner*, which was arranged with all the luxury and elegance now no longer proscribed in France—Sèvres china, gold plate, delicate glass, Saxon linen embroidered with the arms of Orléans according to the fashion of royal and princely houses, everywhere a profusion of flowers, and amongst those present some of the prettiest and most charming women of the Consular Court. Mesdames Récamier, de Rémusat, de Custine, Bernadotte, de Valence, the Princesse de Guémenée, and several others had arrived, when suddenly, to the horror of Madame de Montesson, was announced, unwished for and uninvited, Madame de Stael !

Consternation almost overpowered her politeness, and her reception of Madame de Stael was of the coldest ; but what was she to do ? She expected the First Consul and Madame Buonaparte every moment —he would be sure to be very angry ; and very soon Madame Buonaparte was announced, looking charming and saying that the First Consul would be there in a quarter of an hour, but at the sight of Madame de Stael she said in a gentle but reproachful voice—

" But you know Buonaparte does not like her, and I told you perhaps he would come."

" Eh ! of course I know—but what could I do ? Ask M. de Valence what happened yesterday. She was here (*chez-moi*) and expressed the strongest desire to see the First Consul. I kept silent. She asked me if he often came to see me ; I answered shortly, 'Yes,' and said nothing more, for fear she should ask me directly to come here this morning, but it appears she does not think an invitation necessary. I received her very coldly, and, contrary to my custom, I was almost impolite. If you will listen to me you will not be very cordial to her either ; it is the only way to make her understand that she is *de trop* here."

Joséphine accordingly received Madame de Stael with such stiffness that she became quite confused, and retiring indignantly, seated herself at the farthest end of the room.

Presently the trampling of horses proclaimed the arrival of Napoleon, who dismounted, came rapidly up the staircase, saluted Madame de Montesson, and glancing round the room saw Madame de Stael. Putting his arm round Joséphine, he drew her into the next room, saying to Madame de Montesson, "Is this house yours, Madame?"

Amid the general consternation, Madame de Stael was left alone, deserted by every one, confused by the glances and whispers of the groups around, and not knowing how to escape from the position in which her folly and impertinence had placed her, when Madame de Custine, a beautiful, gentle woman, who greatly admired her, crossed the room and came and sat down by her. Touched by her generous friendship, Madame de Stael eagerly expressed her gratitude, and on asking her name, and being told it was Delphine, told her it should be the name of the heroine of a romance she was writing.

Presently the First Consul, having recovered his temper, came back, and approaching, entered into conversation with her. With her usual impulsiveness she imagined she was succeeding in her wish, and exclaimed—

"Ah! General, how great you are! Let me also be able to say as certainly that you are good!"

"What is required for that?" asked Napoleon.

"Never to speak of exiling me," was her answer.

"That depends upon yourself. Besides, in any

case you would not be *exiled*.   Exiles and *lettres de cachet* have been abolished by the Revolution."

"Ah!" she exclaimed imprudently, "then what was the 18th *Fructidor?* A promenade to Sinnâmasi. The place was ill-chosen, for the air is bad."

Incensed at her beginning to talk in that strain, Napoleon frowned and walked away, leaving her to repent of the folly with which she had defeated her own purpose.

Whilst all these festivities were going on at the Consular Court, and while the power of Napoleon appeared to be daily strengthened and confirmed, plots and conspiracies were from time to time being hatched against him, in one of the most serious of which Bernadotte and Moreau were now concerned.

They had, as has been already mentioned, always been opposed to his ambitious plans, and had seen that he was aiming at the destruction of the Republic and the concentration of all power in his own hands. This they resolved to prevent if they could, and they had begun to prepare the way to do so, reckoning upon the support of a portion of the army, particularly of the Army of the West, of which the troops were then disaffected towards Buonaparte and devoted to Bernadotte and Moreau, Bernadotte especially being adored by his men.   There were at least forty thousand men of the Army of the West favourable to Bernadotte and Moreau, besides forty thousand who were collected in Bretagne, preparatory to being sent to Saint-Domingo to quell the revolt of the negroes under Toussaint-Louverture, the black leader.   The prospect of being sent to the West Indies had filled the troops with discontent:

they called it transportation, and were ready to follow Bernadotte and Moreau. In fact, the state of things was a serious danger for Napoleon if the conspiracy should prove successful, and for all those concerned in it if it should fail or be discovered.

Napoleon, however, had long mistrusted Bernadotte and Moreau, and watched their movements with a vigilant eye. He questioned Désirée, and discovered that she knew nothing of what was going on, but that she was uneasy and frightened, that Moreau had been several times to the house, and that when Bernadotte was with her he seemed restless and preoccupied, slept badly, and talked in his dreams about Moreau and some conspiracy which she did not understand. In admitting all this, incautious as it was, Désirée never dreamed of injuring her husband. She had no idea how far matters had gone, but was afraid he might become involved in some dangerous plot, and thought this the best way of preventing it.

The secret police were now becoming extremely well organised, and it became known to them that some mischief was going on in the army at Rennes, though who were the leaders, how far it had gone, or of what nature it was, they were in ignorance.

But the *préfet* of Rennes received a warning from the minister of police, which by a strange chance happened to arrive on the very day upon which the revolt was to have broken out. The time fixed upon was midday during the parade, and the despatch was only delivered to the *préfet* at half-past eleven. Bernadotte was then at Paris, so the *préfet* sent for the *chef d'état major*, General Simon, who, supposing that all was discovered, lost his head, and in reply to

the questions of the *préfet* betrayed the whole conspiracy and confessed that in a few minutes the
troops in the *Place d'Armes* would rise and proclaim
the fall of the Consular Government. The *préfet*
lost no time, and by his resolution and presence of
mind the outbreak was prevented, the leaders arrested,
and the disaffected troops surrounded by regiments
loyal to Napoleon. To what extent Bernadotte was
involved in this affair it is impossible to say ; at any
rate no proofs implicating him were to be found.

Some French writers accuse him of leaving his
fellow-conspirators in the lurch and ensuring his own
safety ; but where Bernadotte is concerned it is useless to take the opinion of those who are so exasperated by his refusal, when chosen to be King of
Sweden, to sacrifice that country to France, that they
are incapable of doing him justice. His upright,
straightforward, honourable character may lead one
to suppose that his conduct in this matter was not
different from his habitual manner of acting ; but
however that might be, no sufficient proofs against
him were forthcoming : all the officers of the other
regiments disavowed complicity in the conspiracy, a
few arrests were made, and the discontented troops
were hurried off to Saint-Domingo. Napoleon,
though inwardly convinced that Bernadotte was
concerned in the affair, could do nothing against
him. The Council of Ministers declared it would
be impossible to bring such an accusation against a
general so popular both in the country and the army.
Napoleon himself was restrained by Bernadotte being
the brother-in-law of Joseph, who, as well as Lucien,
vehemently took his part.

They persuaded him to leave Paris on the pretext of Désirée's health, for the benefit of which the baths, of Plombières had been recommended, where he remained with her during part of the spring of 1803, not without considerable anxiety and uneasiness. The year 1802 had been characterised by many important events, amongst which were the treaty with England called the Peace of Amiens, and signed at that city in February, confirming to France the possessions she had conquered ; that is to say, Flanders, Brabant, Belgium, all the German territory on the left bank of the Rhine, Avignon, Savoy, Geneva, Basel, Nice, Lombardy, Tuscany, Genoa, and the American colonies of Louisiana and Guiana ; and the Consulate for life being conferred upon Napoleon.

The Concordat, re-establishing religion, had been signed, and on Easter Sunday, 1802, the reopening of Notre-Dame took place with great pomp and magnificence, to the indignation of many fanatical supporters of atheism and Jacobinism. Napoleon took this opportunity of advancing a few steps further also in his social projects. Liveries for the first time appeared in his household ; Joséphine was attended by a brilliant throng of ladies, presenting all the characteristics of a court ; the First Consul wore on the hilt of his sword the famous diamond called the " Regent," which had been bought for the crown by the Regent Duke of Orléans during the minority of Louis XV., stolen in the Revolution, and found afterwards by the Government. It was on the point of being sold for a trifling sum when Napoleon bought it.

The *Comédie Française* was in all its glory, after the terrors of the Revolution from which they had narrowly escaped, for the whole company had been thrown into prison and very nearly been guillotined. The old Comte de Périgord found them there, to his great astonishment, on being sent to share their fate. Mademoiselle Contat, Mademoiselle Mézerai, Armand, Dazincourt, and the rest. Fleury, too, who used to act Frederick the Great to perfection. Even in the terrible position in which they were placed they had not lost their gaiety, and the old Count never met Fleury in the dismal corridor of the prison without stopping to say, "*Comment se porte, votre Majesté.*"

"And in an instant," M. de Périgord used to say in after-years, "the King of Prussia was before me, just as we used to see him in *Les deux pages*, just as he was at Potsdam two years before his death : his back bent but his appearance imposing, the same expression, the same aspect. And all that was the work of a few seconds, in the damp corner of a dungeon, by the dim light from a barred window, and when at any moment a gaoler might interrupt one by saying, 'Come, *citoyen !* go to the revolutionary tribunal ;' that is to say, to death."

They all escaped with their lives, however ; the Comte de Périgord being saved by the cleverness and devotion of his valet,[1] and now prosperous days had succeeded those of gloom and horror ; but though he loved his calling, Fleury would never allow his children to follow it. He said : "I have followed it

---

[1] "A Leader of Society at Napoleon's Court," p. 44 (Catherine Bearne). "Mémoires de la Duchesse d'Abrantès."

through gay and flowery paths, but the thorns which those flowers hide from the public are sharp. I must save my children from the pain of them."

His son became a sailor, and rose to distinction; his daughter married a doctor.[1]

The Opera, the Bouffes, the Vaudeville, and other theatres were also very flourishing. Talma and Mademoiselle Mars were at the height of their fame, so were Mademoiselle Vestris and many others.

There was a constant succession of balls, dinners, and *fêtes*, and the more entertainments were given the better pleased was the First Consul. In fact, he ordered everybody, high and low, to amuse themselves, and they were quite ready to do so. The days were gone when pretty women were obliged to wear the red cap of "Liberty," dare not put on clean linen, and were in danger of being murdered for dancing or playing on a day when the republican army might have met with a reverse, or for carrying a bouquet of flowers to their parents or grandmother on a saint's day.

Never since the Revolution had Paris been so prosperous or so brilliant as during the winter of 1802-3, when, the peace of Amiens having thrown it open to foreigners, it was thronged with those of all nations, especially the English; but the sudden breaking up of that treaty and declaration of war was followed by the treacherous seizure of all the English who had not made their escape in time, and who, contrary to the usages of civilised nations, were detained for years in whatever towns they happened to be in.

[1] " Mémoires de la Duchesse d'Abrantès," t. iii. p. 380.

The cause of the rupture was the refusal of England to evacuate Malta, as they had agreed to do on the stipulation that the Order of the Knights of St. John was to be re-established and restored, an independent sovereign order under the protection of the Holy See, with its priories of different nations exactly as before.

It was, however, discovered that Napoleon had no intention of keeping his part of the agreement, but that the Spanish priories had already been destroyed by his intrigues, and their revenues sequestrated. The treaty, therefore, could not be maintained. Lord Whitworth left Saint-Cloud on May 12, 1803, and the French troops invaded Hanover.

The shops were full of caricatures of the English, especially of the Duke of Cambridge, who was represented as reviewing his troops seated on a crab.

In imitation of the Most Christian Kings of olden times, Napoleon now recommended the success of his arms to the prayers of the faithful through the medium of the clergy, to the ridicule and indignation of his atheist companions, who remarked that Buonaparte needed no prayers to conquer Italy twice over.

He also restored the old days of the week, allowing the absurd and inconvenient names of the months to remain as they were for the present, but remarking, as he ordered the *Moniteur* to be dated " Saturday, such a day of Messidor," " See ! was there ever such an inconsistency? We shall be laughed at! But I will do away with the Messidor! I will efface all the inventions of the Jacobins." [1]

[1] " Mémoires de Napoléon " (Bourrienne).

The Second Consul, Cambacérès, was a remarkably honest and learned lawyer, and apparently a mild, kind-hearted, melancholy man, polite, obliging, formal, very ugly, rather fussy about his health, and very particular about his cook. He gave elaborate and rather dull dinner-parties; there was an atmosphere of gravity and *ennui* about his *salon* and about himself also. His rooms were filled with people whom, as Madame d'Abrantès observed, "you met nowhere else," and many of whom wore the most absurd clothes. As to Cambacérès himself, he persisted in dressing after an obsolete fashion, and would be met walking about Paris in silk stockings, short breeches, embroidered coat, wig with a *queue*, and three-cornered hat, all long out of date. But no one would have supposed that ten years ago he was a rabid, fanatical revolutionist, who had given his vote for the death of Louis XVI., the remembrance of which and the remorse he felt for his share in it preyed upon his mind and haunted him night and day.

Madame d'Abrantès relates the following story, which she says only became generally known at the Restoration, the mention of it being strictly forbidden during the reign of Napoleon :—

Cambacérès had given a most splendid masked ball, in the course of which, feeling tired, he went into a room that was nearly empty, called for an ice, and threw himself into an arm-chair. A masked figure wrapped in a black domino approached in silence, sat down by his side, and, turning towards him, looked fixedly at him. For some minutes he took no notice; then, feeling embarrassed by the presence of this immovable companion, he turned towards him, saying—

"Are you dumb, *beau masque?*"

There was no answer.

"You appear to be not only dumb, but rude," remarked Cambacérès.

The figure shook its head.

"Ah! there is an answer at least. Well . . . do you think my *fête* beautiful?"

"Too beautiful!" replied the figure at last in a deep, hollow voice which made Cambacérès shiver as he answered—

"You think so! But when one receives one's sovereign——"

"You did not know you were going to receive your sovereign," cried the black mask, with an accent growing strangely imperious.

"What! I did not know that the Emperor——"

"Silence, blasphemer!" cried the black mask violently ; and as he spoke he laid upon the bare hand of Cambacérès his own, which, though covered with a white glove, struck an icy chill through him.

"Who are you, monsieur?" asked he, rising. And he raised his hand to the bell, for the room was now deserted.

"Spare yourself the trouble," said his companion. "I will name myself and show myself to you if you wish. Your valets and your flatterers have nothing to do with what will pass between us."

"Monsieur, who are you, then?" And he afterwards told Count Dubois that as he asked this question his tongue seemed paralysed and he could scarcely speak,

"You wish to know who I am? You shall know
—perhaps. Do you recall a day in your life which
you wish to redeem?"

"No," replied Cambacérès after a moment's
reflection.

"No!" repeated the figure in a voice of thunder,
and its eyes seemed to flash.

"No," said Cambacérès again, "for I have always
acted according to my conviction and my conscience.
As a lawyer I may have sometimes arrived at con-
clusions that were painful to me, but I thought I
was right; and then I am only the instrument of
God."[1]

"Do not speak His name! You are not worthy to
do so!"

"Monsieur!" exclaimed Cambacérès, turning
towards the door leading into one of the card-
rooms, "your conduct is too strange to be borne
any longer. You may thank me that I do not have
you arrested. . . . And on no account talk in this
way to the little *masque* I see crossing one of the
salons; he might have less patience than I, and mine
is at an end, I warn you."

"I have nothing to say to that little *masque*,"
replied the dark figure; "he has only followed the
path you and yours opened to him."

Cambacérès shuddered and went towards the door.
Suddenly the figure was by his side, though its foot-
steps made no sound; and leading him back without
his having strength to resist, said—

"Do you remember the 21st of January?"

---

[1] Cambacérès afterwards told Dubois that he thought at first that
it was some *émigré*, who, after consulting him, had lost his case.

Cambacérès was speechless.

"Do you remember the 21st of January?" repeated the figure in a still more solemn voice.

"Yes! yes! it was an unhappy day; but I was not guilty."

"You were a regicide!"

"Monsieur!" exclaimed Cambacérès, striving to shake off the horror that overwhelmed him, "I *will* know who you are!"

"I have told you I would reveal myself to you, and I will keep my word; come, you will know me."

He led the way into another and more solitary room, where only a few lights were still burning. With growing fear Cambacérès followed; an irresistible force seemed to dominate him. The dark figure stood for a few moments by the fireplace, looking at him in silence; then said in a deep voice—

"You wish to see me? You presume on your courage, then?"

"Who are you?"

Slowly the figure raised its hand, unfastened its mask, and threw back its hood. The light of the flickering candles fell upon the face. Cambacérès looked, and with a terrible cry fell senseless to the ground.

He saw Louis XVI.

Cambacérès was deeply affected by this apparition. He related it to Napoleon, who said that it must have been a dream, he must have fallen asleep, but ordered the matter to be hushed up, so that many even of the guests present did not know of it until the Restoration, when, as before mentioned, it was much talked about.[1]

Madame d'Abrantès says that Count Dubois was very anxious to discover more about this ghost-story, but that he told her four years after it was said to have happened that he had never succeeded in finding out anything.

It was supposed by a few that Napoleon had something to do with it, but most people thought it an unlikely subject for him to choose for a practical joke. He looked upon the execution of Louis XVI. with horror.

[1] At the time this was said to have happened Napoleon was Emperor and Cambacérès High Chancellor.

CHAPTER XI

1802—1803

CONSPICUOUS amongst the friends of Désirée and Bernadotte was Madame Récamier, the wife of an elderly Swiss banker, very rich, and much more like the father than the husband of that celebrated beauty, who was one of the most lovely and most admired women in Paris, and who relates in her memoirs the history of the adventure by which she first made the acquaintance of the future King of Sweden.

Her father, M. Bernard, was then *administrateur des postes* under the Consular Government, in spite of which his royalist sympathies had led him to involve himself in a conspiracy, which he assisted by passing the letters of those concerned in it through the post. This being discovered, he was arrested and thrown into prison, where he was in a most dangerous position.

It was one evening in August, 1802, and a dinner-party was going on at Madame Récamier's, for the sister of the First Consul, Elisa Bacciocchi, had invited herself to dine with them; the Buonaparte family having already begun to assume the air of royalty.

Madame Récamier had assented to the request, and the party, besides herself, her parents, and husband, was to consist of Madame Bacciocchi, Madame de Stael, M. de Narbonne, M. Mathieu de Montmorency, and M. de la Harpe.

M. Bernard, however, did not appear, and after dinner, as they passed into the drawing-room, a note was brought to Madame Bernard, upon reading which she gave a cry and sank down half fainting. The note contained the information of her husband's arrest, and the imminent danger of his position was at once apparent.

Madame Récamier, in despair, turned to Madame Bacciocchi, and implored her to help them to obtain an immediate interview with the First Consul.

Elisa hesitated, then told her to go first and consult Fouché, after which she would see what could be done.

"Where shall I find you?"

"At the Théâtre Français, where I am going to join my sister."

Madame Récamier hurried to Fouché, who listened in silence to all she told him, and then said that the affair was most serious, and the only thing to be done was for her to see the First Consul or get some influential person to see him; but it was absolutely necessary to do so to-night; to-morrow it would be too late.

Filled with alarm and anxiety, she drove at once to the Théâtre Français, and went to the Bacciocchis' box, where she found Madame Bacciocchi and Madame Leclerc. The former looked annoyed as she entered, and when she said, " Madame, I come to claim your promise ; I must speak to the First Consul to-night, or my father is lost," replied coldly—

"Well, wait till the end of the piece, and then I am at your service."

As Madame Récamier sat down she observed a tall man in the corner of the box whose dark eyes were fixed compassionately upon her, and who seemed to be irritated by the selfish callousness of the two Buonaparte women.

"Have you seen Lafont as Achille?" asked Pauline presently. "He is very fine in it, but to-day his casque is most unbecoming."

The love-affairs of Pauline and Lafont were just then the scandal of Paris. The distress and anxiety Madame Récamier was suffering all this time were perfectly evident, and the tall stranger could stand it no longer. Turning indignantly to Madame Bacciocchi, he said with an impatient gesture—

" Madame Récamier seems to be suffering. If she will allow me I will take her home, and will undertake to speak for her to the First Consul."

" Delighted to get rid of her and escape the trouble of helping her," Madame Bacciocchi replied eagerly.

"Yes, certainly ! Nothing could be better for you. Trust to General Bernadotte ; no one is more able to help you."

Thankfully Madame Récamier took the arm of her new friend, left the theatre with him, and hastened home, where she found the house full of acquaintances who had heard of her father's arrest and come to inquire about him. Too much overcome to bear the presence of a crowd, she retired to her own room, while Bernadotte proceeded at once to interview the First Consul.

It was well she had found so powerful a protector, for her father was in the greatest danger, having been clearly convicted of allowing the correspondence of the *chouans* to pass through his hands, and it was only by the strongest representations from Bernadotte that Napoleon was induced to promise that M. Bernard should not be brought up for trial. He was in the Temple, and Bernadotte, after his interview with the First Consul, returned at once to tell Madame Récamier of the success of his intercession and his hope of being able soon to get M. Bernard released.

Now Madame Récamier had permission to go to the Temple for the purpose of visiting certain prisoners confined there, and in consequence of these charitable proceedings she knew several of the gaolers ; one especially, named Coulommier, was very devoted to her. She therefore went to the Temple next morning, found Coulommier, and persuaded him to let her see her father, who was *au secret*, and into whose cell accordingly she was introduced ; but she had not been there many minutes when suddenly Coulommier, pale and terrified, rushed back into the cell, seized her arm, and thrust her through a door into a dungeon, where she was left alone in the darkness. As she listened she heard steps and voices, the shutting of doors, then all was silent, and for two hours she remained there,

MADAME RÉCAMIER.
(From the painting by David, in the Louvre.)

until at last Coulommier came back and let her out,
saying—

"I have had a fine fright!   Follow me, and never
ask me to do such a thing again."

The police had at that moment arrived to conduct M. Bernard to undergo an interrogation at the
préfecture de police !

A few days later Bernadotte presented himself at
Madame Récamier's house with an order for her
father's release, and accompanied her with it to the
Temple to set him free.

After all this she and her family were filled with
gratitude to Bernadotte, and this began a lifelong
friendship, about which, however, there was never the
slightest scandal.   Bernadotte cared nothing for the
dissipation and flirtations which were the delight of
so many of his brother-officers, and the confidences
he poured into the ears of Madame Récamier from
this time forth concerned his political hopes, fears,
and plans, and his desire to restrain the ambition of
Napoleon, who was not only aiming at supreme
power for himself, but intended to make it hereditary
in his family.

These were, however, not the kind of confidences
Madame Récamier was accustomed to receive, for she
was by no means a political or particularly intellectual woman.   On one occasion she said laughingly
to Désirée—

" Why, when your husband and I are left alone
together, does he always begin to talk to me about
politics ? "

A woman so strikingly beautiful and so well known
in society was almost certain to have the misfortune

to attract the attention of Napoleon. He had seen
her for the first time at a *fête* given about two years
earlier by Lucien, who was then in love with her
himself, or at any rate showed her great attention
and admiration. His first wife was then living, but
as she was ill, Madame Bacciocchi did the honours of
the evening. Madame Récamier arrived early, and
seeing a man standing by the fireplace, took him for
Joseph Buonaparte, whom she knew, and bowed,
which salutation was eagerly returned by the First
Consul, who looked at her and whispered something to Fouché. Presently Fouché came and stood
behind her chair and said in a low voice, " The First
Consul thinks you charming."

When dinner was announced, Napoleon rose and
walked by himself into the dining-room, followed by
the rest of the company, who sat down just as they
liked. Napoleon was in the middle of the table, his
mother on his right hand, and the left-hand place
was vacant, nobody venturing to take it.

Madame Récamier had come in amongst the rest,
and as she passed her Madame Bacciocchi whispered
something, which, however, she did not understand;
so, not thinking of taking the unoccupied place by
Napoleon, she seated herself several places lower
down the table; upon which, turning angrily to those
who still remained standing, the First Consul said—

"Well, Garat, you sit here," and as Cambacérès
took the chair next Madame Récamier exclaimed—

" Ah! ah! *citoyen* Consul! always by the side of
the most beautiful!"

The dinner only lasted half an hour, at the end of
which the First Consul rose and left the room, fol-

lowed by the rest. Approaching Madame Récamier, he asked if she had not felt cold at dinner, adding—

" Why did not you come and sit by me?"

" I should not have dared," she answered.

" It was your place," rejoined Napoleon; and Madame Bacciocchi exclaimed—

" Why, that was what I told you before dinner."

All the evening his eyes followed her, and after the concert he approached, asked if she were fond of music, and began to talk to her, when Lucien came up and interrupted them, upon which he turned away.

Later on he made overtures to her through Fouché and Caroline Murat, which were unsuccessful, and becoming irritated, he exiled her; ostensibly because she had paid a visit at Coppet to her friend Madame de Stael, whom he had also exiled. Madame Récamier went to Lyons, and as her husband had just lost most of his fortune, she lived there in great discomfort and privation for some time, and only returned to Paris on the fall of Napoleon, 1814.

Madame de Stael was a woman of very different calibre, and was also a great friend of Bernadotte and Desirée, who frequented her *salon*, which was one of the most interesting in Paris. It was not the least like that of Madame de Montesson, or those of the *ancien régime* so much admired and approved by Napoleon, where all political discussions were forbidden, as being likely to give offence and disturb the harmony of society. On the contrary, it was a hotbed of politics and intrigues, and the resort of numbers of clever, influential, disaffected persons who were always opposing and criticising Napoleon and his government, and were too important to be altogether ignored.

Madame de Stael was also herself just the sort of woman he disliked; she had no beauty or grace, in fact was considered rather ugly than not; she was the daughter of Necker, whom she adored and he hated, even going so far as to say that he was the cause of the calamities of the Revolution. Her brilliant talents, restless, enthusiastic disposition, and the influence she had in society were alike distasteful to him, and he could not endure his officers or the members of his court and household to frequent her *salon*,[1] on some occasions forbidding them to do so.

"You owe everything to me," he said to some of them. "I have made your reputation and your fortune, you are sincerely attached to me; well, if I allowed you to visit that woman for three months, you would begin by blaming me with her, next you would pass over to the opposition, at last you would become my enemies, and perhaps I should have the misfortune to surprise you in some flagrant conspiracy against me."

Some of those to whom these sort of remonstrances were addressed, or who were at any rate well aware of the enmity of the First Consul towards the woman whose extraordinary intellectual gifts and influence, both social and political, were so inconvenient to him,

[1] "Vous me devez tout—j'ai fait votre réputation et votre fortune, vous m'aimez avec sincerité ; eh bien ! si je vous laissais fréquenter cette femme pour trois mois vous commenceriez par me blâmer avec elle ensuite vous passeriez à l'état d'opposition, enfin vous deviendriez mes ennemis et peut-être aurais-je le malheur de vous surprendre en conspiration flagrante contre moi."—(Sarrans) "Histoire de Bernadotte."

prudently consulted their own interests and withdrew from her society; but not all the displeasure of Napoleon could prevent her house being frequented by numbers of people who in their different ways were among the most distinguished in Paris.

Talleyrand latterly almost left off going there, in deference to the wishes of Napoleon, but Bernadotte and Lucien Buonaparte were not likely to submit to such dictation; Junot and his wife, in spite of the complaints of the First Consul, persisted in refusing to give up their right to choose their own friends. The Lameths, Barnave, Benjamin Constant, and numerous others of their opinions, MM. Mathieu de Montmorency, de Clermont-Tonnerre, de Narbonne, whose life Madame de Stael had saved during the Revolution, Mesdames de Lauzun, de Poix, de Beau-veau, the Duchesse de Grammont, and many more of the *faubourg Saint-Germain*, besides all the *corps diplomatique*, and all foreigners of any distinction who came to Paris, were to be found at her parties.

It was at the height of the Terror that she saved the Comte de Narbonne. He was hidden in her house, and whilst the revolutionary officials were making a "domiciliary visit" she concealed her fear, indignantly reproached them for violating the privileges of the Swedish ambassador's *hôtel*, and laughed at them as they approached the place where he was hidden. She afterwards saved M. de Montes-quieu in the same place, August 31, 1792. Having obtained passports for Switzerland, she was just going to start on her journey, taking the Abbé de Montesquieu disguised as one of her servants, when she heard that two more of her friends, MM. de

Jaucourt and Lally-Tollendal, had just been arrested and sent to the Abbaye, a few days afterwards the scene of the September massacres. Even then sinister rumours were about, and Madame de Stael put off her departure and resolved to save them. Recollecting that Manuel, Syndic of the Commune, had pretensions to be literary, she wrote to him, asking for an audience, which he fixed for seven o'clock the following morning. He received her with perfect politeness, listened to her representations, promised to do what he could to get her friends set free, and the next morning (September 1st) he wrote to her that M. de Lally had already been liberated by Condorcet, his noble defence of one of his companions having touched the hearts even of the revolutionary tribunal, and that at the request of Madame de Stael, M. de Jaucourt had been set at liberty. It was only just in time, for on the morning of the 2nd, as she was starting on her journey after having been kept awake all night by the agitation in the streets, she suddenly heard the awful sound of the *tocsin*, in spite of which she persisted in going on, and having arranged where to meet the Abbé de Montesquieu, she proceeded on her way in her carriage to which she had six horses. She was soon surrounded by a hideous and furious mob, who stopped the carriage, seized the postillions, and, infuriated by the sight of armorial bearings and handsome liveries, declared she should be taken to the assembly of the section. Madame de Stael got out, managed to tell the Abbé de Montesquieu's servant to warn his master, and went with her horrible escort to the assembly, where she was accused of taking away proscribed persons and as the number of

servants, owing to the place left for M. de Montesquieu, was one short of that given in the passport,
she was sent on to the Commune at the *Hôtel-de-Ville*
where it took her three hours to arrive, her carriage
going foot's pace in the midst of a furious, drunken
mob threatening every moment to murder her. She
appealed in vain to the gendarmes, who added their
threats to the rest, and as on descending from the
carriage and going up under a perfect roof of pikes,
one was levelled at her breast, it was only just pushed
away in time by a gendarme. If she had fallen
down it would have been all over with her. She
was brought before three of the most bloodthirsty
monsters of the Revolution, Robespierre, Billaud-
Varennes, and Collot-d'Herbois; but, fortunately for
her, at that moment Manuel came in, declared he
would answer for her and be responsible, and taking
her by the arm, led her to his own room or office, and
locked her up there for safety with her maid. For
six hours they remained there, not daring to call
any one, though exhausted by hunger, thirst, and
terror. For the air was full of fearful sounds—the
clang of the *tocsin*, the yells of murderers, the shrieks
of their victims; all the tumult of the massacres then
going on—while from the window they could see
the groups of assassins constantly returning from *La
Force* and *L'Abbaye* with bare arms all stained with
blood, howling like cannibals. The carriage, still
loaded, stood before the *Hôtel-de-Ville*, guarded only
by the servants, and was about to be plundered by
the mob when a tall *garde national* sprang upon the
box and forbade them to touch the property of the
Swedish ambassador. He protected it for two

hours, and then, as twilight fell, came in with Manuel, who was pale and trembled violently with the horror of the scenes, exclaiming, " Ah ! how thankful I am to have set your friends free ! " The *garde national* had saved the carriage and luggage out of gratitude to Necker, who had given away corn to the people. When night came on, Manuel conducted Madame de Stael home through the dark, deserted streets, and the next morning Tallien, who was an acquaintance of hers, came, bringing a gendarme to accompany her to the frontier. There were several persons in her room whose names she begged him not to disclose. He gave the promise and kept it. They crossed Paris amidst hordes of murderers, and parted at the *barrière*, he to return to take part in fresh crimes and massacres, she to reach in safety a country where she could rest in peace far from the horrors she had so narrowly escaped.[1]

Although her parents were Swiss, she always considered herself a Frenchwoman, having been born at Paris. She was now five or six and thirty years old. She had been married, by her parents' wish, to the Baron de Stael, a good-looking man much older than herself, who had no talent and no tastes in common with her. He was the Swedish ambassador to France, and died in 1802.

Madame de Stael had been a good friend to Talleyrand as well as to many others, she had even dared to write a defence of Marie Antoinette, for she was a woman full of excellent qualities—courageous, generous, sincere, and kind-hearted ; but she possessed less common sense and prudence than intellectual

---

[1] " Les salons de Paris," t. ii. p. 404–12 (Duchesse d'Abrantès).

brilliancy, and in spite of the cautions of her friends she persisted in encouraging amongst the *habitués* of her *salon* all kinds of abuse, ridicule, and caricatures of Napoleon, which did no good, but only exasperated him and endangered herself and her friends. Joseph Buonaparte himself warned her that she had better be careful, for the First Consul was getting very angry, and had complained to him about her; it was all of no use. Consequently, in 1802, she received an order exiling her from Paris or any place within forty leagues of it.

She had her own place, Coppet, on Lake Leman, and as Napoleon remarked, "all the rest of Europe was open to her"; but it was with grief and despair that she left France to spend the next two or three years in Germany and Switzerland.

Many of her friends who were influential or intimate with Napoleon interceded for her—Joseph, Lucien, Junot, his wife, who was very fond of Madame de Stael and a great favourite with Napoleon, of whom she was not the least afraid, and Bernadotte, who was always ready to help his friends and never forgot them; but it was of no use—Napoleon was inexorable.

Bernadotte, although a republican himself in those days, had never stained his hands with the crimes of the Revolution, but had done his best to protect and save those he could.

On one occasion, hearing that Colonel Ambert, of the regiment of Royal Marines, under whom he had formerly served, had been arrested as an *émigré*, he tried by every means in his power to save him. He went to the Directory, begged them with tears to

PRISON OF THE ABBAYE.

grant him Colonel Ambert's life as the reward of his own services, promising to be satisfied with that alone ; and finding his entreaties useless, he prepared to rescue him himself in spite of them, and would have succeeded if Colonel Ambert had not been one of those obstinate, provoking people whom it is impossible for any one to help.

Bernadotte found out when he was to be brought to trial, bribed his guards to let him escape on the way, conveyed to him the information that all was arranged for his rescue ; but instead of carrying out the instructions for the plan so well concocted, he declined to take advantage of the opportunity offered when the time came, and instead of escaping when his guards gave him the chance, he persisted in going to the trial, trusting to some papers he had to obtain his acquittal ; instead of which he was con-demned and executed.

M. le Chevalier de Jaucourt, one of the friends whose escape from the September massacres has just been related, and who, owing to his pale, rather round face and melancholy manner, was called *Clair de Lune*,[1] had a curious ghost-story attached to him which he was not very fond of telling ; he would relate it, however, when very much pressed by his friends to do so, and to it they used to attribute his melancholy air, saying that it had given him a shock, and the recollection had haunted him ever since it happened.　It was as follows :—

He was born in Burgundy and brought up at the college at Autun, from which, when he was twelve years old, his father sent for him to come home and

' Moonlight.

prepare for his first campaign, which he was to make under the care of one of his uncles.

He arrived at the château, and after having supper with the rest of the family was taken to a large, rather gloomy-looking bedroom where he was to sleep. The valet put a lighted lamp upon a sort of tripod in the middle of the room, and in reply to his remark that he did not want a light left burning, replied—

"Monsieur le Marquis desired that a light should be left you, Monsieur le Chevalier."

So saying, the old man departed, and the boy, looking rather dismally round the great sombre room where dust lay upon antique furniture and grim, ancient tapestry hung upon the walls, undressed slowly, examined the tapestry to see that no one was concealed behind it, and got into bed. Disinclined to sleep, he lay looking by the dim lamplight at the tapestry, which represented a temple with closed gates, before which, upon the steps, stood the life-size figure of a man in a long white robe like that of a high-priest, holding in one hand a key, in the other a bundle of rods.

There was something in the expression of the face which seemed to fascinate the boy; he could not take his eyes from those of the dim figure which hung in the gloom before him. Suddenly he thought he must be dreaming; the figure appeared to move, it came slowly down the steps and stood by his bed; then, raising the hand holding the rods, a sepulchral voice said, "These rods will scourge many of your friends. When you see them move—there is the *clef des champs* [1]—do not hesitate to take it."

---

[1] "Prendre la clef des champs," literally translated "to take the key of the fields," is an expression which means "to escape," "to run away."

The figure then slowly disappeared into the tapestry, and the boy, who all this time had been chilled and almost paralysed with terror, called for the valet, and when he came, not daring to speak to him of what had happened, said he felt ill and did not like to be alone. The old man therefore stayed with him till the morning, when, hastening to his father with fear and hesitation, he related to him the whole story. Instead of laughing at him as he had feared, his father embraced and comforted him, saying—

"My son, your adventure is undoubtedly most extraordinary, but it is less so to me, as my father, your grandfather, had also in this very room one of the most astonishing adventures that could ever be heard of—and—even——"

He stopped suddenly, remembering, probably, the tender age of his son, and would tell him no more ; but the impression of what he had seen, or supposed he had seen, always remained. The rods that struck were supposed to be the perils and calamities of the Revolution, and the *clef des champs* to signify emigration. When asked by the Duchesse de Chartres in after years whether he did not think it was a dream, and that he must have been asleep, he replied—

"No, Madame; I was not asleep. The impression produced by a dream is a different impression from that of reality. I *saw* and I *heard*."[1]

Napoleon afterwards made M. de Jaucourt chamberlain to Joseph Buonaparte.

[1] "Mémoires de Madame de Rémusat."

CHAPTER XII

1803

ON her return from Plombières, where she had remained for some time to take the baths, Désirée went to Mortefontaine to stay with her sister.

There was always a great deal of gaiety going on there, and Joseph was spending enormous sums in beautifying the place and buying up all the land around it. It was already an immense property.

One day in June he gave a superb *fête* to Napoleon and Joséphine, who were about to start upon a tour in Belgium. The earlier part of the day was spent in the gardens, and while they were there Joseph told Napoleon that he intended to take his mother in to dinner and place her on his right hand and Joséphine on his left. Napoleon, whose pretensions to royalty, or to something very like it, were of course ignored by this arrangement, angrily forbade it ; but Joseph, choosing to follow his own wishes in his own house, resisted what, after all, was only a reasonable command of his brother, then First Consul, to all intents and purposes absolute sovereign of France, and whose wife ought certainly to take precedence of his mother. When dinner was announced Joseph accordingly took his mother into the dining-room, leaving Joséphine to follow with Lucien ; but Napoleon, starting up in a rage, seized his wife's arm, and passing before every one, placed her on his right hand and ordered Madame de Rémusat to sit on the left. There was general consternation and confusion—nobody knew where to sit : Madame Joseph Buonaparte found herself at a distant part of the table. Napoleon spoke to none of the family, but only conversed with Joséphine and Madame de Rémusat, to whose cousin, M. de Vergennes, he had just restored his lands. Constraint fell upon every one, the *fête* was spoilt, and Napoleon left next day.

Désirée remained at Mortefontaine for some time, and then went with Julie to Paris, where the Joseph Buonaparte had given up their house in the *rue du Rocher*, which was too far from the Tuileries and too small for their present requirements. They now occupied the old *Hôtel de Marbœuf*, an immense house (since destroyed) in the *faubourg Saint-Honoré*, in a large garden with great trees, lawns, and shady walks, along which Julie and Désirée loved to wander up and down, often accompanied by Pauline Leclerc, now a widow, who had just come back from St. Domingo and lived close by them.

IN AN OLD FRENCH GARDEN.

Copy of a French miniature in the possession of Mrs. Hartcup, Eastwood, Old Catton, Norwich. From the strong resemblance of the taller figure, supposed to have been Désirée, probably with Julie, Queen of Spain.

Affairs in that island had turned out disastrously ;
there had been a frightful insurrection, during which
Pauline was in great danger, and behaved with much
courage and presence of mind ; a fearful epidemic
had broken out, of which General Leclerc had been
one of the many victims, and Pauline, who had not
troubled herself much about him while he was alive,
gave way to violent, frantic grief after his death,
cried and shrieked, and cut off all her hair to put it
on his coffin. When once she had got back to Paris
with her child, however, she soon consoled herself,
and began to complain of being very dull because
Napoleon would not allow her to go immediately
into society.

Julie and Désirée did what they could to comfort
and amuse her, to the great approbation of Napoleon,
who was very fond of Paulette, the prettiest and
silliest of his sisters, but certainly the one who, in the
long run, showed him the most affection and gratitude. Knowing very well what she was, the First
Consul had begged Julie to look after her, and had
arranged that she should live near Joseph Buonaparte.

That Napoleon should have liked and esteemed
Julie was natural enough, for besides her many
virtues [1] and her amiable, inoffensive disposition, she
was the wife of his favourite brother, and they
opposed his wishes less and gave him less trouble than
any of his brothers and sisters. But, considering all
that had passed between him and Désirée, her early

---

[1] On one occasion when, at a family party, they were speaking of
a legendary Buonaparte Saint, Julia said to Napoleon, " *Mon frère*,
tell us about him " : to which the First Consul replied, " *Ma sœur*,
you need feel less curiosity about him than any of the others, as
you are certain to see him in heaven."

love for him, her anger at his desertion of her, her marriage with the man who was his rival, the constant associate of his enemies, and more than once engaged in conspiracies against him, it is surprising that the extremely friendly terms upon which they were should always have remained unbroken. It is true that Désirée did not like Joséphine, and did not go to La Malmaison oftener than her position at court required, but she never seems to have been concerned in the spiteful attacks made upon her by the Buonaparte family, nor to have done anything worse than to speak of her as *La Vieille*, and to find a certain triumph in displaying to her and Napoleon the young Oscar Bernadotte, of whom she was not a little proud.

When Pauline Leclerc began again to enter into society, she made the acquaintance of Prince Camillo Borghese, head of the great Roman family of that name ; a remarkably handsome and stupid man, with whom she carried on a flirtation which soon became the scandal of the court. Camillo Borghese was eager to marry Pauline, and as she imagined herself to be in love with him, and was besides delighted to be what she called " a real princess," and to take precedence of her sisters, Napoleon's consent was asked for and obtained, on condition that the marriage should not take place until the proper time of mourning had passed.

Pauline and Borghese, however, persuaded Madame Letizia to allow a private religious marriage to be celebrated at Mortefontaine,[1] which they kept secret from Napoleon for two months, and which caused him

---

[1] " Napoléon et sa famille," t. ii. p. 204 (Masson).

great irritation when it came to his knowledge. He refused to be present at the civil marriage, also celebrated at Mortefontaine in the presence of Joséphine, Madame Letizia, Joseph, Louis, Elisa, Caroline, Bernadotte, their husbands and wives, Madame Clary, and one or two old friends. Lucien was in America, and Cardinal Fesch in Rome, where Lucien had gone with his second wife after a violent quarrel with Napoleon.

He was a great loss to Bernadotte, to whom he was a firm friend.

"They are dupes," he remarks in his memoirs,[1] "who think that my friend, Bernadotte, owes his throne to the Emperor Napoleon, and consequently very unjust to accuse him of ingratitude towards him."

It was with triumphant delight that Pauline paid her first visit at Saint-Cloud, covered with the Borghese jewels, looking radiantly beautiful, and whispering to her friend, Madame Junot, who was present, her spiteful joy at the envy she supposed she excited in Joséphine. Suddenly, in the midst of her reluctant admiration of Madame Buonaparte's exquisite costume of white and gold, harmonising so admirably with the blue and gold of the great *salon*, she stopped, glanced at the white and gold dress, then at her own, which was of a soft, delicate green, heaved a deep sigh, and murmured—

"Ah! *mon Dieu! mon Dieu!*"

"What is the matter?" asked Madame Junot.

"Why did I not remember the colour of the drawing-room furniture! And you, Laurette—you, who

---

[1] "Mémoires de Lucien Buonaparte," t. ii. p. 214 (Jung).

are my friend, whom I love as my sister (which, as Madame Junot remarks, was not saying much), why did not you warn me?"

"Eh! of what, then, once more! That the *salon* at Saint-Cloud is blue? But you knew it just as well as I do!"

"Of course; but at such a moment one is troubled, one does not know what one knew before; and see what has happened to me. I have put on a green dress to come and sit in a blue armchair!"

And with a look of despair, exclaiming that she must appear hideous, she rose and took leave, insisting on Madame Junot going back to Paris with her.

"Thank you," said the latter, "but I have my carriage here. And you, your husband——"

"That is to say, I am alone."

"What! and your honeymoon only just beginning!"

"What nonsense are you talking, *chère amie!* A honeymoon with that *imbécile!* You are joking!"

Accordingly they left the palace together, Pauline giving herself the most ludicrous airs as she paced slowly along between the double line of servants, trying to look royal, and by no means succeeding, followed by Prince Borghese, who stumbled over his sword and fell down as he got into the carriage.

The next day Madame Junot met the Princess Borghese at the house of her mother, Madame Permon, a beautiful woman of the Comnenus family, who was very fond of Pauline, but had the greatest horror and contempt for the new society, and for whom Pauline and her family had great respect and affection.

"Well," she said, speaking of the presentation at Saint-Cloud, "so you looked very charming?"

"Oh, *Maman Panoria!* ask Laurette."

"But," continued Madame Permon, "you must now behave like a princess, with dignity, and above all with *convenance*, Paulette; and when I say *convenance*, I mean politeness. You are a spoilt child, we know that. For instance, dear child, you don't return visits; that is not right. I don't complain because you are at my house every day, but other people complain."

Pauline looked sulky, and as Madame Permon continued her reproofs, Madame de Caseaux and Madame de Bouillé came in, and to them she referred the question, in which they agreed with her.

"You are now *une grande dame*," they said to her, "*by your marriage with Prince Borghese.* Therefore you must be like the *grandes dames* of the Court of France. What distinguished them was, above all, an extreme politeness. Therefore to return the visits made to you, to re-conduct, with the correct degree of consideration for their rank, those who come to see you; never to walk first when you find yourself at a door with a woman who is your superior or equal, or older than you; never to step into your carriage before the woman who is with you unless she is your *dame de compagnie;* never to forget to place every one in your *salon*, or at your table, according to their rank, to offer to those women seated near the prince two or three times during dinner the dishes near you; to be polite and agreeable with dignity—in fact, that is the code of politeness for you to follow if you wish to place yourself in the world."

When they spoke of getting into a carriage, Madame
Junot smiled, and her mother, seeing this, said to
the Princess Borghese—

"When you brought Laurette back in your
carriage, did you get in before her?"

The princess blushed.

"Is that what happened yesterday?" asked
Madame Permon hastily.

The princess, who feared as well as loved Madame
Permon, threw an imploring look at Madame Junot,
who, sacrificing truth to good-nature, answered—

"No, no; the princess had the politeness to make
me get in first."

"Because, you see," proceeded Madame Permon, "it
would be much more serious yesterday than any
other day.   My daughter and you, Paulette, have
always been, as you are still, almost equal in my
heart as you are in that of Madame Letizia.   You are,
therefore, so to speak, sisters, sisters in affection.
Therefore I could not endure to think that some day
Paulette would forget that affection because she was
called princess, and had diamonds and all the luxuries
of a new life.   But since it has not been so that is all
right."

"But," said Pauline coaxingly, leaning against
Madame Permon's shoulder, "I am the sister of the
First Consul!   I am——"

"Well! what is the sister of the First Consul?
What was the sister of Barras to us?"

"But it is not the same thing, *Maman Panoria!*"

"Absolutely the same as far as etiquette is concerned.   Your brother has a temporary rank, which
is only personal; and indeed, to say the truth, it

does not justify him in taking the liberty of returning nobody's visits.   He came to the ball which I gave for my daughter's marriage, and he has never left his cards at my house!"[1]

This conversation, as Madame d'Abrantès remarks, shows the state of French society at this time; the ceremonious politeness and good breeding of those belonging to the *ancien régime*, the utter ignorance or neglect of the usages of society of the newly-risen members of the Consular Court.   It was then a time of transition between the vanishing Republic and the Empire; which in the following year brought order and magnificence into the arrangements of the court.

Soon after this episode the Prince and Princess Borghese left Paris and took up their abode in their great Roman palace, where, in spite of the displeasure of Napoleon, both they and Cardinal Fesch received Lucien and his wife with friendship and affection.

The history of this marriage of Lucien, which caused such a commotion and division in the family, was rather a romantic one.

Alexandrine de Bleschamps, daughter of a *bourgeois* of Calais, had been married at nineteen to a rich broker at Paris.   He had a large house, lived in an extravagant, reckless way, and in a short time was ruined, deserted his young wife, and went to the

[1] Madame Permon, mother of Madame Junot, afterwards Duchess d'Abrantès, having been an intimate friend of the Buonaparte family, and known Napoleon from childhood, could never realise his extraordinary change of position.   When reminded of his greatness, she replied, "Well ! what does that signify ?   Marshal Saxe was very great too, and he returned visits."—" Les Salons de Paris," t. v. pp. 75-81 (Duchesse d'Abrantès).

West Indies, leaving her with an infant daughter to get on as she could.

Left alone at Paris under these disastrous circumstances, Alexandrine made the acquaintance of Lucien Buonaparte. She was exceedingly beautiful, and he fell violently in love with her. It was not a caprice like one of Napoleon's love-affairs, nor a calm pro-

LAURE JUNOT (NÉE PERMON), DUCHESSE D'ABRANTÈS.
(Quaglia.)
From "La Generale Junot," with the permission of
the author, M. Joseph Turquan.

tecting, reasonable affection like that of Bernadotte for Désirée, but a deep, passionate, unchanging love, such as one occasionally meets with, which they both shared, and which from henceforth altered and regulated the whole course of their lives. Alexandrine, telling Lucien that she placed her fate in his hands, went to live at his country place, Plessis-

Chamans, during the summer of 1802, and when
Lucien returned to Paris for the winter he bought for
her a small *hôtel* which had a private communication
with his own, in which a son was born to them in
May, 1803, and baptized by a priest, from whom
Lucien received a certificate declaring the child to be
the offspring of a legitimate marriage celebrated by
himself between Lucien and Alexandrine, who had
taken an oath before him that they were prevented
by political reasons from going through the civil
form and publishing their marriage, which they promised to do as soon as it could be done without
danger.

The reason was, in fact, the delay in procuring the
certificate of the death of Jouberthon, which had
taken place at Port-au-Prince, June 15, 1802.

Meanwhile Napoleon was beginning to be anxious
that his brothers and sisters should marry into the
different royal families of Europe, and so support
and carry out what he called his "system," which was,
in fact, to get all the power in Europe into his own
hands by means of his relations, who would, he
imagined, act as his prefects and satellites in the
countries where he had placed them.

The idea of Napoleon being that his brothers and
sisters were his property, and that their marriages
ought to be made, not for their happiness, but for his
advantage; it was very annoying to him that there
were, now that he had some chance of success, only
two available. The marriage of Elisa had been made
without his knowledge, he had been unable, or at
least had not thought it advisable, to withhold his
consent to that of Caroline, that of Louis had been

forced on by Joséphine, and turned out badly in every way. The other two were better ; for Joseph's marriage had been most useful to the whole family in former days, and Pauline's, though it did not satisfy his ambition, was still a much greater one than any of the rest, the rank, fortune, and position of the Borghese being very distinguished, although it fell short of the royalty at which he aimed.

But now he thought he saw an opportunity for Lucien, who after marrying once against the wish of his powerful brother, was a widower, and might be made useful. The King of Etruria had just died, his widow was to be Regent of the absurd kingdom recently created and called Etruria ; she was remarkably plain and by no means attractive, but she was a Bourbon, a queen, and daughter of the King of Spain, therefore she would be a most excellent marriage for Lucien.

The latter gives an account of a conversation between himself, Joseph, and Napoleon upon this subject. Lucien and Joseph were breakfasting together one day when Napoleon arrived, apparently in excellent spirits.

"'Well, *messieurs les gourmands !*' he exclaimed, 'not finished yet ? No, no, sit still and finish, or you will say like every one who has dined with me, that you are dying of hunger.'

"Joseph and I rose from the table, assuring him that we had finished a moment since.

"Napoleon made some joking reference to the long dinners of constitutional kings, and on Lucien observing that they had as yet never tried one, he replied—

"'Whether it would be for good or for evil, I can tell you that you will never try one if it depends on me. That is a hollow notion, and all stupidity and nonsense. Come home with me.'

"'Let us sit down,' he said, when they had arrived. 'I am very glad to get you both here this morning, because I have to communicate to you a family project of some importance. It has occupied me for some days, and concerns Lucien.'

"'Concerns me!' exclaimed Lucien. '*Citoyen* Consul, I am much obliged—but—really—however, I am glad of it, for I flatter myself you would only occupy yourself with me for my good.'"

Napoleon. "Certainly, you shall judge of it. What is in question would be Joseph's right if he were in a position to profit by it, but as he is not a widower, I will not say, unfortunately—"

Joseph, hastily. "I should think not! No, happily I am not a widower. My little Julie is the best wife in the world."

Napoleon. "That is saying a good deal, in general. For you in particular we all know that, besides her well-known goodness, she has the greatest indulgence for your little conjugal transgressions. God knows that upon that point—"

Joseph. "Ah well! for that matter I think all husbands are very much in the same case, and wives too sometimes, but not mine."

Napoleon. "Very well, so much the better for you. But you will allow that Madame Julie tolerates many things from you that most wives would not stand. I don't except my sweet Joséphine."

Joseph. "Oh, come! Tell us at once what you

have to say. But remember that I love my wife, that I love and respect her very much, very much indeed, and that whoever says anything against her, were it—"

Napoleon. "We know that, we understand that you love her, you respect her, and she deserves it; although Madame Julie has the one great fault in my eyes of which I have told you a hundred times, to your great annoyance. But you don't imagine you are going to frighten me now?"

Joseph. "Then you must not speak to her again, as you were not afraid to do before, about this particular fault."

Napoleon. "However, if she goes on having nothing but girls—"

Joseph. "You need not trouble yourself about that. I am the principal person concerned, and I assure you not only that it is all the same to me, but that I prefer girls to boys."

Napoleon. "Girls are of no use except to contract alliances."

Lucien. "And that is no advantage except for reigning families: and even history proves that they do not do much good. All the dethroned kings are examples of that. For a long time the few families who reign over the world only marry amongst each other."

Napoleon. "It may be so, but you, who are Corsicans to the tips of your fingers, know perfectly well that we only care for boys."

Joseph. "That's an exaggeration. We like the firstborn to be a boy, because we have such a strong *esprit de famille*, and the more a race is established the more consideration one has."

Napoleon. "Meanwhile not one of us has a son yet."

Joseph. "Which proves it is as much my fault as Julie's."

Napoleon. "That may be. If I have none I can't blame Joséphine. Eugène and Hortense are the proof of that. . . . Anyhow, I would just as soon have no children as have only daughters."

Joseph. "And I am quite content to have mine."

Napoleon. "You are like Lucien. He has nothing but daughters either, but he is a widower, and we may hope that he will marry again and have sons. For that reason I have resolved to marry him. I hope he will not complain of my choice."

Lucien, laughing. "*You* have resolved! *You* have made a choice! Thank you, *citoyen* Consul, but it seems to me that it is I who should make this choice, since it concerns me so closely. In fact, if I am to marry it must be as *I* wish."

Napoleon. "I understand that, but I say that it is impossible you should not wish it when you know who it is. Joseph shall judge."

Joseph. "I am quite willing to judge, but it will be according to my ideas, whereas it is in the first place Lucien who must judge by his own."

Lucien. "Undoubtedly. And with all the gratitude I owe you, *citoyen* Consul, I beg you to understand that I am of an age and position to arrange my own marriage. I should never care for a wife chosen by any one but myself."

Napoleon. "Come, Joseph, help me to make him hear reason in his own interest."

Lucien. "My interest! It is quite satisfied.

citoyen Consul, and I keep to the profession of matrimonial faith which I have made you."

Napoleon. "I see how it is. What I have been told is true. This is not, perhaps, the moment to speak to you of my project. To talk and argue one requires sense, and that people in love never have, even if they had any before. However, I don't wish to have to reproach myself with not using all possible means in circumstances so favourable to you and which certainly will not recur."

Joseph, impatiently. "Let us know what it is, then."

Lucien. "*Mon Dieu !* it's no use, my dear Joseph. Don't you see the Consul is joking? Let us talk of something else."

Napoleon. "Be it so, let us say no more about it. But I must tell you one thing, and that is that I am afraid they will cost you very dear, *citoyen* Lucien, the *beaux yeux* of your Madame Jo—Madame Jou— Madame Joubert—what do you call her?—some devil of an outlandish name no one can remember."

Lucien. "If I knew what you wanted to say I would help you to pronounce it."

Napoleon. "Yes! I believe you don't know! *I* know! A handsome woman—for I don't deny it. . . . Does Joseph know her?"

Joseph. "I don't know who you are talking about, *mon frère.*"

Napoleon. "You know quite well, and Lucien still better, of whom I am speaking. Well! let him love this lady, it is right and natural. Let him idolise her if he thinks her worthy of it ; but not so blindly—or rather let us say so foolishly—as to give up the best *parti* in Europe."

14

Joseph. " But who is it, then? "

Lucien. " Patience! till you have done amusing yourself at my expense, *citoyen* Consul."

Napoleon. " *Ah ça!* once for all, *citoyen* Lucien, understand, I do not joke—the matter is serious. You don't guess? You have no idea? Well, *messieurs*, it is a king's daughter of whose hand I can dispose, and who will take no husband except from me. Oh! don't laugh, there is nothing to laugh at—it is the Queen of Etruria."

Lucien declined to entertain the idea, saying that he was a republican, and did not want to marry a queen, especially an ugly one. Napoleon observed—

" Believe me, Lucien, it is not necessary that our wives should be handsome. Our mistresses are different ; an ugly mistress is monstrous—she fails in her chief, we may say her only, duty. Do you not agree, Lucien? "

Lucien. " Entirely ; and it is for that reason that I consider that one's wife should be pretty, so that she may always remain the mistress of her husband."

Napoleon. " One could not argue with stricter morality. If my memory is correct, you did not always say that."

Lucien. " I have never changed as to that, and now less than ever."

Napoleon. " Ta, ta, ta! Ta, ta, ta! Since when have you become such a pattern? There was a time when you would have been sorry to be, and especially to appear so."

After some discussion Napoleon desired Joseph to try to influence Lucien, and the interview closed.[1]

[1] " Mémoires de Lucien Buonaparte " (Jung).

Joseph therefore began, as they went towards Lucien's house, to persuade him, if not to marry the Queen of Etruria, at least to make a marriage suitable to their rank; saying that they were now in a very different position from the time when he married Mademoiselle Clary, who was then a very good *parti* for him.

But Lucien cut all this short by informing his brother that [1] he was already legally married to Alexandrine, whereupon Joseph's opposition came to an end, and he accompanied Lucien to his *hôtel* to make the acquaintance of his new sister-in-law.

The Buonaparte family was now divided. Napoleon was furious, and not only refused to receive or acknowledge Lucien's wife, but did all he could to prevent the rest from doing so. Louis and Hortense called on them, and then were forbidden by the First Consul to repeat their visit—Joséphine could not, of course, oppose the will of Napoleon.

But the Signora Letizia vehemently took the side of Lucien, who was her favourite son,[2] and whom she adored; Joseph and Julie did the same. Elisa, who loved Lucien better than any of the rest, declared she should do as Joseph did, and went to see her sister-in-law and nephew, whom Joseph promised to betroth to one of his own daughters.

Bernadotte and Désirée showed them the most cordial, affectionate friendship, and were continually at their *hôtel*, where the little Oscar Bernadotte was

---

[1] The civil marriage took place Oct. 28, 1803.

[2] Lucien was the one of all her sons most like his father.

the constant playfellow of Charlotte [1] and Christine [2] or, as they were called, Lolotte and Lili, the daughters of Lucien by his first marriage.

Napoleon's quarrel with Lucien was, in fact, more likely to draw Bernadotte nearer to him, for besides his sympathy with his friend and indignation at the way he was treated, the antagonism between him and the First Consul was growing stronger on both sides ; indeed, on one occasion, in a discussion between the latter and Joseph about Bernadotte, Napoleon had exclaimed angrily, " Understand that if that headstrong southerner goes on disputing the acts of my government,[3] instead of giving him the command he asks for I will have him shot in the Place du Carrousel."

" Is that a message you wish me to give him ? "

" No, it is a warning I give you, his friend and brother-in-law, that you may prudently advise him to be more careful."

Joseph shrugged his shoulders, said nothing to Bernadotte, but told Lucien, who was much troubled on hearing it. It would not, however, have been easy even for Napoleon to get rid of Bernadotte, he was too powerful and popular, and the knowledge of this was still more irritating to the man whose wonderful genius had already raised him from obscurity to such a pitch of power that any opposition infuriated him.

He had one violent quarrel with Lucien about the colony of Louisiana, which he proposed to sell to

[1] Married Prince Gabrielli.
[2] Married first, Count Arved de Possé (Swède) ; second, Lord Dudley Stuart.
[3] " Mémoires de Lucien Buonaparte," t. ii. p. 107.

America. Lucien protested against this being done
without the consent of parliament, declaring that
it was unconstitutional, to which Napoleon replied
angrily—

"Constitution !   Unconstitutional !   Republic !
Sovereignty of the nation !   Fine words !   Fine
phrases !   Do you think you are still at the club
at Saint-Maximin ?   We have got beyond that, understand it clearly.   Ah, *parbleu !*" . . . And the scene
ended by his throwing down a snuff-box on which
was a portrait of Joséphine painted by Isabey.   The
box did not break, but the portrait came off, to the
great alarm of Joséphine when she heard of it, as
she thought it a bad omen.

When Napoleon recovered his temper he laughed
at the snuff-box and remarked to Lucien—

"You see I am not the only one of the family
inclined to get angry."

The one who oftenest fell into a rage was, in fact,
Joseph, but he was also the one whose anger was
soonest over and signified least.   In any. quarrel
between him and Napoleon the latter was always
the first to make overtures of peace, so strong was the
Corsican feeling of respect for the eldest brother which
he, perhaps unconsciously, retained.   In a Corsican
family the elder brothers and sisters addressed the
younger ones with the familiar "*tu,*" of which the
younger ones did not venture to make use when
speaking to their seniors.[1]

---

[1] Napoleon did not at this time, if ever, *tutoyer* Joseph, but
preserved the habit of calling him *vous*, using the familiar "*tu*" to
all the rest.   Joseph, in consideration of Napoleon's rank, had
lately begun to use the second person plural in addressing him.
—"Mémoires de Lucien Buonaparte," t. ii. p. 229.

It was to Joseph that Napoleon appealed, begging him to prevent their mother from calling him *Napolion.* "It is a name that sounds bad in French," he said· "In the first place it is an Italian name. Let mamma call me Buonaparte, like everybody else; not *Buonaparti* above all; that would be still worse than *Napolion.* But no, let her say the 'First Consul,' or 'the Consul' simply. Yes, I like that best. But Napolion, always that Napolion! it irritates me."

A discussion followed between Napoleon, Joseph, and Lucien, and then Napoleon said that, after all, "Napoleon" was a fine name.

Lucien. "Then why don't you want mamma to go on calling you so?"

Napoleon. "Well, in the first place because she pronounces it like the Italians and that is disagreeable. And however she tries to Frenchify it she can't succeed. Between ourselves, our mother has never known how to speak either French or Italian. It is annoying."

Joseph and Lucien, together. "But our mother speaks the Italian they speak in Corsica."

Napoleon. "That is exactly what I tell you. Do you think I am likely to feel flattered when M. Lucchesine, for instance, the first diplomatist and linguist *par excellence,* whom we receive at the Tuileries, should hear my mother reply in *patois* to a phrase in pure Tuscan?"

Joseph and Lucien. "*Patois!* But — but in Corsica—"

Napoleon, interrupting. "But—but --confess that it is disagreeable."

Lucien. "I see nothing disagreeable in it."

Joseph. "There we are! Yes, there we are. The only thing that is disagreeable about it is that you don't like people in Paris to remember that our family is Corsican."

Napoleon. "To a certain point that is true; and you ought to feel the same, for it is only reasonable. Above everything in France ridicule is to be avoided, and our mother with her Corsican jargon, *Corsican* I admit—"

Joseph, hastily, with a red face. "You admit! But it *is :* it *must* be!"

And the discussion increased in warmth, Napoleon declaring that Corsica was an insignificant little island (*une petite île de rien du tout*), half French, half Italian, and that it was no use for them to be angry, as that would not make it any different, and ending by saying that he was very sorry he had been born a Corsican.[1]

[1] "Mémoires de Lucien Buonaparte," t. ii. p. 225.

CHAPTER XIII

1803—1804

AFTER the breaking of the peace of Amiens
Napoleon's attention was strongly concen-
trated upon the great camp at Boulogne, where the
troops that he called the "Army of England" were
then quartered, and near which lay anchored the flotilla
intended to convey them to the shores of that country,
the conquest of which he and they imagined they
were soon to add to their other triumphs.

The First Consul was furious at a caricature which
appeared in London, was sent to Paris, and diligently
sought for by the police. The French fleet was represented by a number of nutshells which an English
sailor, seated on a rock, was dispersing by whiffs
from his pipe.

In the month of November, 1803, Napoleon went
to visit the camp, and remained there for some time in
order to inspect the preparations going on for that

purpose.   He was accompanied by his *préfet du palais*
—M. de Rémusat, who, shortly after their arrival, was
seized with typhoid fever and sent to his wife, who
came immediately from Paris to nurse him.   Now
Madame de Rémusat was one of the most attractive
women of the present court.   Both she and her
husband belonged to old royalist families,[1] ruined by
the Revolution, and Napoleon had been delighted to
place her as *dame du palais* to Joséphine, who was
very fond of her.   She was only twenty years old,
handsome, clever, and although a general favourite,
far above any of the intrigues or scandal of the court,
the mutual devotion of her husband and herself being
well known to everybody.

On hearing of her arrival in the camp Napoleon
sent for her at once.   She was in the greatest anxiety
about her husband, and could not restrain her tears,
but Napoleon kissed her, assured her that her
husband would be cured by her presence, tried to
console her, and said she was to breakfast and dine
with him, as he must take care of a woman of her age,
alone, among so many soldiers.   Madame de Rémusat
knew very well that for that matter she would have
been safer without his chaperonage than with it, but
she had no choice, she must obey.   Besides, she cared
nothing about the First Consul, and was only occupied with her husband, consequently no harm came
of all the time she passed alone with Napoleon except
a certain amount of gossip and suspicion, the falseness
of which her whole life and character successfully
refuted ; though it was probably no thanks to
Napoleon that such was the case.

[1] She was Mademoiselle de Vergennes.

He was in the habit of finishing his breakfast in a quarter of an hour, but would sit for a long time at and after dinner, especially when, as often happened, they were alone. He knew better than to begin to make love to her, as he did to the women without brains or character by whom he was chiefly surrounded, but he passed the time pleasantly enough *tête-à-tête* with a young, beautiful, charming woman, to whom he could talk on any subject that interested him.

He asked after Joséphine, with whom he had lately had another quarrel about his *liaison* with the actress Mademoiselle Georges.

" She troubles herself much more than there is any need to do," he said. " Joséphine is always afraid of my becoming seriously in love; she does not understand that love is not made for me. For what is love? A passion which makes one abandon everything in the whole universe, to see and care for nothing but the person one loves. And I am assuredly not of a nature to give myself up to any such exclusion. Therefore why should she concern herself about these distractions, into which my affections do not enter at all?"

Their conversations were not, however, by any means confined to the gossip of the court or the scandals of the household of the First Consul. It was the interest he had felt in a conversation about Shakespeare and English poetry in general, in which Madame de Rémusat had taken a leading part, that had first attracted his attention to her; and as they lingered over their dinner on those winter evenings or sat together afterwards, they discussed art, literature, science, even political matters; and, growing more and more confidential, Napoleon would talk to her of himself, his past life, his ideas and feelings, in a way than which there is none more easy and certain of drifting from an indifferent acquaintance into an intimate friendship, a serious love-affair, or a decided flirtation, according to the circumstances or the individuals concerned.

"At first," said Napoleon, "I did not understand much about the Revolution, but it suited me. The equality by which I was to rise fascinated me. I was at Paris on the 20th of June. I saw the mob marching upon the Tuileries. I have never liked the movements of the populace, and I was disgusted with the coarse brutality of those wretches. I saw the imprudence of the leaders by whom they had been aroused, and I said to myself, 'The advantages of this Revolution will not be for them.' But when I heard that Louis had put the red cap on his head, I knew that he had ceased to reign, for in political affairs one can never rise again from what has been degradation. On the 10th of August I felt that if I had been called upon I would have defended the King; I recoiled from those who were founding the Republic by the mob; and then I saw those fellows in blouses attacking men in uniform; it shocked me!"

He told her also that he had always been reserved and melancholy. "When I was at the École Militaire," he said, "I had a little chosen corner where I could sit and dream in peace, for I was always fond of reverie, and when I entered the service I was bored at the barracks, and I used to read novels which interested me immensely. I tried to write some, and

that gave a sort of vagueness to my imagination. . . .
I threw myself into an ideal world, and sought to discover in what it differed from the realities amongst
which I found myself. . . . I liked Ossian for the
same reason which makes me find pleasure in listening
to the sound of the wind or the murmur of the sea."

In her memoirs Madame de Rémusat describes
Napoleon as short, not well made, with chestnut-
coloured hair, deep greyish-blue eyes, and a most
fascinating smile, which, when angry, would change
into a menacing frown. His dreamy temperament
delighted, as he told her, in surroundings which
appealed to the imagination : melancholy music, twilight, stories of apparitions, Ossian's poems, wild,
romantic tales. Sometimes he would come into the
drawing-room at Saint-Cloud or La Malmaison, have
the lights covered with gauze, and not allow any one
to talk, while slow, plaintive music was played or
ghost-stories told.

In spite of his colossal intellect, she says, he had
not a great soul ; he possessed neither truth nor
generosity, and was incapable of admiring or understanding a noble action. He spoke with approbation
of any one who was a skilful liar. Later in life he
became *triste;* and later still, when cares, anxieties,
and misfortunes overwhelmed him, his temper was
bad.

At no time of his life, she says, had he any
manners ; he never knew how to enter or leave a
room, to sit down or rise, to salute any one politely or
gracefully ; he was always brusque, and no language
he spoke ever seemed easy to him.

After a sojourn of some weeks in the camp at

Boulogne, Madame de Rémusat had the joy of seeing her husband sufficiently recovered to go back to Paris. The *aides-de-camp* and other officers who knew of the long hours which, in the intervals of her nursing, she and Napoleon had spent together, did not believe the time was passed only in conversations on art and literature, or even in sentimental reminiscences, and various reports got to Joséphine, whose suspicions were sufficiently aroused to cause her reception of Madame de Rémusat to be colder than usual. The latter, however, soon succeeded in convincing her that these suspicions were unfounded ; and she confessed that she had reproached Napoleon on the subject, and he had only amused himself by leaving her in doubt and refusing to give any explanation. For the rest, no one of any weight or whose opinion was worth having attached any belief to the malicious gossip in question, the character of Madame de Rémusat raising her above any such slanders.

Napoleon had one or two *liaisons* while at Boulogne, which he kept as secret as he could, saying that otherwise his example would be quoted and followed by all his officers, married or single ; whereas he wished austerity to prevail, for licentiousness would corrupt and enervate the army—that wonderful instrument of his power, whose strength and vigour it was his great desire to preserve.

Although possessing that light-hearted, easy temperament which is not given to magnify or anticipate troubles or dangers, Désirée could not feel otherwise than anxious and uneasy as time went on and the antagonism between her husband and the First Consul seemed to increase rather than diminish,

It was perfectly apparent that Napoleon's intention to establish himself permanently as the supreme power in France would very shortly be carried out if it were not vigorously opposed ; and even if it were, it seemed doubtful if any opposition would be successful against one who was not only the greatest genius of the age, but the hero and idol of the army and the people. At the same time his enemies were many and various. The royalists, of course, were always on the watch, and the old-fashioned, steady republicans were asking each other what was the use of the Revolution, and beginning to say that it was not worth while to have shed all the blood and made all the sacrifices of the last few years merely to put the Buonaparte in the place of the Bourbons.

A certain number of generals, united in this opinion, were secretly consulting together, hoping to form a party strong enough to raise their voices against the destruction of the Republic ; and the head of the malcontents was Moreau, the victor of Hohenlinden—a gallant soldier, but a most unsuitable leader of a conspiracy.

It was in firmness and decision of character that he was wanting ; indeed, so undecided and uncertain was he that for some time he was claimed both by the royalists and republicans as a supporter.

There is a Chinese proverb, " He who deliberates sufficiently before every step will pass his life standing upon one leg." And in private life when one suffers from people who cannot make up their mind, or who, if they appear to have done so, are always liable to have their opinions entirely altered by the next person to whom they talk, one is almost inclined to prefer

the thoroughly obstinate persons, who are generally
stupid and probably wrong, but who have the single
advantage that one knows exactly what they will say
and do.

It was impossible to persuade Moreau to act in
this matter. He hesitated, procrastinated, changed
his mind, left Paris, and went to his country place,
Grosbois, where Bernadotte followed him, but returned
without having succeeded in prevailing upon him to do
or say anything. His wife and her mother, who were
royalist in their sympathies and also very jealous of
Joséphine, did their best to influence him, but for
some time things went on in the same dilatory
manner, without coming to any crisis.

Désirée saw and knew that something was going
on around her. There was an air of mystery and
agitation ; her husband seemed anxious, preoccupied,
and absorbed in some affair in which he appeared to
be involved with Moreau and others ; but he told her
nothing about it, and the meetings and consultations
did not take place at her house, but at that of Madame
Récamier, who was also a friend of Moreau. The
emissaries of the Comte d'Artois were using every
endeavour to draw Moreau into the great royalist
conspiracy which was being formed under Cadoudal
and Pichegru, under the latter of whom, Moreau, a
Breton by birth, had served in 1793-4.

Pichegru was an old schoolfellow of Napoleon, had
fought with success and renown under the banner of
the Revolution, but had, after some years, been
suspected of royalist sympathies and of certain transactions with the Prince de Condé, for which he was
deprived of his rank of general, and after living in

retirement for two years had been elected member of the Council of Five Hundred. Again mixing himself up in a royalist conspiracy, he was transported to Sinnamari, escaped to England, where he became one of the most active agents of the Bourbons.

During the winter of 1803-4, under cover of all the gaieties and amusements going on as usual, most dangerous plots were concocted; the royalists and republicans being sometimes even inclined to unite in opposition to Napoleon and the present Government.

" Madame Moreau gave a ball," writes Madame Récamier in her memoirs; "all Europe was there except official France; the only French element was the republican opposition. Madame Moreau, young and charming, did the honours with the perfection of grace. In spite of the crowds with which they were filled, the rooms seemed empty to me; the absence of all connected with the government struck me forcibly. This absence, which seemed to place Moreau in a sort of menacing isolation, was to me like a melancholy foreboding. I noticed how pre-occupied Bernadotte and his friends appeared, and how Moreau himself looked like a stranger at the *fête.*

" My thoughts were far from the ball. I sat down often, and during a *contredanse* that I did not wish to dance, Bernadotte offered me his arm to get some fresh air. It was his thoughts that wanted space. We came to a little room, where only the distant sound of the music followed us, to remind us where we were.

" I confided my fears to him; he did not yet despair

of Moreau, whose position he thought so well suited to direct and moderate a movement, but he was irritated by the thought that all these advantages might be thrown away.

"'If I were in his place,' he exclaimed, 'I should be at the Tuileries this evening to dictate to Buonaparte the conditions upon which he should govern.' Just then Moreau passed. Bernadotte called him, and repeated all the reasons and arguments which he had used to persuade him. 'With a popular name,' he said, 'you are the only one amongst us who can come forward supported by the whole people—decide at last!'

" Moreau replied to Bernadotte with what he had often said, that he felt the dangers with which liberty was threatened ; that Buonaparte must be watched, but that he dreaded civil war. He held himself in readiness ; his friends might act, and when the time came he would be at their disposal ; they might count on him at the first movement made ; but at this time he did not consider it necessary to provoke one. . . ."

In March, 1804, the Duc d'Enghien was treacherously seized outside French territory and shot at Vincennes on the pretence that he was concerned in or knew of some plot of the royalists, of which he was entirely innocent. This atrocious murder, for it was nothing less, aroused a universal cry of horror and indignation, not only throughout Europe but in the Buonaparte family. Joséphine lavished tears and entreaties, assuring Napoleon that vengeance would certainly overtake him—that he would some day be guillotined and she with him ; his brothers, and at any rate Elisa, expressed their reprobation in the plainest terms : his mother overwhelmed him with indignant reproaches, assuring him that this atrocious action would be for ever an ineffaceable stain upon him.

But already, in February, the plot of Pichegru and Cadoudal had been discovered by the secret police, and Moreau, with a number of others, many of whom were probably innocent victims of the remorseless Fouché, were arrested and thrown into prison.

It has always been thought that the friendship of Napoleon for Désirée, and his connection with Joseph, had now and at other times been the safeguard of Bernadotte. It was a moment of terror for Désirée unless she was assured of his immunity, for Bernadotte was sent for to the Tuileries when Moreau was arrested. However, no accusation was brought against him, and when a very short time afterwards the Empire was proclaimed, Napoleon said to him in a short and peremptory manner—

" You see how it is ; the nation has declared for me ; but she wants the concurrence of all her children. Will you march with me and with France, or will you hold yourself aloof ? "

" I do not promise you affection, but a loyal support," was the answer of Bernadotte.

CHAPTER XIV

1804

THE departure of Lucien and his wife was
deeply regretted by the Bernadottes. The
former had returned from Rome only to find Napoleon
inexorable. He would do everything for Lucien if
he would sacrifice his wife and declare his children
illegitimate ; nothing if he refused. Lucien should
not live in Europe, or at any rate only in a distant
part of it ; certainly not in France.

Lucien declined to give up his wife and children,
or to accept invitations to family festivities where his
wife was not invited ; and, horrified at the murder of
the Duc d'Enghien, he exclaimed to her—

"Alexandrine, he has tasted blood, let us get
away."

In a fragment left at his death, written in 1837, he

says : " The details of this evening, the last I was to pass in France, are ever present to my mind. . . . It was Easter-eve, 1804, the four travelling carriages were ready and loaded in the courtyard of the *hôtel, rue Saint-Dominique.* . . . The servants went to and fro, the post-horses were ordered to be harnessed at daybreak. . . . My dear brother Joseph, with a sorrowful expression on his kind, handsome face, was walking with me up and down the long gallery of pictures for which I then had such a passion, and which were to begin to be packed for Rome after my departure. My mother and my wife were sitting on a little sofa by the fire, . . . a number of *chiffons* were scattered over the divans, &c., they were presents from my wife, mother, and sisters to our sister Pauline, lately become Princess Borghese, . . . who was expecting their arrival as eagerly as ours. . . . My wife looked sorrowfully at these fashionable trifles which my mother, with equal sadness, was having packed up by Mademoiselle Sophie, my wife's maid, who was in despair at leaving Paris. . . . The clock on the chimney-piece struck eleven. . . . My mother advanced and took Joseph's hand with an evident nervous tension, and forcing back her tears, said—

" ' Come, my sons, you must separate, it is time.'

" ' No, mother, not yet,' replied Joseph. ' Lucien will let me wait till midnight. I still hope *he* will recall him.'

" ' No, my son, Napoleon will not recall your brother. He does not want him near him. . . .'

" ' Mother, it is only half-past eleven. The Consul does not go to bed till twelve ; suppose I went back

and asked him for another letter for Lucien, telling
him——'

"'What, my dear brother?' interrupted I.

"'Why, not to go?'

"'Your kind heart misleads you, *mon frère;* he
wishes it, I *must* go.　Do you want the same thing
to happen to me as to the Duke ——?' and I
stopped.

"'Shall I go and ask the Consul, mother?' repeated Joseph three times.　Then, rising from her
seat, my mother said—

"'Yes, my son, yes; you, his elder brother, go and
beg him to let Lucien stay, so that he may answer
you in anger as he did me and even his Joséphine.
Let those who are so grieved at his departure go with
him. . . . I shall go, I shall go, not with you, Lucien,
but after you.　In that way I shall spare him the
embarrassment of my obstinacy.'

"She sank back suffocated with tears into the arms
of my wife, my dear Alexandrine. . . .

"Midnight approached.　Joseph seemed on thorns.
He walked up and down the room ; I was sitting on
a low seat at the feet of my mother and wife.　Presently Joseph said—

"'Lucien, if you loved me, you would give me a
great proof of it.'

"'My good Joseph! you know whether I love you,
it is almost filial love that I have for you.　You have
stood in my father's place. . . . What shall I do?
What do you want me to do?'

"'Well! suppose you were to go yourself before
he goes to bed, and ask to speak to him before you
set off?'

"'Well! *après, mon frère;* what shall I say to him?'

"'Oh, you would tell him that—that you are sorry to go away on bad terms with him, and then——'

"I took my mother's hand and kissed it.

"'Am I to go and tell him that, *ma bonne mère?*'

"'No, my son, you ought not. Besides, it would be perfectly useless. I know what he said to me in his anger.'

"'If that's all I am not afraid of his anger. I know that one does not always act upon what one says in a passion.'

"'Yes, that is true,' replied my mother; 'but you are both hasty. Napoleon is powerful--more so than you are, my poor Lucien. Decidedly, I would rather you left without seeing him. . . .'

"Midnight struck. . . . My mother went up to embrace our sleeping children. Lolotte, the eldest, was the only one who awoke. Poor little thing! she was sorry to hear it was not morning, for she was delighted to take this long journey. Happy age! she rejoiced, and we—*nous avions la mort dans l'âme.*

"The door of the *hôtel* was opened to let in the carriage which came for my mother and Joseph; it had just been closed again; we were thinking of going to get some rest.

"As we came out of the gallery to go up to our bedroom, we were stopped between the two doors by somebody who suddenly stood before us. My wife clung to my arm, and I felt her tremble.

"Shall I confess that for a moment I had the hope that it might be the First Consul himself, come, if not to stop my departure, at least to say goodbye, and tell me to change the exile to which he had condemned me into a short journey? His daily ill-treatment of me, his dreams, even, which his wife Joséphine had the simplicity or the perfidy to repeat to me, and the infamous calumnies of his police, could only lead to a tragic scene between us. Our mother foresaw this and dreaded it exceedingly, which was the reason she was so anxious for me to take advantage of my letter of recommendation to the Pope.

" I had asked the First Consul for this letter after a violent scene, which had been followed by a reconciliation due to the entreaties of mamma. She persuaded me to make the first advances, because she said it was I who was in the right. But the peace did not last long. Every time I was not of his opinion, there was a new quarrel, new threats. It was, above all, to our mother that he complained. He repeated to her that I should do well to make use of my letter to the Pope, and that if I stayed he would not be responsible for himself, *and still less for me*.

" ' *Enfin*, Madame,' he added one day ; ' do you want there to be a tragedy between your sons? . . .'

" But to return to the person we left between our two doors, who seemed to want to keep us prisoners. At the first words I was agreeably surprised to recognise the voice of my friend General Bernadotte ; it was impossible to mistake when, with his energetic, *piquant*, southern accent, he came up to me, saying—

" ' *Comment !* You oblige me to force your door? You intend to escape me without *adieux* and without my trying once more to persuade you not to go? To go away? What folly! Resist, resist, as you ought: he who quits the game loses it. After all, what do you fear?'

" 'I? Nothing for myself, but it's much worse.'

" ' *Bah! bah! les carmagnoles de Fouché! Parbleu!* we should see about that! In your place, my dear Lucien, I should not go.'

" 'Nor I either if I were General Bernadotte, for then I should not risk a fratricidal war and all that might follow.'

" 'Well! if you have that to fear, be it so; go, then, but recollect what I tell you, he who leaves his place, loses it.'

" No, *mon cher*, there is no longer any place for me to gain here, the price is too high. And then—and then——'

" My wife, dreadfully tired and overdone, took an affectionate leave of the general and retired.

" ' At least,' he said, looking after her, ' no one can say that the First Consul has not chosen a beautiful pretext for his quarrel with you.'

" My conversation with Bernadotte lasted till daybreak, which was the hour fixed for our departure, and we only separated at the sound of the horses' bells as they entered the courtyard.

" That night I saw and embraced for the last time my illustrious friend. Since then, removed far from each other, we have never met again, and doubtless we never shall."

Bernadotte wrote a long letter to Lucien in Italy, in which he deplored his absence, recalled old memories and affections, prophesied the destruction of liberty and the establishment of an autocratic power; said that he did not intend to vegetate in the shade of the laurels of others, and that he thought of retiring to America, where they might meet ; begging Madame Lucien not to fret about what had happened, as he heard she was doing ; for she was too good and too pretty to excite the dislike of any one, and too clever not to understand that it was only a pretext which, if he dared, Napoleon would thank her for furnishing ; ending—

" *Adieu, Lucien, au revoir*—when and where it shall please God."

One day at the beginning of the year 1804, Colonel Gérard, one of his *aides-de-camp*, proposed to Bernadotte that they should go and see a *clairvoyante*, or person who had second sight, and was just then a good deal talked about on account of the strange things she was said to have seen and foretold. He remarked that at the present time everything was so extraordinary, who could tell what she would be able to show them ?

Bernadotte consented, and they went together to the house of the *clairvoyante*, to whom Gérard presented Bernadotte as a rich merchant who wished to consult her about the success of a commercial enterprise. The woman, looking at Bernadotte, replied—

" Monsieur, you are not a merchant, but a soldier, and among the highest in rank."

On their persisting in their assertions, she shook her head incredulously, remarking—

" Well ! if you engage in commercial transactions they will not succeed, but you will find yourself forced to give them up and follow your destiny."

She then pretended to consult her cards, and said with surprise and emotion—

" You are not only of high military rank, but you are, or will be, related to the Emperor."

" What Emperor ? " cried they both together.

" I mean the First Consul, but you will soon see him Emperor."

Then appearing to see a vision, she continued, dreamily—

" Yes, he will be Emperor, but I see clouds that will separate you. He does not dislike you, and you have affection for him. Ah ! how his star rises ! "

Again the old woman paused, her countenance became filled with astonishment, and she went on—

" Monsieur, beware of quarrelling with him, for he will be very powerful, he will see the world at his feet. And you, far away from him, you will be a king—yes, you will be a king——"

There was silence, and then she exclaimed—

" I can tell no more—I see no more," and fell back exhausted in her chair.[1]

The principal events occupying the public during the spring and summer of 1804 were the war with England, the trial of the royalist conspirators, and the approaching establishment of the Empire, all of which were going on at the same time.

Napoleon displayed great anxiety about the regulation of the court, which was now to be arranged with the utmost splendour, and according to the rules of courtly etiquette, so far as they could be discovered ; and this was not altogether easy with the

[1] " Histoire de Bernadotte " (Sarrans).

materials of which it was at this time principally composed.

Napoleon consulted Talleyrand and Madame de Montesson ; and Joséphine sent for Madame Campan, to tell them what was customary at the court of Marie Antoinette. There was, as Madame de Rémusat remarks, a perfect fever of etiquette at Saint-Cloud. Enormous volumes of the " Règlements de Louis XIV." were got out of the State libraries, from which instructions were taken and copybooks full of extracts made. Madame Campan was overwhelmed with questions about the arrangements of the household, intimate circle, and daily life of the last Queen of France ; the Buonaparte family were in a ferment of anxiety and excitement about what titles and honours were to be bestowed upon them, how their households were to be formed, &c., &c.[1]

On the 18th of May the accession of the Emperor was proclaimed by the Senate, who proceeded in State to present to Napoleon the *sernatus consultum* relative to the foundation of the Empire.[2]

For the first time Napoleon was addressed as *Votre Majesté* by Cambacérès in his speech ; and his first act on the same day was to make Joseph Grand Elector and Louis Constable, each with the titles of Imperial Highness. Cambacérès was made Arch-Chancellor, and Lebrun Arch-Treasurer. Elisa, Caroline, and their husbands were at Saint-Cloud, also Joseph, Louis, their wives, and Eugène de Beauharnais.

The Emperor desired them to stay and dine, and

[1] " Mémoires de Madame de Rémusat."
[2] " Mémoires de Bourrienne."

before dinner, which was at six o'clock, Duroc announced the titles they were to bear. Neither Julie nor Hortense were particularly elated on being informed that as wives of the brothers of the Emperor they were to be princesses—and "Altesses Impériales." Julie cared nothing about such matters, and Hortense was too unhappy to care much about anything except to get away from Louis Buonaparte ; but Elisa and Caroline, finding that they were not made princesses, were in despair and furious.

The Emperor came in, saluted every one by their new title, and they proceeded to dinner. That repast was by no means a pleasant one ; the day was very hot, and a violent thunderstorm going on. Caroline was nearly crying the whole time and kept drinking large glasses of water, as Napoleon spoke of the " Princess Joseph," and the " Princess Louis "; while Elisa, being older and possessing more self-control, did not cry, but was only very disagreeable, until the Emperor, irritated by all this, became angry, and talked in a mocking, sarcastic way on purpose to annoy them. After dinner, in a private *salon*, there was a violent family quarrel. Caroline especially gave way to as bitter complaints and reproaches as if Napoleon had, according to his well-known remark, been dividing with them the inheritance of the King, their father. But neither reason nor common sense ever made the slightest impression in these matters upon the sisters of Napoleon. He himself showed wonderful kindness and indulgence to them on this and many other occasions ; at first he was very angry, which was not surprising ; but when Caroline, in a passion of tears, sobs, and rage, threw herself upon the floor and fainted, or nearly fainted, the Emperor relented, and a few days afterwards his sisters also appeared in the *Moniteur* as " *Altesses Impériales.*" [1]

Next day there was a creation of marshals, the following being the names of the generals raised to that rank: Berthier, Murat, Moncey, Jourdan, Masséna, Augereau, Bernadotte, Soult, Brune, Lannes, Mortier, Ney, Davoust, Bessières, Kellerman, Lefèbre, Pérignon, and Serrurier.

Delighted at the concurrence of Bernadotte, Napoleon publicly shook hands with him, thanking him for his support and the sacrifice of his wishes to the good of France, and bestowing upon him various honours and decorations.

His address to the Emperor on this occasion preserved the just medium, avoiding equally the slavish adulation of Murat and the almost insolent tone of Augereau.[2]

Napoleon bought from Moreau his estate of Grosbois and his *hôtel* in the *rue d'Anjou*, of which he gave the former to Berthier, the latter to Bernadotte.

The conspiracy which had been gathering for some months, and the discovery of which had spread suspicion and alarm throughout Paris, was both dangerous and perplexing. From that time to this, divers and opposing theories and opinions have always existed as to the nature and extent of it, the individuals by whom it was carried on, their aims and intentions.

---

[1] " Mémoires de Madame de Rémusat. Napoléon et sa famille " (Masson), pp. 400–401.

[2] " Bernadotte," p 62 (Pingaud).

It was even asserted by some that a serious conspiracy never existed at all, but was the invention of Napoleon and Fouché, who wished to destroy certain persons they believed to be hostile to them, and took that means of doing so.

The only thing that could lend colour to such a supposition of iniquity seems to be the theory advanced by certain fanatical partisans of Napoleon, who did, and do, not only condone but justify the illegal seizure and murder of the Duc d'Enghien, on the plea that he considered it the best way to ensure his own safety, against which he thought the unfortunate prince had designs, and the death of whom would at any rate remove one enemy from his way and terrify the others into inaction.

One of them even seeks to excuse it by saying that, having seized their prisoner in a manner undoubtedly illegal, they did not know what else to do with him !

Now, it is in such sentiments as these and in such reasoning as this that we see the germ of all tyranny and cruelty alike of the despotic rulers of former ages, and of the bloodthirsty tyrants of the Terror, who, if they feared or suspected any person, and it was in their power to do so, caused him to be accused and put to death without hesitation, remorse, or consideration, of justice, or legality.

For it is never denied that it was absolutely illegal for the French to arrest the Duc d'Enghien at all in German territory; and that they only did so because the country in which he chanced to be was weaker than their own. The Duc d'Enghien knew nothing about the plot, and if his murderers had really believed him to be concerned in it, he would, of course, have been tried with the rest, who were not sentenced until the 10th of June.

Bourrienne remarks in his account of what took place—

"It is absolutely impossible any reasonable person can regard the Duc d'Enghien as an accomplice of Cadoudal ; and Napoleon basely imposed on his contemporaries and posterity by inventing such false-hoods and investing them with the authority of his name."

After relating how Duroc expressed to him his belief in the guilt of Moreau, and how he in reply advised Duroc that it was better to be cautious ; for it was no joke to accuse the conqueror of Hohen-linden ; Bourrienne goes on to say—

"No person possessing the least degree of intel-ligence will be convinced that the conspiracy of Moreau, Georges, Pichegru, and the other persons accused, would ever have occurred but for the secret connivance of Fouché's police. Moreau never for a moment desired the restoration of the Bourbons. I was too well acquainted with his intimate friend, M. Carbonnet, to be ignorant of his private sentiments. It was, therefore, quite impossible that he could entertain the same views as Georges, the Polignacs, Rivière, and the others ; and they had no intention of committing any overt acts. These latter persons had come to the Continent solely to investigate the actual state of affairs, in order to inform the princes of the house of Bourbon with certainty how far they might depend upon the foolish hopes constantly held out to them by paltry agents who were always ready to advance their own interests at the expense of truth."

Napoleon, however, was convinced that his life was threatened, and many of his friends and supporters were of his opinion ; the greatest alarm prevailed at Paris on all sides and amongst all parties. It was declared that the assassination of Buonaparte was the object of the plot, that he was in extreme peril, for never had a conspiracy been better organised, that its members belonged to all classes of society, and were to be found amongst his officers, his household, his *préfets*, and the women of his acquaintance ; and it was, of course, true that Napoleon's life had already been repeatedly threatened.

It has already been explained that for some months attempts had been made to reconcile Moreau with the royalists and draw him over to their assistance, and Bourrienne confesses that it was not at all impossible for Napoleon to have believed them to have been successful. The conspiracy was revealed to Napoleon by Fouché, and forty-nine persons, several of whom were women, arrested and thrown into prison.

Pichegru had at first contrived to evade the police, who for some time searched for him in vain, but a scoundrel named Leblanc, after agreeing to receive him in his house, went to Murat and betrayed him, demanding and receiving as the price of his infamy, 100,000 francs. He afterwards had the impudence to ask for a decoration ; but this was refused, and he was ordered to leave Paris.

Pichegru was arrested in his bed, from which he started up, tried in vain to reach his pistols, and was only overpowered after a desperate resistance, in which he severely injured a gendarme and was himself wounded. He was taken to the Temple, which he never left alive. A son of M. de Lagrenée, formerly director of the French Academy at Rome ; a young man who had been Pichegru's *aide-de-camp*, had resigned on the banishment of his general, and become an artist. When concealed in Paris, Pichegru went to see him, but refused to allow him to risk giving him shelter as he wished to do. His disinterested friendship very possibly cost him his life. Most of the accused were confined in the Temple or La Force. Cadoudal was in the Conciergerie.

One of the conspirators, named Bouvet de Lozier, who was in the Temple, tried to hang himself with his cravat, and had nearly succeeded when the gaoler came in. He declared that he could face death but not the cross-examination of the trial, and had resolved to kill himself lest he should be persuaded to make any confessions ; which, however, he was ultimately induced to do.

The agents of Fouché had given Pichegru, Georges Cadoudal, and some of the others to understand that they might depend upon Moreau, who was prepared to join them ; but on appealing to Moreau himself they found that he had never been spoken to on the subject, and that they had been led into a trap. Most of them were about to leave Paris when they were arrested.

When Pichegru was required to sign his interrogations he refused, saying that he knew all the secret machinery of the police, who by some chemical process would erase all the writing except his

signature, and then fill up the paper with false statements. All the prisoners displayed a courage which
caused much alarm as to what would be the result of
the trial.

On the 28th of May, ten days after the Empire had
been declared, the trials began. Paris was in a
ferment of excitement. Some of the prisoners were
very well known in society, and the most intense
interest was displayed in their fate—above all in that
of Moreau. For if Rivière, the Polignacs, and Charles
d'Hozier had influential friends and relations at court
and in the *faubourg Saint-Germain*, Moreau was the
idol of the army and the people ; in fact, it was considered very likely that there would be a rising in his
favour.

During the twelve days the trials lasted, an
immense crowd thronged the avenues of the Palais
de Justice : every one wanted to be present. At one
of the sittings General Lecourbe, a friend of Moreau,
entered the court leading Moreau's little son, whom
he lifted up in his arms, saying in a voice of emotion,
" Soldiers ! behold the son of your general."

All the soldiers in court immediately rose and presented arms, and a murmur of applause ran through
the crowded court.

Georges Cadoudal, the Chouan leader, who did not
inspire so much interest, was a rough soldier, but had
the soul of a hero. When it was suggested to him
by M. Réal that he might be offered a pardon if he
would promise to renounce the conspiracy and accept
employment under government, he only replied—

" My comrades followed me to France, and I shall
follow them to death."

THE PRISON OF THE CONCIERGERIE.

The French newspapers did all they could to
injure the prisoners in the opinion of the public by
mangling and misrepresenting their defence in a
most malignant manner ; but so great was the
sympathy for the accused, who were all young
and behaved with undaunted courage and loyalty,
that the court was dissolved in tears when M. de
Rivière pressed to his lips and heart the medal given
him by the Comte d'Artois ; and Armand and Jules
de Polignac each tried to assume the whole guilt, and
entreated that his brother might be saved. None of
them denied the conspiracy, but all repudiated the
idea of an intention to assassinate Napoleon or anybody else.

On the 10th of June the sentences were pronounced. Twenty were condemned to death,
amongst whom were Georges Cadoudal, Jean
Cadoudal, MM. Armand de Polignac, de Rivière,
d'Hozier, and Coster-Saint-Victor ; Moreau, Jules de
Polignac, and three others to two years' imprisonment ; the rest were acquitted. Consternation and
horror filled the city at these sanguinary proceedings. Pichegru had been found dead in his bed,
having either committed suicide or been strangled in
the night ; which it was could never be proved.
Bourrienne declares that Buonaparte caused him to be
murdered for fear of what he might say at the trial
respecting the doings of the secret police and the
treacherous way in which he and his companions had
been ensnared. Amongst other reasons for dis-
believing in his suicide, Bourrienne states that he had
never abandoned the religion of his youth. Many
believed in this murder though it was indignantly

denied by the supporters of Napoleon, and by himself, but it was never proved either way.

When the sentences were made known there was a cry of horror. It was Sunday, but all the usual places of amusement were deserted ; a deep gloom hung over the city. The friends of the condemned were using all their endeavours to get pardons ; Murat went to Napoleon and implored him to forgive them all, observing that such an act of clemency would honour him in the eyes of all Europe, but his representations were useless. In a few cases the intercessions were successful, eight of those condemned to death were reprieved, the other twelve were executed June 25th. They met their death with the greatest heroism. Georges Cadoudal refused all overtures and offers, and only asked to be allowed to die the first, that his comrades might know that he had not survived them.

The one man amongst them whose death Napoleon regretted was Georges Cadoudal.

" Among the conspirators," he said afterwards to Bourrienne, " for example, there was an individual whose fate I regret. This Georges in my hands might have achieved great things. I can duly appreciate the firmness of character he displayed, and to which I could have given a proper direction. I caused Réal to intimate to him that if he would attach himself to me, not only should he be pardoned, but I would give him the command of a regiment . . . Georges refused all my offers ; he was as inflexible as iron. . . . What could I do ? He underwent his fate, for he was a dangerous man ; circumstances rendered his death a matter of necessity. Examples of severity were called for when England was pouring into France all the offscourings of the emigration ; but patience ! patience ! I have a long arm, and shall be able to reach them when necessary. Moreau regarded Georges merely as a ruffian. I viewed him in a different light. . . . Réal told me that when Moreau and Georges found themselves in the presence of Pichegru they could not come to any understanding because Georges would not act against the Bourbons. Well, he had a plan, but Moreau had none ; he merely wished for my overthrow without having formed any ulterior view whatever. This showed that he was destitute even of common sense." [1]

The names of those who were spared were Bouvet de Lozier, an *émigré*, who had made various disclosures under promise of pardon, the Duc de Polignac, the Marquis de la Rivière, Charles d'Hozier, Rochelle, Rusillon, Lajolais, and Armand Guillard.

Madame de Rémusat declares in her memoirs that the Duchesse de Polignac and her aunt, Madame d'Andlau, came to her in tears, begging her to obtain them, through Joséphine, an audience of the Emperor, that she did so after infinite trouble, and that when all was over they never showed her the slightest gratitude ; that the duchess made her a few forced visits, which gradually ceased ; that when, at the Restoration, the King sent the Duc de Polignac to La Malmaison to thank Joséphine for having tried to save the Duc d'Enghien, and he took that opportunity of thanking her for saving his own life.

[1] Bourrienne.

Joséphine said that he would, of course, go also and thank Madame de Rémusat for her exertions in his behalf; but that he did nothing of the kind. That when shortly after she met the Duchesse de Polignac at a great party at the Duchesse d'Orléans' she appeared to have entirely forgotten her, and when she recalled herself to her recollection, seemed very stiff and embarrassed, and after a few short sentences moved away without a word of thanks.

But whatever were the efforts made, and the sympathy and kindness shown by Madame de Rémusat for the Duc de Polignac and his brother, and although Caroline Murat was declared to have interceded for the Marquis de Rivière, and various persons for others of the condemned, it was in fact Madame de Montesson who saved the two Polignacs, M. de Rivière, and M. d'Hozier.

Her health was already failing, she frequently suffered violent pain, and was rather more ill than usual, when one day her friend Madame de la Tour came to her at Romainville in the greatest distress, imploring her to save her nephews, the Polignacs, saying that she was the only person who could do so from her great influence with Joséphine, for whom she begged her to give her a letter.

But Madame de Montesson, ill as she was, ordered her carriage, sent for her dress, saying that when the life of a man was at stake an interview was better than a letter, and drove to Saint-Cloud without loss of time.

On arriving at Saint-Cloud she was at once shown into the *salon* of Joséphine, and urgently with tears begged for the pardon of her friends.

"Alas!" cried Joséphine, "what can I do for them?"

"Everything," replied Madame de Montesson earnestly. "You have a powerful reason for persuading the Emperor to spare you these three heads that are to fall at his desire. It is his own glory you

MARQUISE DE MONTESSON,
WIFE OF LOUIS PHILIPPE, DUC D'ORLÉANS.

will save with them. What does he want? To be king? Well, does he desire that our hearts, which would always be for him, should be alienated by this act of cruelty? Does he wish the steps of the throne he ascends to be stained with innocent blood?"

"But they are guilty!" said Joséphine gently.

"No, they are not guilty!" exclaimed Madame de Montesson passionately.

"They are not guilty? What oaths have they taken? What faith have they broken? Ever faithful to their sovereign, they came back to France for his interests, it is true. Well, let them be watched; let them be imprisoned. But not death! no bloodshed! My God! has not blood enough flowed in France?"

And overpowered by her agitation she sank back on the sofa.

"Calm yourself," said Joséphine, embracing her. "You make me blush for my fears. I will speak; Buonaparte will hear me. And I swear to you that he shall grant me the pardon of MM. de Polignac and de Rivière or I will have no more affection for him. You open my eyes. Undoubtedly they are not so guilty as that, Moreau!"

"Oh, him! I leave him to you! Although, to say the truth, the first act of your hero in the road his glory has opened to him ought to be altogether great and glorious. Ah, Joséphine! mercy becomes a sovereign so well!"

"I promise to do all that I could do to save my brother. Trust to me."

"Could not I see him?" asked Madame de Montesson.

"I will go and find out," and Joséphine hurried away, but returned with a dejected air.

"I cannot see him *myself*," she said. "Go back, but count upon me."

However, in spite of the entreaties of Joséphine, the death sentences were passed, and Madame de

Montesson, leaving her friends crying and lamenting, again took the road to Saint-Cloud.

Napoleon had been much irritated because Moreau had not been condemned to death, although he always declared he should not have allowed the sentence to be carried out, which even the base and violent Hemart and Thuriot were afraid to pronounce in view of the popular feeling.[1]

" I have spoken," said Joséphine," directly she saw her, " but I have very little hope.   He is more angry this time than I ever saw him yet about conspiracies, even that of the infernal machine, when, if it had not been for poor Rapp,[2] Hortense and I would have been blown into the air, to say nothing of Madame Murat.   I spoke to him with all the interest that was due to an affair of such importance, and I fear——"

" But I want to see him !" interrupted Madame de Montesson.   " Let me see him, and you will be an angel."

" You shall see him, *mon amie !* you shall see him. Calm yourself.   But for your own sake, if you want to influence him, don't let me fear what he calls scenes.   I know him, and I know that is the way to do no good.   Calm yourself."

" Eh !   How can I be calm ?   If you knew what grief, what desolation I leave behind me ! "

---

[1] Hemart was President of the Court, and Thuriot also one of the judges   They were both regicides, and at this trial they showed the grossest malignity and unfairness, trying by all means to influence unfavourably to the prisoners   Judge Mavier was an honourable exception

[2] They were going to the opera, and it was a remark of Rapp's about Joséphine's shawl that made her stop to change it, and thus arrive a few minutes late and escape the explosion.

"But be tranquil—at any rate, outwardly! Wait for me ; I will come back directly."

In a few minutes she came in hurriedly.

"Come, come!" she exclaimed, and offering her arm to Madame de Montesson she drew her towards the study, or private room, of the Emperor, which was some distance off. As she entered and looked at him she trembled and lost hope. He was walking up and down with his hat on, and he did not take it off as they came in.

"Well, Madame," he exclaimed brusquely, "so you also are in league with my enemies? You come and ask me for their lives when they are only planning my death! when they are seeking it, and making me see it in the very air that I breathe! They make me fearful—*me!* Yes, they prevent me from going out, because I dread to see half Paris the victims of their barbarity. They are monsters!"

Madame de Montesson was silent, which irritated the Emperor.

"You are not of my opinion, it seems?"

She looked down.

"You will not do me the honour to answer?"

"What can I say to you, Sire? You are agitated ; you are, above all, offended, and you will not listen to me. What I can assure you is that I have a horror of blood, even of the guilty. Judge what I think of those who would shed yours."

"Then why, if you have any friendship for me, do you come and intercede for men who, if I forgave them now, would kill me to-morrow?"

"No, Sire," replied Madame de Montesson, "you have been deceived. MM. de Polignac may have one absolute idea which rules their lives and guides them in all they do and say. They desire the return of the princes, as General Berthier and General Junot would desire yours under the same circumstances, but they are not assassins. They may have employed a man to whom any means are allowable, but they are incapable of imagining, still more of committing, an infamy."

Joséphine. "What did I tell you, *mon ami?* You see Madame de Montesson says just the same as I do. What do I say besides? That MM. de Polignac will in future be bound in gratitude to you if they owe you their lives."

Madame de Montesson. "Add to this consideration, which is immense, that you are at a point, Sire, which you ought to mark by mercy rather than by severity. You know that I almost predicted to you this epoch at which you have arrived. In consideration of this prophecy be still my hero. Be more, be the guardian angel of France. Let that be said of you which has never yet been said of any sovereign, ' He was brave as Alexander and Cæsar, and good as Louis XII.' "

Napoleon, in a gentler voice. "But I am not King. As Emperor I am only the First Magistrate of the Republic."

Madame de Montesson. "You are, and will be, all you wish to be. At any rate, as First Magistrate of your Republic, as you call it, you can pardon, and you must."

Napoleon. " And who will guarantee not only my life, but the lives of all around me, if ! grant this pardon ? "

Madame de Montesson. "The word of honour of those condemned, which I will answer for their never breaking."

Napoleon. "You appear to know those very little for whom you answer, Madame. MM. de Polignac are doubtless men of honour, but they will regard their plighted word as an oath taken in prison, and they will get themselves released from it by the Pope."

Joséphine. "Well, if you do not think them strong enough to resist their dominant wish, imprison them, but not death, *mon ami*, not death."

Madame de Montesson rose and took his hand, saying—-

"Sire, what is to be done? Must I implore you on my knees? Save MM. de Polignac, save the accused, save them all! Oh! I entreat you!" and she knelt before him.

The Emperor raised her hastily, and made her sit down, saying—

"You afflict me, Madame, for I really cannot grant you the lives of all these men, for whom the peace of France is nothing, and who trifle with the blood of her sons as they would with that of a tribe of savages."

Joséphine. "Buonaparte, I have already asked you, and I will go on asking as long as there is a shadow of hope. But if you refuse me, I will not love you any longer."

Napoleon, embracing her. "But since you love me how can you ask the pardon of these men, who, I repeat, not only desire my death, but the confusion of France?"

Madame de Montesson, gently. "That is not what they want."

Napoleon. " Eh, Madame ! What else can they hope for ? The revolutionary agitation which I have had so much difficulty in controlling myself, would it be kept under by an unskilful hand ? A government cannot be improvised, Madame, and popular feeling would not now answer to their royalist anger against the Revolution and the Republic. However, while blaming MM. de Polignac and de Rivière for wishing to bring back events perhaps even more bloodstained than those of '93, I find them less guilty than republican generals, men like Moreau " (and his voice trembled) " and Pichegru, who will clasp hands like brothers with the Chouan Georges."

He threw himself back upon a sofa ; he was pale, and appeared to shudder ; his lips were white and his face convulsed. Madame de Montesson made a movement of alarm, but Joséphine signed to her to remain quiet, and going up to Napoleon, took his hands in her own, embraced him, and spoke to him in a low voice, till gradually his features regained their accustomed calmness.

" Yes," he continued, rising and walking quickly up and down in the room, and in and out of the garden ; " these men of France are more guilty than the servants of the family of Louis XVI.—the unhappy Louis XVI. ! But Moreau, the victor of Hohenlinden, to become a conspirator ! He thinks I am jealous of him ! And why ? *grand Dieu !* My portion of renown is brilliant enough ! I want no other to make it brighter, and, with God's help, I hope to deserve one as great as there can be under heaven."

Joséphine and Madame de Montesson. "Well, then, be merciful to MM. de Polignac, commute their sentence. But not death! oh, not death!"

Napoleon to Joséphine. "To-morrow will you come to speak to me for Moreau? Would you believe," to Madame de Montesson, "that after being for four years subject to the impertinence of the wife, she has been importuning me to get the pardon of the husband? She is really good, my Joséphine." And he drew her to him and embraced her.

Madame de Montesson. "And I must also embrace you to thank you."

Napoleon. "To thank me? What for?"

Madame de Montesson. "Why, for the pardon of my friends. Have not you just said so? Did not you say that Moreau was more guilty than they?"

Napoleon. "Undoubtedly."

Madame de Montesson. "Well! if that is so you cannot condemn them while you pardon the most guilty."

Napoleon. "Eh! who told you, Madame, that I should pardon any one?"

Madame de Montesson. "My heart, which knows you and feels assured you will not condemn Moreau. He will not be condemned."

Joséphine. "*Mon ami, grâce, grâce!*"

Madame de Montesson. "Come! say the word; it it will do you good."

Napoleon. "But I cannot give a full pardon, I must have a guarantee, and that can only be against the freedom of these gentlemen."

Madame de Montesson. "Ah! thanks! thanks! you are as good as you are great."

Napoleon. "But let them be circumspect in their prison ; no intrigues, no plots."

Madame de Montesson. "I will answer for them. In speaking of the accused, I mean *all* those accused for the royalist cause?"

Napoleon, hastily. "No, Madame. In granting to you and to Joséphine the lives of MM. de Polignac and de Rivière I only understood and included those two names ; the rest must submit to their fate."

Madame de Montesson. "Even M. d'Hozier?"

Napoleon. "M. d'Hozier like the others."

Joséphine. "*Mon ami !*"

Napoleon. "They are quite right who say that a statesman should never let a woman come near his study (office of government). What do you both want of me? You have been tormenting me for the last hour to obtain a thing which will perhaps be fatal to me. God grant that one day you may not remember this conversation with horror."

"Well! be it so ; I will give you him too (M. d'Hozier). That is to say, I will speak to Cambacérès and the chief judge, for I have not the power alone."

The health of Madame de Montesson seemed to revive after this, and for the remainder of the year 1804 her house at Romainville was more than ever the resort of all the pleasantest and most distinguished people in Paris. Her friendship with the Emperor was deepened by her gratitude for the pardons he had granted her, her affection for Joséphine was always the same, and she was also on very friendly terms with several of his generals—Duroc, Junot, and some others, but she detested Savary, and would never consent to receive him.

She died in 1806, and was buried with the Duc d'Orléans, at Seine-Assise. A curious incident took place at her funeral. As her body was carried down the steps of the church of Saint-Roch to be placed on the hearse which was to convey it to Seine-Assise, the procession of about a hundred persons was met by another, for whom the same requiem was chanted, the same tapers burned, the same hangings draped the church. It was that of Mademoiselle Marquise, the opera-dancer, once adored by the Duc d'Orléans, the mother of his sons, the Abbés de Saint-Far and Saint-Albin, and his daughter, Madame de Brossard, whom he had deserted for Madame de Montesson.[1]

Moreau was pardoned, but banished from France. He went to America, and only returned to Europe to enter the Russian service in 1813. He was killed before Dresden fighting in the army of the Allies, August 26, 1813.

[1] "Salons de Paris," t. iii. p. 72 (ed. Gavarnie), Duchesse d'Abrantès.

CHAPTER XV

1804

THE advantages of the friendship and connection between the Clarys and Buonaparte which at first seemed to be all on the side of the latter family, had now turned to the benefit of the former. Julie and Désirée surrounded themselves with their relations ; not only their brothers and sisters shared in their brilliant fortunes, but good appointments, civil and military, were given to their nephews and cousins, and splendid marriages found for their nieces. Their sister-in-law, the wife of their eldest brother Etienne, with whom Désirée had gone to the Maison Commune on the evening she made the acquaintance of Joseph Buonaparte, the first step in the rapid ascent of the family to riches and power, had formed a deep and lasting friendship with the Signora Letizia, and when the Clary family flocked to Paris to share the fortunes of their youngest sisters, she was attached to the household of the mother of Napoleon, if not by any official title, at any rate as an intimate and confidential friend. Without distinction or much education, she was a woman of good sense and capacity, anxious to direct with propriety the altered prospects of the family, but in the spring of 1804 she had an illness which permanently affected her health, and although she recovered sufficiently to go with the Signora Letizia to Rome, and was named *dame d'honneur* with her husband as chamberlain in the future household of Madame Mère, she did not live long enough to occupy that post. During the absence of the Signora Letizia at the baths of Lucca, she was taken ill in Rome, the Signora Letizia hurried back to her in great anxiety, and M. Etienne Clary set off from Paris on hearing of her illness, but arrived too late to see her before she died. She left seven children.

The coronation of the Emperor took place on the 2nd of December, shortly before which Pope Pius VII. arrived at Paris to perform the ceremony. He was lodged at the *Pavillon de Flore*, and by the desire of the Emperor treated with the highest respect and honour. His presence in that capital, where only four years ago the churches were closed, and those who still kept their faith were obliged to receive the sacraments of the Church in secret and in peril, was an extraordinary circumstance and created great interest and excitement. There was a perfect rush to see him, not only by the Parisians and the foreigners who crowded into Paris for the coronation, but numbers of country people who came in from the provinces. Amongst others came a swarm of those officials called "presidents of cantons," whose appearance with the costumes and swords they were unaccustomed to wear, was extremely ridiculous. A certain number of them was selected to be presented to the Pope, and, as they were very poor, they resolved to save the expense of hiring carriages by walking to the Tuileries, putting on gaiters to protect their white silk stockings.

The Pope gave them an address so touching that many people present shed tears. One of the presidents, putting his hand into his pocket, drew out his gaiters and wiped his eyes with them, smearing his face with mud to the general diversion.

The coronation in Notre Dame was a magnificent spectacle, but, as M. de Bourrienne remarks, "The glitter of gold, the waving plumes, the richly-caparisoned horses of the imperial procession, the mule which preceded the Pope's *cortège*," . . . have already been frequently described.

The sisters of the Emperor were furious at being obliged to bear the train of the Empress, but Napoleon's orders were not to be trifled with ; he desired that Elisa, Pauline, and Caroline, as well as Hortense and Julie, who made no objection, should follow Joséphine and carry the long mantle of crimson velvet, embroidered with golden bees and lined with ermine, the weight of which was so great that she could scarcely walk under it even when thus supported. Observing this, the three spiteful women contrived to drop it just as the Empress was about to ascend the steps of the throne, and very nearly caused her to fall backwards ; whereupon as she turned to remonstrate, the Emperor, perceiving what was going on, addressed to them a few sharp, stern words, which put a stop to their malicious proceedings for the time.

During the magnificent ceremonial Napoleon, wearing the imperial robes, the crown on his head, the sceptre in his hand, turned to Joseph, who stood near him and said—

" If our father could see us now ! " [1]

A less picturesque incident during the function was that, wishing to attract the attention of Cardinal Fesch, the Emperor struck or pushed him in the back with the sceptre.

The proceedings were so long that it was getting dusk when the Emperor and Empress returned to the Tuileries.

Next day took place the imposing ceremony of the distribution of the imperial eagles, for which all the troops in Paris were assembled in the Champ de Mars, where a throne was erected for the Emperor, from which he rose and gave the following address—

" Soldiers ! behold your colours ; these eagles will ever be your rallying point. They will always be where your Emperor may think them necessary for the defence of his throne and his people. Swear to sacrifice your lives to defend them, and by your courage to keep them constantly in the path of victory. Swear ! " [2]

[1] When Charles Buonaparte, their father, was dying he cried out in delirium that nothing could save him since that Napoleon, whose sword would some day triumph over Europe, tried in vain to deliver his father from the dragon of death.—" Fragment Historique," Joseph Buonaparte, t. i. 29.

[2] Bourrienne, " Mémoires de Napoléon."

The households of the Empress, Madame Mère, as the mother of Napoleon was now called, and the Princesses were immediately formed. That of Pauline was the most magnificent of the sisters; Napoleon always had a weakness for her and wished to give her something to pacify and amuse her. The number of her ladies and officers of the household was excused by Prince Borghese being governor beyond the Alps. She had made the acquaintance at Rome of the Duc de la Rochefoucauld, who was quite ready to admire and flirt with her, but when she asked him to be her grand chamberlain declined at once. But the *ci-devant* Duc de Clermont-Tonnerre, who was so poor that after his campaign as volunteer in the army of Condé, he was obliged to hire his court-dress, but was full of spirit and gaiety, and eager to get his lands restored, accepted the post, to her great delight.

An anecdote which delighted the *faubourg Saint-Germain* and happened shortly afterwards, concerned Madame Mère, and was widely circulated in Paris.

The Baron Desmousseaux, on his way to dine with Cambacérès in the *rue Saint-Dominique*, got out of his carriage in the courtyard of the *hôtel* into which his coachman had driven, and, following the servants up the great staircase, entered a *salon* in which, by the fire, sat two not very *distinguée*-looking women, one of whom, Madame de Fontanges, rose as he was announced. The other remained immovable.

Slightly bowing, he went to the fire, stood before it, warming one foot after another, and remarked—

" I was afraid I was late, but I see *Son Altesse* has

not come in, nor most of the guests arrived, so dinner will not be ready yet."

"Of whom are you speaking, Monsieur?" said Madame de Fontanges. "Who are you, and where do you suppose you are?"

"I am the Baron Desmousseaux, *préfet* of the Haute Garonne. Is not this the palace of the Prince Cambacérès?"

"No, Monsieur, it is not. You are not in the house of the *Archi-chancelier*, but in that of Madame Mère."

"*Mère de qui? Mère de quoi?*"[1] cried the astonished *préfet*.

"I tell you, Monsieur, that you are in the house of Madame, mother of the Emperor, who desires you to retire, not being at this moment in the humour to accept your respectful compliments."

Monsieur Desmousseaux hastened to offer apologies and excuses which the Signora Letizia was not well bred enough to know how to receive; and appeared at Cambacérès' just as every one had sat down to dinner. In order to account for his unpunctuality he related his adventure, which was greeted with peals of laughter, and for weeks afterwards people asked one another—

"Have you been to see *Madame Mère de qui, Mère de quoi?*"

There was much bitter feeling in the *faubourg Saint-Germain* for such amongst their set as accepted any office at the Imperial Court at this time.

"Congratulate me, Madame," said M. de Brissac

[1] Mother of whom? Mother of what?—('Mémoires d'une Femme de qualité," t. i. p. 199.)

to a woman of his acquaintance. "The Emperor has made me Count."

"Ah. Monsieur!" was the answer. "I have less pleasure in doing so than my grandmother had in congratulating your ancestor when the King made him Duke. You are really too modest in lowering yourself so far."

The Emperor had, notwithstanding his indulgence to Pauline, been much displeased with her proceedings in Italy, especially with her restless discontent and desire to get back to France ; he had in the spring addressed to her the following letter of admonition :—

"MADAME ET CHÈRE SŒUR,—I hear that you have not the good sense to conform to the manners and customs of the city of Rome ; that you show contempt for its inhabitants, and have your eyes perpetually turned towards Paris. Although occupied with important affairs, I have nevertheless wished to make you acquainted with my intentions, hoping that you will conform to them.

"Love your husband and his family, be polite, adapt yourself to the Roman customs, and understand clearly that if at the age you are, you allow yourself to be guided by bad advice, you can no longer count upon me. As to Paris, you may be certain that you will find no support there, and that I will never receive you except with your husband. If you quarrel with him it will be your own fault, and then France will be forbidden to you ; you will lose your happiness and my friendship." [1]

---

[1] "Napoléon et sa famille," t. ii. p. 407 (Masson).

Napoleon was the only person to whom Pauline ever paid the least attention in matters either great or small. Amongst other trifling affairs which the Emperor did not consider beneath his notice, were the lists of guests invited by his sisters to their parties, over which he exercised a strict supervision. One day, Duroc, Grand Marshal of the Palace, appeared with a list of persons desirable to be invited, amongst whom, after various objections, Pauline came to that of Madame Regnault de Saint-Jean d'Angely

" I will not have her at my house," she exclaimed.

" Her conduct is certainly very light," replied Duror, " but on account of her husband——"

" Eh! What do I care about her conduct or her husband! *(je me moque bien de sa conduite et de son mari). Pardi!* she is too pretty, I tell you, and that does harm to other women."

" Madame, allow me to tell you that you do them much more harm. There are prettier women in your household than Madame Regnault—Madame de Barral, amongst others—and I can assure your Imperial Highness that when your Highness is there, no one looks at any of those ladies."

" That is different—quite different: but scratch out Madame Regnault as I ask you."

" But, Madame, can there ever be too many pretty women?"

" I shall be there, *pardi!* isn't that enough? Will you not see me quite at your ease?"

" Madame, it is the Emperor's order."

" Eh! Why didn't you tell me that at first? *Pardi!* if it is the Emperor's order I shall not dispute it.

But what an idea to invite that great brunette, who poses for a Greek profile and never lets one see anything else! Have you noticed how she enters a room?—walking like a crab." And she proceeded to imitate her.[1]

The household of Julie, Princess Joseph, was not very numerous, and was to a great extent composed of her own relations and early friends, with the exception of her *dame d'honneur*, the Comtesse de Girardin, who had been formerly Duchesse d'Aiguillon, a very charming person. During the Terror she had been imprisoned with Joséphine, then Vicomtesse de Beauharnais. One day a gaoler came in to take away a piece of furniture belonging to Joséphine, whose companions asking in terror if she was condemned, and receiving an equivocal answer, began to cry and lament.

"What are you afraid of?" asked Joséphine. "It is not possible for me to die—am not I to be Queen of France?"

"By this remark she referred to the prophecy, now so well known, of an old negress in Martinique, that she would be Queen of France, but would die in a *hospice*.

"Well!" exclaimed the Duchesse d'Aiguillon irritably. "Why not name your household at once?"

"Yes, I will!" replied Joséphine; " and I will appoint you my *dame d'honneur* when I am Queen of France."

After the coronation the Empress remembered this, and asked Napoleon that she might fulfil her promise; but he replied—

[1] " Les sœurs de Napoléon," p. 208 (Turquan).

" No ; she is divorced."

Relenting, however, he consented to the Duchesse d'Aiguillon, or rather the Comtesse de Girardin, being appointed to the household of the Princess Joseph.[1]

There was a tone of liberalism about the *entourage* of Joseph and Julie not pleasing to the Emperor, who had remarked to him—

" My household and yours, in order to be well constituted, can only be composed of soldiers and the ancient nobility . . . The rest, with their wives, should be excluded. You must choose your officers and ladies-in-waiting amongst the old *noblesse*, and especially that of those countries recently united to France, such as Belgium and Piedmont. Imitate me : there are still plenty of great names amongst whom you can find what you want."[2]

The social surroundings of Joseph and Julie, however, rather resembled a *société de château* than a court, and had also an exceedingly domestic character. The Clarys and their relations swarmed at Mortefontaine and the *Hôtel de Marbœuf*—eight brothers and sisters, most of whom had children, an innumerable company of uncles, aunts, cousins, and connections, besides many old friends of Joseph, to whom he remained firmly attached, and whom in his prosperity he was eager to help. For one of the reasons which made Joseph and Julie so much loved in their family and amongst those around them, was their great kindness. They never in their altered

---

[1] "Salons de Paris," t. iii. p. 225 (Duchesse d'Abrantès). New edition. Garnier frères, Paris.

[2] " Napoléon et sa famille," t. ii. p. 415 (Masson).

fortunes forgot or neglected the friends of less
flourishing days, who were always welcome at their
luxurious home, at the extravagant, sumptuous
entertainments they gave, and to whatever support
and assistance they could bestow upon them. Julie
was perpetually arranging marriages, and giving
trousseaux and *dots* to her nieces and cousins, and
Joseph found posts for their husbands and for the
nephews and cousins and friends of his wife and
himself, and pushed them on by all means in his
power. They were an invaluable uncle and aunt.
They married the daughter of Julie's half-sister,
Madame Lejean, to General Maurice Mathieu, and
a daughter of her sister, Madame Anthoine de
Saint-Joseph, to General Salligny, for whom they
obtained the title of Duc de San Germano;
another Clary was married to a Tascher; another
daughter of Madame Anthoine de Saint-Joseph to
General Suchet, afterwards Duc d'Albufera: there
was no end to the riches and honours showered
upon the Clary family.

Désirée was still the first and dearest of all to
Julie, and was constantly with her, especially as
Bernadotte was now made Governor of Hanover,
where his administration was most successful, and
where he formed and trained a splendid body of
troops, at whose head he won still more glory
during the next campaign.

Plain and retiring as a young girl, Julie preserved
the same characteristics as a woman at the head of
a great household. Knowing full well that she was
not formed to shine in society, feeling embarrassed
and ill at ease in the costly dresses and jewels in-

dispensable to be worn in public, she avoided, as far as possible, all occasions necessitating such display, finding plenty of occupation and interest at home in the intimate society she had gathered round her, in the education of her daughters, and in the charities she dispensed with unfailing generosity. Whilst the consciousness of her want of attraction rendered her shy and insignificant in general society, and whilst she was called stupid, prudish, and *dévote* by those who were slightly acquainted with her, Julie was, in her home, sensible, merry, capable, and deeply religious. She never took offence, never spoke against any one, never noticed injuries or slights except to laugh at them, and far from being narrowly prudish, she received into her household and circle several women who had histories attached to them. Her influence with Joseph was very great, and his respect and affection for her never altered, in spite of his numerous infidelities. Julie cared nothing for rank or state; in fact, would have infinitely preferred that her husband should be a rich merchant of Marseille, like her father. She did not care much for any of her husband's family except Madame Mère; of the rest she saw very little, as their ways and tone did not suit her.

Désirée, on the contrary, liked society, dress, and amusements of all kinds, and was rather a friend of the Buonaparte, though she had now a circle of her own, consisting of persons very superior to them. To her *salon* came Madame de Genlis, MM. de Cabre, Sabran, de Choiseul, and others connected with the ancient court, amongst whom Bernadotte was always anxious she should make friends.

The Abbé de Cabre called himself the poet of the Maréchale, and when one evening Désirée asked him to make her portrait in verse, he at once replied [1]—

> "Pourquoi me demander ce que c'est qu'une femme
> A moi dont le destin est d'ignorer l'amour ?
> De l'aveugle affligé vous dechireriez l'âme
> Si vous lui demandiez ce que c'est qu'un beau jour."

Another *habitué* of her *salon* was the Cardinal Maury, a well-known figure in Parisian society. Talented, literary, very ugly, very immoral, extremely amusing, he had more than once found his wit stand him in good stead. Once during the Revolution he was surrounded by a crowd of ruffians who threatened to hang him, shouting—

" *A la lanterne !* '

" *Imbéciles !* " he exclaimed, " would that make you see any better?" They laughed and let him go. Another time he was surrounded by two or three hundred Marseillais, one of whom called out—

"Stop, dog of an abbé ; I will send you to say mass in hell!"

"Take care I don't send you before me to serve it," retorted he. " Here are my *burettes.*"

And he advanced towards him taking out the pistols he always carried.

He was of obscure birth, and when a young man made his way to Paris on foot with a small bundle and a few crowns, to seek his fortune. On the way he fell in with a youth of about his own age, as pale and sickly as he was strong and vigorous. They made friends, continued their journey together, and on arriving at Paris took a lodging between them

[1] " Désirée Clary." p. 135 (Comtesse d'Armaillé).

where they pursued their studies.   Maury wrote ser-
mons ; the other, whose name was Portal, studied
medicine.   They always preserved their friendship,
after one had become a cardinal, the other one of
the first physicians in Paris.   Finding himself obscure
and unknown, Portal had imagined a singular way
of advertising his name.   A servant arrived one day,
out of breath with running, at the door of a large
hôtel in a fashionable street, at which he knocked
violently three or four times.

"M. Portal, the doctor, is here, is not he?   Will
you tell him he is wanted immediately?"

The reply was that they did not know him.

"What? you don't know M. Portal, the first
doctor in Paris?   Ah! *mon Dieu!* what will Monsieur le Duc say?   He has no confidence in any
one else!"

And he ran on to another door, repeating the
same thing, and waking people up all night, till the
idea became fixed in their minds as they began to
inquire about and send for the doctor who seemed
to be so important and so run after.

The pickpockets of Paris were as skilful at this time
as in that capital or in our own at the present day.

M de Limoges, a rich banker, with a pretty wife,
had a miniature of her with their child of two years
old, painted by Augustin, and mounted on a tortoise-
shell snuff-box lined with gold, which he usually
carried in his pocket.   One evening, coming out of
the *Théâtre Favart*, he felt some one push against
him, and turning round saw a very good-looking,
gentlemanly young man, who apologised politely ;
but when he arrived at home, M. de Limoges found

that his snuff-box was gone. He sent advertisements to all the papers offering a reward of ten louis for the recovery of it, and then left Paris on business for Bordeaux. On his return two months later, he found a little packet addressed to him, on opening which, he discovered, not the snuff-box, but what he more valued, the miniature, with the following letter :—

"MONSIEUR,—I can understand your regret at having lost the miniature which I have the honour of sending you. So charming a child and so beauful a woman must be the delight and pride of the man who has the right to have them painted. But allow me to make one remark : when one has a wife and child like yours, has them painted by Augustin and mounted on a snuff-box, one has a gold box, and sets the miniature in diamonds of the first water ; that would have been more honourable to you and more profitable to me.

    "I have the honour to salute you,

        "THE ROBBER."

"PS.—You promise ten louis reward to whoever will bring back your miniature. In good faith this promise is a little *gasconne*, for you cannot suppose that I am so simple as to make the trial ; but I shall see whether you promise with the intention of fulfilling. Put the ten louis in your pocket the day after to-morrow and come to the *Théâtre Favart*, I will pay myself with my own hands."

The letter and packet having been sent to his house during his absence some time had passed before he received them ; but, true to his promise, M. de Limoges put ten louis in his pocket, and went to the appointed place. It was in vain, for the thief had probably been arrested for some other exploit, and thereby prevented from taking his reward, as he said, with his own hands.

Both Julie and Désirée were friends of the celebrated Comtesse de Genlis, niece of Madame de Montesson, who, however, was not very fond of her, and of whom in her *Mémoires* she frequently complains.

The social existence of Madame de Genlis was, as Madame d'Abrantès observes, full of contradictions. Her family was noble, she was a *chanoinesse* at eight years old, and was called Comtesse de Lancy until she married the Comte de Genlis, younger brother of the Marquis de Genlis, whose family was noble, ancient, and allied to most of the great names in France. The Comte de Genlis perished in the Revolution in 1793. The Comtesse, having attached herself to the Orléans family, had charge of the education of the children of Philippe Egalité, then Duc de Chartres. Her friendship with that individual and the unbounded influence she exercised over him and over his children was the cause of much unhappiness and uneasiness to the Duchess de Chartres, a woman of angelic character, with a reputation as unstained as that of her husband was infamous.

Philippe Egalité, as he had the baseness to have himself called, became Duke of Orléans in 1785, on the death of his father (the husband of Madame de Montesson). In spite of all her discourses upon

18

virtue, propriety, and duty, many were the stories and reports circulated about Madame de Genlis, by no means in accordance with her precepts; but it seems probable that these were mostly, though not entirely, gossip and scandal spread by her enemies, or by those whose envy she had excited. The most suspicious circumstance was the presence of a child she called Pamela, and brought up with her own daughters and the Orléans children; whom she declared to be an English orphan she had adopted in order to teach the other children to speak English, but of whom no relations were ever forthcoming, and who was, and still is, supposed by many to have been her daughter and that of the Duc d'Orléans. However that might be, the child was very beautiful and talented. She afterwards married the unfortunate Lord Edward Fitzgerald.

After Philippe Egalité had reaped the reward of his crimes, and met himself the death he had voted for his cousin and King, Madame de Genlis spent some years wandering about in exile, and returned to France in 1800. Her connection with the Orléans family had alienated from her the sympathies of many of the Legitimists, but she never lost the affection of her old pupils, the Duc d'Orléans afterwards Louis Philippe, his brothers and sister; and although she did not meet with the enthusiastic affection with which her rival, Madame de Stael inspired her friends, she had a large circle of acquaintances and admirers amongst the leading people of the day—political, intellectual, and social. The eldest of her daughters was married to a Belgian, the Marquis de Lawoestine; the second to the Comte

COMTESSE DE GENLIS.

de Valence, one of the most dissipated, extravagant men about the Court.

His father, who resembled him in these characteristics, had a mistress whom he adored, and who gave birth to a son at the same time that a dead daughter was born to the Comtesse de Valence. The Count caused the son of his mistress to be substituted for the dead child, and brought him up as his heir. The Countess, however, always suspected the truth, would never acknowledge him as her son, and left nearly all her fortune away from him. He was very handsome and a brave soldier ; he emigrated, but always refused to fight against France.

The intimate friendship which lasted so many years between him and Madame de Montesson was not supposed to have been always a platonic one ; it was, indeed, said that the Duc d'Orléans, her husband, coming suddenly into a room one day, found him on his knees before her, but that she had the presence of mind to say, without any embarrassment—

" See this *fou de Valence!* he has been at my feet for the last hour to obtain the hand of my niece." Upon which the Duke replied—

" Well, you must grant it to him. Come, I will promise I will promise you."

And the marriage was thus decided. It did not turn out happily.

Madame de Genlis was certainly one of the most remarkable women of the day. Very handsome, brilliantly clever, a celebrated harpist, a good actress, she spoke several languages, had led an interesting, wandering, adventurous life, and her literary talents were well known. Everybody read her books, many distinguished persons corresponded with her. The Emperor, on hearing that she had returned from emigration, and was badly off, sent M. de Rémusat to inquire what he could do for her, gave her a pension and an apartment at the Arsenal, where she held her *salon* and wrote several of her novels and biographies. She had a passion for education, and besides the Orléans princes and princess, had brought up her own two daughters, her niece, her nephew, Pamela, and other children. She also took it into her head that she would like to educate the daughters of Joseph and Julie, and wrote to the Emperor upon the subject. But Julie was not of the same opinion. She had, of course, heard a great deal about that gifted woman which might not signify in an acquaintance or friend for herself, but would not be desirable in a governess for her daughters. At any rate, she refused, and her husband also, but she gave Madame de Genlis a pension of 3,000 francs, and they continued on excellent terms.

Madame de Genlis speaks enthusiastically of the kindness and charity of Julie and the absence of all ostentation she always showed. On one occasion the priests of Saint-Sulpice, finding every day pieces of gold in the alms-bag, and observing that they were put in by a lady who wore a veil, and sat by a column in a corner of the church, and who came alone and unattended every morning, followed her, and discovered that it was Julie (the Queen of Spain).

Madame de Genlis first met Désirée at a dinner-party given by M. de Cabre, and remarks that she had all the attraction of beauty and charming manners, and that her conversation and *esprit* were equally agreeable.

"I sat by Marshal Bernadotte," she writes, "who resembles in the most astonishing manner the portraits of the great Condé. His good looks, aristocratic air, and politeness increase this glorious resemblance, which is completed by his great military talents. As we left the table I whispered to M. de Cabre that he had the manners of a king."

CHAPTER XVI

1805—1806

THE power of Napoleon was now at its height, and he was more than ever determined to follow the extraordinary "system" which he had imagined, and which, if carried out as he intended, would have made him absolute ruler of the civilised world—at any rate, in the eastern hemisphere. With his brothers, brothers-in-law, stepson, and other relations upon the different thrones of Europe; any prince of a reigning family who might retain the crown of his ancestors only doing so as the husband of a wife belonging to the Buonaparte; and supposing, of course, all these crowned relatives to be ready to act as his prefects, and submit to his dictation; he would undoubtedly have achieved a position unheard of in the history of mankind. His marvellous successes caused him to see no impossibility in such a prospect.

His ideas of the kind of obedience due to him may
be gathered from the following extracts from a catechism revised by his directions, and taught in the
schools :—

"*Q.* What are the duties of Christians towards
the princes who govern them? and what are our
special duties towards Napoleon I., our Emperor?

"*A.* Christians owe the princes who govern them,
and we especially owe to Napoleon, our Emperor,
love, respect, obedience, military service, and the
taxes ordered for the preservation and defence of
the Empire and of his throne. Therefore, to honour
and serve the Emperor is to honour and serve God
Himself.

"*Q.* Are there not special reasons which ought
to attach us more strongly to Napoleon, our
Emperor?

"*A.* Yes ; for it is he whom God has raised up
under difficult circumstances to re-establish the public
profession of the holy religion of our fathers, and to
be the protector of it. He has restored and preserved
public order by his active and profound wisdom ; he
defends the State with his powerful arm ; he has
become the Anointed of the Lord by the consecra-
tion he has received from the Sovereign Pontiff,
head of the Universal Church.

"*Q.* What ought one to think of those who fail in
their duties towards our Emperor?

"*A.* According to St. Paul, they would be resisting the order of God Himself, and would render
themselves worthy of eternal damnation."

When Madame de Stael saw this catechism she
said, "Is one to believe, then, that Buonaparte will

have hell at his disposal in the next world because he can make us experience it in this one?"

One of the fancies of Napoleon, which at the time caused Joséphine most uneasiness, was for Madame Duchâtel, a lady-in-waiting of her own, a fair, pretty woman of twenty-four, whose husband, a highly-placed official about the court, was old enough to be her father, and whose reputation until now had been unblemished. She could not, however, resist Napoleon, but at first they kept their *liaison* secret, at any rate from Joséphine. However, she soon suspected that something of the kind was going on, though who the subject of the new caprice might be she could not imagine. At first she suspected Madame Ney, a most harmless, rather shy person, against whom there was never anything to be said, and who could not understand why Joséphine would not speak to her. Madame Duchâtel pretended to flirt with Eugène de Beauharnais, who was in love with her, and with Murat, who carried letters between her and the Emperor. At last Joséphine found out, and reproached Napoleon, which only made him angry. He used to play cards in the evening with Mesdames Murat, de Rémusat, and Duchâtel, all the time talking in the most extraordinary way about love and jealousy, while Joséphine sat melancholy and tearful at the other end of the room. Madame Duchâtel, who had not sense enough to take warning by all the other women who had been Napoleon's mistresses, thought she was going to be a powerful favourite, and gave herself airs accordingly. Joséphine watched her, and one day at Saint-Cloud, seeing her leave the room where she was sitting with several other people, and not return, followed her. She first went to the Emperor's study, which was empty, and opened on the garden. She then went up a little private staircase to some rooms Napoleon had furnished above. The door was locked, but she heard the voices of the Emperor and Madame Duchâtel inside, and knocked until it was opened. She broke into indignant reproaches, Madame Duchâtel began to cry, and Napoleon was so furious that she ran away and took refuge with Madame de Rémusat, who had vainly tried to prevent her from acting in this way, but who now assured her that she must meet the Emperor alone, and retired into the *salon*, where were several other persons, amongst whom Madame Duchâtel, looking much disturbed. Presently, in the other room, loud voices were heard, that of the Emperor like thunder. No words could be distinguished, but the sound of crashing and breaking of furniture were heard as Napoleon smashed everything around him. Horses and carriages were hastily ordered, and every one dispersed and went back to Paris in dismay. Napoleon declared he had no peace, that this spying was intolerable, that he would get a divorce; but very shortly he and Joséphine made friends, and though the affair went on a little longer, causing great discomfort and endless quarrels, Napoleon suddenly got tired of it, came to Joséphine, and said—

"Don't cry, it's all nothing. Have I given you pain? Well, forgive me, and I will tell you all about it."

He declared he was tired of Madame Duchâtel, who seemed to think she was going to rule him; he

told Joséphine many malicious remarks she had
made, and various inexpedient details, and begged
her to break off the affair. Joséphine sent for the
culprit, reproved her for her folly, assuming that it
was nothing more. Madame Duchâtel denied everything, and the affair was finished. The Emperor was
scarcely civil to her afterwards, and she could not
retire from her service on account of her husband's
position.

But when Joséphine was divorced, she remembered
her kindness, and there was no one more assiduous
at La Malmaison or more anxious to show her
gratitude than Madame Duchâtel.[1]

Meanwhile one great obstacle to the "system,"
which was beginning to be realised by Napoleon, was
the kind of *personnel* upon which it was to be formed.
Lucien, of whom he would have preferred to make
use before all the others, was as obstinate as ever.
Napoleon had succeeded in inducing all or nearly all
the rest of the family, including even their mother
and Cardinal Fesch, not indeed to quarrel with
Lucien, but to try to persuade him to divorce his wife
--without the slightest effect, except that of making
Lucien very angry, and eliciting from him an indignant letter reproaching his uncle, a prince of the
Catholic Church, for giving him advice which was
neither honourable nor Christian.

The correspondence upon this subject is very
voluminous, for during several years Napoleon
continued to make frequent overtures to Lucien,
whose letters were manly, sensible, and honourable

---

[1] "Mémoires de Madame de Rémusat, Napoléon amoureux"
(Turquan).

in the highest degree. He steadily refused to divorce his wife for any advantage that was offered him, or, as he said, to sacrifice his wife to his children. For it is to be remarked that in all the correspondence, not only Napoleon, but all the rest of the family, seemed to think it a matter of course that the interest of the children should come before the wife ; and to be quite astonished that Lucien should not be of that opinion.

Jérôme had also married without the consent of Napoleon an American girl, daughter of a merchant named Patterson, and being a minor this would have been illegal without the permission of the heads of the family, *i.e.*, his mother and Joseph. They, however, had not withheld their consent, but when Napoleon heard of it he was furious, and insisted that the marriage was illegal. Jérôme at first resisted, Lucien supported him, assuring Mr. Patterson, brother of Jérôme's wife, that all the family recognised the marriage except Napoleon, and that he would relent ; or that, if he did not, Jérôme could become a naturalised American, and settle in America, where he would very likely join him, as he had no intention to submit to his brother's tyranny. But between Lucien and Jérôme there was no resemblance. The youngest brother soon yielded to the threats and promises which had failed to move the elder ; he consented to give up his wife and child and marry the Princess Catherine of Wurtemberg, in return for which he was made King of Westphalia.

The Emperor seized Parma, Piacenza, and Lucca, which he gave to his sister Elisa, and began a new campaign in Germany.

Bernadotte, at the head of the splendid troops he had trained, conquered all the country about Salzburg, and re-established in Munich the Elector, whom Napoleon soon after made King of Bavaria.

The battle of Trafalgar was fought in October near Gibraltar, and the fleets of France and Spain nearly destroyed by Nelson, whose glorious death saddened the triumph of England. It was a severe blow to Napoleon, who did all in his power to prevent the extent of the disaster from being known ; in fact, for some time it was only rumoured in France, and it was a foreign paper which first revealed the calamity to the nation.

The surrender of Mack and the Austrian troops at Ulm, however, went far to console them, and in December came the great victory of Austerlitz, " the battle of the three Emperors," in which Napoleon defeated Alexander of Russia and Francis Joseph of Austria, and which was followed by the peace of Presbourg.

Bernadotte was opposed to the Russian centre at Austerlitz ; his friends declared that he greatly contributed to the victory ; his enemies, that if, after he had forced back the Russian troops he had allowed the pursuit to go on longer. they would have been annihilated.

But at any rate after this battle he was made Prince of Ponte Corvo ; rather to the uneasiness of Désirée, who was dreadfully afraid lest she should be obliged to leave Paris to go and live at a place she had never heard of before.

A deputation from the little Italian principality soon arrived, and Désirée was called upon to receive

them ; which, not being accustomed to such representations, she did with much shyness, and was still
more nervous when they expressed a wish that she
should come and live amongst them. She was, however, reassured by her friends, who explained that
this would not be necessary, but that " Princess of
Ponte Corvo " would merely be a title of honour.

The wives of Napoleon's officers, both civil and
military, had to resign themselves to long and frequent separations from their husbands, who, even if
they were not fighting, were sent about by Napoleon
to all parts of Europe. It is well known that French
women have a stronger dislike than most others to
leaving their own country ; seldom are they to be
found living, as Russians and Americans do, in
foreign lands, or accompanying their husbands to
far-off colonies and remaining there for many years,
like the English.

In this respect both Julie and Désirée were
thorough Frenchwomen ; to live anywhere but in
Paris, or at the very least in France, appeared to
them a misfortune too great to contemplate ; and yet
the fate of each of them was to spend the later part
of their lives far away from the scenes now so
beloved and familiar.

Bernadotte was away for a considerable time,
during which he kept up a constant correspondence
with Désirée, whose association with Joseph enabled
her to inform him of everything going on in the
political world. Early in the spring of 1806,
Napoleon made Joseph King of Naples, for which
kingdom he departed, unaccompanied by Julie,
who dreaded a foreign country and could not bear

to leave Mortefontaine, Paris, and all her friends there.

The Emperor, however, insisted on their leaving the *Hôtel de Marbœuf* and taking up their abode at the Luxembourg, as being a more suitable residence for royalty. Joseph did not at all wish to go, and begged to be allowed to "reign at Mortefontaine," but the Emperor was inexorable : he was beginning his system. He had just married Eugène de Beauharnais to the daughter of the King of Bavaria, and this marriage, unlike most of those he made, turned out very happily. Eugène fell in love with the Princess Auguste, who was both pretty and charming, and she returned his affection. A proof that Napoleon was far less generous to his stepson than to his brothers and sisters was that Eugène distressed himself because he could not give the princess a wedding present he considered sufficiently magnificent. His mother, however, who had come to Munich for the marriage, had a splendid tiara made for him, which put an end to the difficulty.

The Emperor was delighted with this alliance, with the Princess Auguste, and with everybody ; and his attentions to the Queen of Bavaria were so marked that Joséphine became jealous and rejoiced when the festivities were over and they returned to Paris.

Some time afterwards the Emperor wrote to Eugène— [1]

"My son, you work too much, your life is too monotonous. That is all very well for you, because to you work ought to be a recreation ; but you have a young wife, who is expecting her confinement.

---

[1] Eugène de Beauharnais was then Viceroy of Italy.

I think you ought to arrange so as to spend your evenings with her, and form a little society around you. Why do you not go to the theatre once a week, to the State box? I also think you ought to have a small hunting establishment, and hunt at least once a week. I will gladly set apart a sum in the budget for that purpose. You ought to have more gaiety in your house; it is necessary for the happiness of your wife and your own health. A great deal of work can be done in a very short time. I lead the life you lead, but I have an old wife who does not require me to amuse her; and I have also more business, but yet I can truly say that I take more pleasure and diversion than you do. A young woman requires to be amused, especially in the state she is in. You used to be fond enough of amusement; you must resume your former tastes. What you might not do for yourself, it is right that you should do for the princess. I have just established myself at Saint-Cloud. Stéphanie and the Prince of Baden get on tolerably well. I spent the last two days with Marshal Bessières; we played like children of fifteen. You used to get up early in the morning, you must resume that habit. It would not disturb the princess if you both went to bed at eleven o'clock; and if you finish your work at six o'clock in the evening, you still have ten hours to work if you get up at seven or eight o'clock."

His marriage delighted his mother, who said that the Princess Auguste was "*une très-grande dame*"; she and Eugène always showed the greatest kindness and affection to Joséphine, in fact, their family remained one of the brightest spots in her life.

Eugène was an absolute contrast to the Buonaparte ; he never asked for anything, was always
satisfied, and never complained of the difference
between the riches and honours showered upon the
Buonaparte, Murat, and others, and the provision
made for himself; though he did confide to his
mother his annoyance that Napoleon, jealous of the
love of the people under his government, was forcing
him to impose oppressive taxes in order to alienate
their affections.[1]

And yet Napoleon had as much affection for
Eugène as he was capable of feeling.

"They (the Buonaparte) are jealous of my wife,
of Eugène, of Hortense, of every one around me!
Well! my wife has nothing but debts and diamonds.
Eugène has not 20,000 *livres de rentes.* I love those
children because they are always anxious to please
me. If a shot is fired, it is Eugène who goes to see
what it is; if I have a ditch to cross, it is he who
gives me a hand. The daughters of Joseph don't yet
know that I am called Emperor : they call me Consul ; they think I beat their mother ; while the little
Napoleon,[2] when he passes the grenadiers in the
garden, calls out ' *Vive Nonon le soldat !* '

"They say my wife is false, and the *empressements*
of her children studied. Well! I like it ; they treat
me like an old uncle, and that makes the charm of
my life ; I am getting old, I am thirty-six, I wish for
repose."

The first royal marriage celebrated at Paris was
that of Stéphanie, daughter of Claude, Comte de

[1] "Mémoires" (Madame de Rémusat).
[2] Son of Hortense.

Beauharnais, who cared very little about her, but had sent her to a convent to be brought up. Joséphine was sorry for the neglected child and showed her a great deal of kindness, and Napoleon, taking a fancy to her, for she was very pretty, adopted her, placed her at Madame Campan's, and after the battle of Austerlitz negotiated her marriage with the grandson of the Grand-Duke of Baden.

The prince was heir to the Grand-Duchy, and his mother, widow of the Grand-Duke's eldest son, violently opposed the connection, declaring it to be a *mésalliance* to which she would never consent. But Napoleon, to whom this marriage was a part of his "system," had offered a considerable aggrandisement of territory to Baden as the price of the alliance, to which both the Grand-Duke and his grandson willingly agreed ; and the bridegroom-elect came to Paris, where preparations were made on a splendid scale for the wedding.

Unluckily, Stéphanie, who was exceedingly pretty, attractive, fond of flirting, and whose head had been turned by her sudden change of fortune, by the indulgence of Napoleon, and by the flatteries of the courtiers, did not like the Prince of Baden when she saw him. She had set her mind upon a slight, dark man, whereas the prince was not only fair, but rather inclined to be stout, very shy, and somewhat awkward.

He, on the contrary, fell desperately in love with Stéphanie, who, in spite of the airs she gave herself and the flirtations she carried on, had no harm in her, but was full of good qualities, and only seventeen years old. All his attempts to please her failed in

STÉPHANIE DE BEAUHARNAIS, GRAND-DUCHESS OF BADEN. (Schroeder.)

inducing her to be even civil to him, and he began
to be displeased at, and suspicious of, the marked
attentions shown her by the Emperor, who ordered
her to be called "Princess," to be placed upon the
right hand of the Empress, and given precedence of
his own family and every one else.

He reprimanded her about her conduct to her
fiancé, but the lecture resulted in a pronounced
flirtation with himself. Joséphine was very angry,
and complained bitterly to Napoleon, who always
assured her she ought not to be jealous of him,
as he was not like ordinary men, nor bound by the
common laws of morality.

Joséphine reproved Stéphanie, asking indignantly,
"What do you think you were placed at Madame
Campan's for? To learn to flirt? And with whom?
The husband of your aunt!"

Stéphanie listened, promised amendment, and confessed the advances of the Emperor, saying that she
meant no harm; if she had she would have kept matters more secret, and then no one would have known
anything about it; but she promised, with many
apologies, to be more circumspect, only nothing
would reconcile her to the prospect of the Prince of
Baden as a husband.

However, the wedding was celebrated with great
pomp by the legate Cardinal Caprara, in the chapel of
the Tuileries in the presence of the *corps diplomatique*
and all the fashionable society in Paris. The Emperor gave a *dot*, splendid diamonds, and 1,000 louis,
for pocket-money to the bride, who looked very
pretty, but the melancholy air of the bridegroom
caused general comment.

Notwithstanding all the attention which had been devoted to the arrangement of the Imperial Court in general, and this ceremony in particular, things did not go altogether smoothly. The Emperor did not know whether to give this bride his right or left hand on leaving the chapel, the Empress would always walk slowly. and the procession pressed behind her as the chamberlains kept hurrying it on, saying, "*Allons, allons, mesdames, avancez donc,*" which was very difficult, owing to the long heavy mantles worn by the ladies. The Comtesse d'Arberg, who was present, and had been accustomed to the etiquette of the German courts, and in that of an archduchess, was exceedingly scandalised, and remarked that they might as well all wear short petticoats, and "*on devrait nous appeler les postillons du palais.*"

For a long time the *ménage* was by no means a happy one, the dislike of Stéphanie for her husband continued, the marriage was one only in name, and Napoleon, hearing but complaints from the grand ducal family, who were in despair at there being no possibility of heirs of Baden, wrote in vain to Stéphanie, and then sent a confidential envoy to remonstrate with her. But his representations were equally ineffectual in reconciling Stéphanie, the inclinations of whom had not changed, with her husband, who was now estranged and offended.

Napoleon gave Pauline and her husband the small principality of Guastalla, with which she was much dissatisfied.

Murat was made Grand-Duke of Berg and Clèves and Berthier, Prince de Neuchâtel ; upon which occasion Napoleon ordered him to marry. Now Berthier had ever since he had been in Milan, 1796, been devotedly attached to a certain Signora Visconti, a beautiful Italian, tall, dark, imperial, with all the grace and fascination of the South. The widow of Count Sopranzi, she had married M. Visconti, separated from him, and began a *liaison* with Berthier which lasted till his death. Berthier could not endure the idea of marrying, and represented to Napoleon that his affections were already engaged, to which the Emperor paid no attention, except to remark that Berthier, being now fifty years old, such a passion was ridiculous, and that unless he married the daughter of the Duke von Birkenfeld, he would never see him again. Berthier being of a different calibre from Lucien and Bernadotte, was afraid to disobey the Emperor; on the other hand, he did not choose to sacrifice himself or the Signora Visconti; therefore he married, and the person he sacrificed was his unfortunate wife, who was ugly and rich, and to whom he behaved meanly and badly. She was a meek, spiritless person, who resigned herself to her fate, and always lived on terms of affectionate friendship with Signora Visconti; whose relations to Berthier remained unaltered.

Bernadotte, meanwhile, was still in Germany with the Grande Armée; Désirée, who kept aloof as far as she could from the court of Joséphine, was obliged to follow her to Mayence during the war, where she found herself amongst surroundings and under circumstances she did not like, and was said by those around her to give herself airs. In her friendship with the Emperor there was always mingled a sentiment of pique and opposition; she made use of this friendship for the benefit of her husband and family, but it did not prevent those who were secret enemies of Napoleon and his Government being welcomed in her *salon*.

Besides the splendid *hôtel* in the *rue d'Anjou*, she had the country house at La Grange, bought by Bernadotte soon after their marriage, and another at Auteuil, where she spent part of the summer; but she always put off her departure from Paris as long as she could, and returned directly the heavy dews and early twilights of autumn began, to the cheerful shelter of the *rue d'Anjou*. There, and in the country also, she was more and more surrounded by friends old and new. Truguet, the Corsican admiral, to whom the Buonaparte had once been anxious to marry Elisa, and who was now a *frondeur* against them, and the *ex-conventionnel* Chiappe, whose intimate friendship for herself sometimes gave rise to gossip, although there was really no cause for scandal, and he was as much a friend of Bernadotte as of his wife.

Chiappe was a Corsican, of which nation, as a rule, those who did not adore the Emperor were his most ardent enemies; and Chiappe disliked Napoleon even more than did Bernadotte. Three times the Emperor had tried to remove him out of the way by appointing him to some distant post, but he always evaded it or returned, and his friendship for Désirée never changed.[1]

On the 7th of November, 1806, Bernadotte gained a brilliant victory at Lübeck, where he made 6,000 prisoners, stormed the city, and captured Blücher, in spite of the attempts to rescue him by 1,600 Swedes,

[1] "Bernadotte," p. 80 (Pingaud).

who were on board their ships in the harbour, and who fell into the hands of the victor. Little did Prince de Ponte Corvo foresee the consequences to the future of himself and his family, of the kindness and generosity with which he treated his prisoners. He entertained all the officers as his guests, restored their property and horses to them, and when they returned to Sweden they spread the fame of his military glory and chivalrous courtesy throughout the land.

CHAPTER XVII

1807—1808

IN spite of his victories and successes, Bernadotte felt always the same secret distrust of Napoleon which the Emperor entertained for him. Even after the capture of Lubeck, the official bulletin gave an unfair share of the honours of the day to Soult and Murat; while some one repeated to him a remark of the Emperor's which had been overheard : "*Bernadotte ne doute de rien . . . quelque jour le Gascon y sera pris.*"

However, the command of the Polish contingent was added to what he already held, and the campaign against the Russians was pushed on in the depth of the winter. On the 25th of January, 1807, his quarters were surprised by the enemy at Mohrungen, and though with inferior numbers, he rallied his troops, and by his resistance saved the army, and Napoleon himself from defeat and capture, all his baggage fell into the hands of the enemy.

But so well had Bernadotte treated his German prisoners that General Bennigsen sent him back all his personal property as a mark of gratitude for the kindness he had shown them.

Bernadotte took no part in the battles of Eylau and Jena. The battle of Eylau was fearfully sanguinary, and the victory was claimed by both sides. The Emperor declared that if Bernadotte's army corps had arrived in time the issue of the battle would have been very different, and tried, in his usual way, to lay the fault on Bernadotte, although the officer sent to convey to him the order to march upon Eylau had been taken prisoner by the Cossacks before reaching him. Bourrienne says : " Buonaparte, who always liked to throw the blame on some one, if things did not turn out exactly as he wished, attributed the doubtful success of the day to the absence of Bernadotte ; in this he was right ; but to make that absence a reproach to the Marshal was a gross injustice. . . ."

" Bernadotte was extremely disinterested, but he loved to be talked about. The more the Emperor endeavoured to throw accusations upon him, the more he was anxious to give publicity to all his actions. He sent to me an account of the brilliant affair of Braunsburg, in which a division of the 1st Corps had been particularly distinguished. Along with this narrative he sent me a note in the following terms : 'I send you, my dear minister, an account of the affair of Braunsburg. You will perhaps think proper to publish it. In that case I shall be obliged to you to get it inserted in the Hamburg journals.'   I did so.   The injustice of the Emperor and the injurious way in which he spoke of Bernadotte obliged the latter, for the sake of his own reputation, to make known the truth."[1]

At the bridge of Spanden, which he was defending Bernadotte received a dangerous wound in the head.   The Emperor then wrote him an approving, even affectionate letter,[2] containing friendly allusions to Désirée, who, on hearing of her husband's danger, set off immediately to join him, and nursed him until he was well.

The victory of Friedland and the peace of Tilsit closed the campaign.

General de Marbot relates in his memoirs that while the French troops were on the left bank of the Vistula he was sent with despatches to the strong fortress of Graudenz, situated upon that river, where he had to wait for two days.   There were about a hundred and fifty French prisoners, employed on different works in the fortress.

A certain Harpin, of the 3rd Dragoons, who was employed by the head carpenter to pile up wood, had managed secretly to make himself a little raft, and, having stolen a rope, had let himself and the raft down from the ramparts to the Vistula, which flowed beneath, when he had the bad luck to be surprised by a patrol, brought back, thrown into a dungeon, and the next day, according to Prussian law, condemned to receive fifty lashes.

Just as he was led out into the *place d'armes*

[1] "Mémoires de Napoléon" (Bourrienne).
[2] "Bernadotte," p. 77 (Pingaud).

Marbot happened to come up to fetch a book out of a carriage standing in the *place d'armes*, belonging to Duroc, who was conducting the negotiations. Seeing Harpin led out, and hearing the story, he drew his sword, rushed forward, and swore he would kill any man who should dare to dishonour by blows a soldier of the Empire. Duroc's carriage was guarded by a soldier named Moustache, well known for his fearless courage and herculean strength, who had followed Napoleon in twenty battles, and who now, taking four pistols from the carriage, hurried to the assistance of Marbot. They disengaged Harpin, gave him two pistols, and told him to get into the carriage with Moustache. Marbot then turned to the soldiers and declared that this carriage belonged to the Emperor, whose arms were upon it, that it was sacred everywhere, that any Prussian attempting to violate the sanctuary of it should be shot, and that he ordered Moustache and Harpin to fire upon any one who should attempt to enter it.

The Prussian *Major de place* went to his superiors for orders, and Marbot, entering the castle, sent for Duroc, who was then in the King's cabinet but came out at once. Hearing what was going on he hurried back to the King and indignantly protested against the flogging of a French soldier, declaring that if this sentence were carried out the Emperor would order the Prussian officers who were his prisoners to be flogged. The King ordered Harpin to be set free, and proposed to exchange the hundred and fifty French prisoners for the same number of Prussians. This was done; the

French soldiers joyfully embarked on the Vistula to join their comrades on the other side, and Napoleon, on being informed of the incident, announced to the Russians and Prussians that if any French prisoner were flogged he would shoot every officer of theirs who fell into his hands.[1]

There was just at this time an idea of restoring the ancient kingdom of Poland, and great were the hopes and expectations founded by the Poles upon the supposition.   In the early days of the Consulate[2] Napoleon had deeply at heart to avenge the dismemberment of that unhappy country, the re-establishment of which would have formed a barrier between Russia and the rest of Europe. In the end, however, the plan proved impracticable, and the Emperor contented himself with establishing a part of it upon the Vistula as Grand Duchy of Warsaw, which he gave for the present to the King of Saxony.

But the dream of Murat was to be King of Poland ; it was at this time his favourite subject of conversation ; he would compare himself to Sobieski, of whom he was never tired of talking and hearing. A certain number of the soldiers and people admired him ; Poniatowski gave him the sword of Bathori, Prince of Transylvania, he wore the ancient Polish costume, and gave himself such ridiculous airs of majesty that he was the laughing-stock of all the *salons* of the great houses in Warsaw, where they called him a *comedien qui joue les rois*. But his hopes and self-complacency were alike shattered

---

[1] " Mémoires " (Marbot).
[2] " Mémoires de Napoléon " (Bourrienne).

at Tilsit, when at the interview on the Niemen he appeared before Napoleon in all the glory of his fantastic costume. "Go away!" exclaimed the Emperor, "and put on your general's uniform. You look like Franconi!"[1]

The kingdom of Westphalia was made out of territory taken from Hesse-Cassel, Hanover, and Prussia, and given to Jérôme. After the campaign the Prince of Ponte Corvo received enormous sums of money and vast domains in Poland, Hanover, and Westphalia—a magnificent share of the spoils of conquest.[2] He was also made governor of the Hanse towns.

By the peace of Tilsit all German rivers and ports were closed to English commerce: a dangerous blow aimed by Napoleon at the country against which his most deadly hatred and least successful attacks were now directed. He, and many others also, believed that the ruin of England was now only a question of time, and that what was called the "Continental blocus" was the weapon at last found for her destruction.

But it soon appeared that the blocus did not injure England alone; it aroused a general clamour of disapprobation. It was odious to all the Baltic powers. Sweden was entirely sacrificed to it; Holland was in a ferment; the order to destroy all English goods in the harbours was execrated, and, when possible, evaded; hatred of Napoleon and revolt against his system were spreading amongst all who were being ruined by this decree; amongst others

[1] " Napoléon et sa famille," t. iv. p. 92 (Masson).
[2] " Bernadotte," p. 77 (Pingaud).

the Hanse towns, where Bernadotte, respected and liked as he had been in Hanover, mitigated as much as he could the general distress, and refrained from carrying out the oppressive law to its full extent, by which again he incurred the anger and dislike of Napoleon.[1]

Neither the social nor political arrangements made for Louis were answering at all. He had been made King of Holland much against his will, and instead of proving the submissive, obedient French prefect Napoleon expected, he had taken a great affection for his new kingdom, declared he was now a Dutchman, that Holland was and ought to be a free country, and objected to sacrifice her interests to those of France, especially in the matter of the blocus.

As to his marriage with Hortense, it had turned out deplorably. Louis had certain good qualities and tastes which, if he had had a wife who suited him, could such a being have been found, might have been developed ; but though not without principles, kindness of heart, and intellectual tastes, he was morbid, partly on account of his bad health, suspicious, obstinate, fidgety, and tiresome to an irritating degree. He changed perpetually from one palace to another, spied into everything, took offence at everything, tyrannised over his wife, meddled with the merest trifles, gave way to ill-temper, estranged all around him, and then declared he had no friend but his dog, whose death was a new grief to him, for he was kind to and fond of animals. His life was certainly not happy, he made

[1] " Bernadotte " (Sarrans).

his wife still more wretched, and the Emperor
became more and more irritated, as may be seen
by the following letter :—

"4 *April*, 1807.

"Your quarrels with the Queen penetrate the
public. Adopt in your home the paternal, effeminate
character you display in your government, and in
public affairs the rigorism you show in your household. You treat a young wife as one commands a
regiment. You have the best and most virtuous
wife in the world, and you make her miserable.
Let her dance as much as she likes, it is natural
at her age. I have a wife who is forty; from the
battlefield I write to her to go to balls. And you
expect a woman of twenty, who sees her life passing,
who has still all its illusions, to live in a cloister!
To be like a nurse, always washing her child! You
are too much in your household and not enough in
your administration. I should not tell you all this
unless I took an interest in you. Make the mother
of your children happy; there is only one way to
do so, which is to show her great esteem and confidence. Unfortunately you have too virtuous a wife;
if you had a coquette she would lead you by the nose.
Your wife is proud; the very idea that you can have
a bad opinion of her revolts and afflicts her. You
ought to have had a wife like some I know in Paris.
She would have deceived you and would have kept
you at her feet. It is not my fault, I have often told
your wife so."

To this sensible letter, however, Louis paid no
attention, and Lucien was as determined as ever

to take his own way. With Joseph the Emperor had certain disagreements, but Joseph was always his favourite brother, and the quarrels between them were few and easily appeased.

He insisted on marrying Stéphanie Tascher, a niece of Joséphine's, to the Prince d'Aremberg, whom she could not endure; but although Stéphanie could not help so far obeying her formidable uncle as to go through the ceremony she refused to live with her husband afterwards, at Brussels, returned to Paris, and after the fall of Napoleon got a divorce and married somebody else.

Strange to say, the marriage of Jérôme with the Princess Catherine of Wurtemberg, notwithstanding the unfortunate circumstances preceding it and the contemptible behaviour of Jérôme to his first wife and child, turned out much more happily than three-fourths of those arranged by Napoleon.

For although Jérôme was more selfish, extravagant, and dissipated than any of Napoleon's brothers, and less attractive than Joseph and Lucien, although he was perpetually carrying on some love intrigue, yet, if he was unfaithful to his wife, he was at any rate not rude or disagreeable or tyrannical to her, as Louis was to Hortense. On the contrary, he was always exceedingly anxious she should be pleased and happy; he gave magnificent *fêtes* in her honour, loaded her with costly presents, was always courteous and considerate, and never allowed any of his numerous *liaisons* to interfere with the deference and attention due to her.

And Catherine, seeing this, and finding that her influence with him was never diminished by his love-affairs with other women, neither did these *liaisons*, while they were going on, make him behave to her with the discourtesy Napoleon showed to Joséphine under similar circumstances, regarded with a certain amount of indulgence these proceedings, when she noticed them at all, attached herself with great affection to Jérôme, and got on well with his family, especially Madame Mère and the Emperor.

At the beginning of their married life there were, however, occasional disputes and commotions caused by Jérôme's conduct, and one of them happened while they were at Fontainebleau, where the court was established at the end of the summer.

The Prince and Princess of Baden, whose domestic affairs had not become any more satisfactory, were staying there, and Stéphanie, finding that the Emperor thought no more of his former fancy for her, had fallen into a flirtation with the King of Westphalia, which caused a great deal of gossip and scandal, besides irritating the Queen and making her unhappy.

Matters came to a climax at a ball, where Jérôme and Stéphanie danced so much together and made themselves so conspicuous that every one was talking about them. The Queen of Westphalia could not dance, being *enceinte*, so that she had all the more opportunity of watching all that was going on, and what she saw so displeased her that she began to cry and then fainted.

There was general consternation; the music stopped, people pressed round with remedies, and the Queen was carried into another room accompanied by the Empress, who did all she could to console her.

The Emperor was very angry, and sternly reprimanded Jérôme, who, always in awe of his brother, was now frightened and repentant, hastened to Catherine, overwhelmed her with excuses and caresses, and stayed with her till she recovered, when they retired together.

The Emperor desired Joséphine to speak to the Princess of Baden, which she did; she also sent Madame de Rémusat to remonstrate with her.

Stéphanie, as thoughtless and good-natured as ever, listened with attention to the representations of her friend, who assured her that that sort of conduct would never do in Germany, and that as she would have to live there and not in France it was necessary to alter her ways; that the line she was now taking could only bring her into troubles and misfortunes, and the best thing she could do would be to make friends with her husband and adapt herself to the country which must now be her home.

Stéphanie had the good sense to see that Madame de Rémusat was right, and to follow her advice; she promised that she should be satisfied with her behaviour, and at the next ball made herself so pleasant to her husband that he was surprised and overjoyed at the change, especially when Stéphanie, who found her position at the French Court less delightful now that she was no longer spoilt by the Emperor or treated with such distinction as formerly, turned her thoughts to Baden, where a beautiful home and high position awaited her, and where she contentedly returned and lived happily with the Prince. Stéphanie was greatly beloved in after years, not only by her husband and children, but by the people and those around her.

The Queen of Naples was the only one of the princesses who gave no balls or large entertainments; it was Joseph who liked them, and in his absence she preferred to be quiet. She occupied herself very much with the education of her two daughters; and expecting, naturally enough, that they would both be queens, she remarked that she felt responsible for them to their future subjects. One of them, after the fall of their family, married the eldest son of Lucien, the other the elder of the two remaining sons of Louis.

The Emperor disapproved of the dislike of the Queen of Naples for society, as he desired, for the encouragement of trade, that entertainments should be frequent; and Joseph wrote to complain to his brother that Cambacérès had borrowed the Luxembourg to give a ball in. The King of Naples observed that it looked very odd, and that either the Queen ought to have given the ball herself or M. l'Archichancelier should have found some other place for his *fête*. To which the Emperor replied that he also thought it ridiculous, and would have prevented it if he had known in time, but as it was then too late to stop it he had said nothing, but let it alone, and Joseph had better do the same. "It was the fault of the Queen, who is too kind; she ought to have said she did not like it."

Julie had given the *Hôtel de Marbœuf* to Mademoiselle Anthoine de Saint-Joseph on her marriage with General Suchet, and Désirée, who was particularly fond of this niece, was delighted to have her close to her. But she had always of late, hanging over her, the fear of being separated from Julie, as the Emperor disapproved strongly of her remaining at Paris while Joseph was at Naples, and from time to time he said so, both to her and to Joseph. But Julie could not endure the idea of leaving France, her friends, and her peaceful summers at Morte-fontaine and comfortable winters in the Luxembourg to go and lead the sort of life she hated at Naples ; besides which she was not then in very good health, so she excused herself for a long time, until at last in September came the following letter from Napoleon :—

"MADAME MA SŒUR ET BELLE-SŒUR,—I desire you will start for Naples. The present season is the best. I think, therefore, that you had better set off on the 15th of September, so as to arrive on the 23rd or 24th at Milan, and be at Naples between the 1st and 10th of October. This being the only object of this letter, I pray God, *Madame ma sœur et belle-sœur*, to have you in His holy and mighty keeping."

Julie wrote to Joseph explaining that she was really not well enough for the journey, and he represented this to the Emperor ; therefore Julie was allowed to stay a little longer, but in November she had the imprudence to go to Fontainebleau, where Napoleon declared she looked quite well, and that he was scandalised that she had not set off on her journey, adding that he was accustomed to see wives anxious to be with their husbands.

The fact was that Napoleon wished Julie to be at Naples, not considering that that court could be properly conducted without a queen; besides this, he knew that her presence would put an end to certain proceedings of the King, her husband, which he did not think altogether creditable; for he had always a horror of scandal. And Julie was no use to him in Paris, where she would do nothing to increase the attractions or splendour of his court; refusing even to attend those family dinners which took place every Sunday, and were so intolerable, and living surrounded by all the Clarys, who were becoming every day more rich and powerful, and who appeared to form a sort of opposition, not only to the rest of the Buonaparte, always excepting Madame Mère, but to the Beauharnais as well. It was almost a political clique in his eyes, for the Princesse de Ponte Corvo now influenced her sister, and was of course guided by Bernadotte.

However, Julie managed to put off her journey until March, 1808,[1] when she reluctantly departed to her new kingdom.

On the way to Naples she proposed to pay a secret visit to Lucien and his family; not daring to set Napoleon at defiance by going openly; but Lucien declined to receive anybody at his house by stealth; so the interview did not take place.

The absence of Julie from her beloved France was, however, of short duration, for that same year broke out the Peninsula War, of which, in a work like the present, it is impossible to treat. Napoleon seized upon the Spanish crown, which he gave to Joseph, offering Murat either Naples or Portugal. Delighted to have a kingdom at last, Murat and Caroline chose

---

[1] "Napoléon et sa famille," t. iv. p. 88 (Masson).

Naples, which was just as well, Portugal not being in the Emperor's possession.   But in the eager pursuit of his "system," Napoleon moved his brothers and other relations about like pieces on a chessboard. He offered Portugal to Jérôme, but the Princess Catherine was a Lutheran, and objected to leave Germany or change her religion; he offered Spain to Louis, who had complained that the Dutch climate did not suit him, and who would not carry out the blocus to the detriment of Holland.   But Louis refused, saying he was now a Dutchman, and had taken oaths which he could not break to the states of Holland.

Joseph having accepted the crown of Spain, made his entry into Madrid, June 25th, and Julie, who utterly refused to go to Spain, returned to Paris.

In the latter part of 1807 the Emperor made a journey to Venice and the other Italian provinces which, by the treaty of Presburg, had been annexed to the kingdom of Italy; returning to Paris on the 1st of January, 1808.   Stopping at Chambéry on his way back, he was told that a young man had been waiting there for several days to see him.   A letter from him was given, amongst others, to the Emperor, who opened them all before beginning his breakfast, looking at the signatures and laying them aside.

"Ah!   Ah!   What have we here?" he cried. "A letter from M. de Stael?   What can he want?"

"Sire," replied Lauriston, the *aide-de-camp* on duty, "he is a very young man, and there is something very prepossessing in his appearance."

"A very young man?   Then I will see him.   Rustan, tell him to come in."

The object of Auguste de Stael, who was only seventeen years old, was to claim two million francs which he declared the French Government owed his late grandfather M. Necker, and to induce the Emperor to allow his mother to return to France. His interview lasted during the whole time Napoleon was at breakfast. He began by asking where M. de Stael came from.

" From Geneva, Sire."

" Where is your mother ? "

" She is either in Vienna or will soon be there."

N. "Vienna? Well, that is where she ought to be ; and I suppose she is happy. . . . She will have a good opportunity of learning German." To the reply that she was not happy, he answered, " Ah! bah ! Your mother unhappy, indeed ! However, I do not mean to say she is altogether bad. She has talent— perhaps too much—and hers is an unbridled talent. She was educated amidst the submerged monarchy and the Revolution ; and out of all these events she makes an amalgamation of her own ! All this is very dangerous ; her enthusiasm is likely to make prose- lytes ; I must keep watch upon her. She does not like me ; and for the interests of those she would compromise I must forbid her coming to Paris. If I were to allow your mother to return to Paris, in less than six months I should be obliged to send her to Bicêtre or the Temple, which I should be very sorry to do, for the affair would make a noise and injure me in public opinion. Tell your mother that my determination is formed, my decision irrevocable. She shall never set foot in Paris as long as I live."

M. de S. "Sire, I cannot believe that you would

arbitrarily imprison my mother, if she gave you no reason for such severity."

N. "She would give me fifty . . . I know her well."

M. de S. "Sire, permit me to say that I am certain my mother would live in Paris in a way that would afford no ground of reproach : she would live retired, and only see a very few friends. . . . I venture to entreat that your Majesty will give her a trial, were it only for six weeks or a month."

N. ". . . I tell you it cannot be. She would enrol herself under the banner of the *faubourg Saint-Germain.* She see nobody, indeed ! . . . She would visit and receive company ; she would commit a thousand follies. She would say things she might consider as very good jokes, but which I should take seriously. My government is no joke : I wish this to be well known by everybody."

After a long discussion, in which he could gain nothing, young de Stael alluded to a work of his grandfather's.

"Yes, certainly!" exclaimed Napoleon. "Your grandfather was a fool ; an idealist, an old madman. At sixty years old to be forming plans to overthrow my government ! States would be well governed under such theorists, who judge of men from books and of the world from the map!"

S. "Sire, since my grandfather's plans are, in your Majesty's eyes, only vain theories, I cannot conceive why they should so highly excite your displeasure. There is no political economist who has not traced out plans of constitutions."

N. "Political economists are nothing but visionaries, who dream of plans of finance when they are not fit to be schoolmasters in the smallest village in the Empire. Your grandfather's work is that of an old man who died abusing all governments."

S. "Sire, may I presume to suppose from the way in which you speak of it . . . that you have not read it?"

N. "That is a mistake. I have read it from beginning to end."

S. "Then your Majesty must have seen how my grandfather rendered justice to your genius."

N. "Fine justice, truly! He calls me the indispensable man, but judging from his arguments the best thing that could be done would be to cut my throat! Yes! I was, indeed, indispensable to repair the follies of your grandfather and the mischief he did to France. It was he who overturned the monarchy and brought Louis XVI. to the scaffold!"

S. "Sire, you seem to forget that my grandfather's property was confiscated because he defended the King."

N. "Defended the King! A fine defence, truly! You might as well say that if I give a man poison, and then when he is in the agonies of death present him with an antidote, I wish to save him. For that is the way your grandfather defended Louis XVI. As to the confiscation you speak of, what does that prove? Nothing. Why, the property of Robespierre was confiscated! And let me tell you that Robespierre himself, Danton, and Marat have done less mischief to France than M. Necker. It was he who brought about the Revolution. You, M. de Stael, did not see this, but I did. I witnessed all that passed in those

days of terror and public calamity, but as long as I
live those days shall never return. Your speculators
trace their Utopian schemes upon paper, fools read
and believe them, everybody babbles about general
happiness, and presently the people have not bread
to eat. Then comes a Revolution. That is the result
of all those fine theories. Your grandfather was the
cause of the saturnalia which desolated France."
And he uttered these last words in a voice of fury,
but calmed himself, continued the conversation, and
presently asked M. de Stael—

"And you, young man, what are you doing? How
do you distinguish yourself? You must be something in this world. What are your projects?"

S. "Sire, I can be nothing in France; I could not
serve a Government which persecutes my mother."

N. "That is true. But since by your birth you
may be somebody out of France, you should go to
England, for look you, there are only two nations,
France and England; the rest are nothing." As he
rose from breakfast, Napoleon went up to young
de Stael, pinched his ear, and said, kindly—

"You are young. If you had my age and experience you would judge of things more correctly.
I am far from being displeased with your frankness.
I like to see a son plead his mother's cause. Your
mother has given you a difficult commission and you
have executed it cleverly. I am glad I have had this
opportunity of conversing with you. I like to talk
with young people, especially when they are un-
assuming and not too fond of arguing. But I will
not hold out false hopes to you. Murat has spoken
to me about this, and I told him what I now tell you,

that my will is irrevocable. If your mother were in prison I should not hesitate to liberate her, but nothing shall induce me to recall her from exile."

M. de Stael declared that his mother was as unhappy as if she were in prison, to which the Emperor replied that she had all Europe for her prison, that she could go to Rome, Vienna, Berlin, or still better, to London, where they liked wrangling politicians. As regarded the debt, the de Staels must appeal to the law. He then got into his carriage with Duroc, and after a long silence, in which he seemed absorbed in deep thought, said—

" I am afraid I was rather harsh with that young man . . . but no matter, it will prevent others from troubling me. These people calumniate everything I do. They don't understand me, Duroc ; their place is not in France. How can the Necker family be for the Bourbons, whose first duty, if ever they returned to France, would be to hang them all ? "

Bourrienne, in his memoirs of Napoleon, declares that although Joséphine had neither taste for nor knowledge of political affairs, yet she had a curious intuition which never failed to be justified whenever any misfortune was about to befall Napoleon ; and that with this foreboding of evil she was strongly imbued when the Emperor seized upon the Spanish crown. She frequently said, with evident distress, that no good would come from Joseph being King of Spain ; and before long her fears began to be realised, for with the Peninsula War came reverses to the hitherto victorious armies of France ; the first successful resistance of a people resolved at any cost to preserve their national independence.

The rumours prevalent of the approaching divorce also were received with disapproval by the people. They liked Joséphine, and her melancholy looks excited their compassion ; besides which there was always an idea current amongst them that her fate was so bound up with the Emperor, that if he separated from her it would bring misfortune upon him. She had spent the summer of 1807 with him at Bayonne, where he was occupied with the affairs of the Peninsula ; and whilst there he showed her undiminished affection, walking and driving with her, often playing and laughing with her in the presence of the escort. On one occasion he seized her shoes, threw them to a long distance, and forced her to get into the carriage without them, while he admired her pretty feet. At other times he would seem torn between conflicting feeling, his love for her and pain at a separation, and the ever-increasing longing for an heir, a son of his own. The question of succession had been, ever since the declaration of the Empire, a source of never-ending quarrels and perplexities in the family, who treated the matter exactly as if they had a right to be aggrieved by his choice. Joseph declared that his was the first right, and Napoleon, in fact, always retained to a remarkable degree the respect for the claims of seniority in his family. On one occasion Caroline was filled with indignation, which she dared not show to the Emperor, because, when she was Queen of Naples, he ordered her place at the dinner-table to be put below that of her eldest sister, Elisa, then Grand-Duchess of Tuscany. And Jérôme, when King of Westphalia, thought himself injured because Napoleon made him

sit with his back to the horses while he placed
Lucien, Prince of Canino, by his own side.

But as Napoleon remarked, Joseph was older than
he would probably die first, and had only daughters.
Lucien was excluded. For a long time he looked
upon the eldest son of Louis as his heir; in fact, the
resemblance of the child to himself and the extraordinary love he had for him, encouraged the false
and injurious reports as to their real relationship.
He wished to adopt and educate the boy himself; but
Louis, suspicious and jealous, violently opposed the
idea, declaring that it would give colour to the reports
about Napoleon and Hortense: that his own right to
succeed came before that of his son, whom he would
not have exalted above him or made independent of
him: and that if the Emperor insisted he would leave
the country with the boy, whose death, however, put
an end to these projects, and about whose brothers
the Emperor cared little.

There was a plan of inducing Joséphine to feign an
accouchement, and to impose upon the nation as the
legitimate son of the Emperor, the child of one of his
mistresses. Joséphine consented, and the matter was
broached to Corvisart, the celebrated doctor, who
refused to have anything to do with it.

The birth of his two illegitimate sons, one by a
lectrice of his sister Caroline, the other by the Polish
Countess Walewski, increased in the Emperor the
desire to have a legitimate heir, and the idea was
fostered by his family, whose spite against Joséphine
overpowered the consideration they might have been
supposed to have for their own interests, for as long
as Joséphine remained his wife there would be no

legitimate son for Napoleon, and one of themselves would be his successor; whereas, if he took a young wife he would probably have an heir.   But such was the dislike of the Buonaparte to the Beauharnais, that it extended even to the children of Louis, because they were also those of Hortense.   Even Madame Mère showed scarcely any affection for these grandsons, though she was devoted to all her other grandchildren.

One day, in the lifetime of the little Napoleon, son of Louis, the Emperor, who was playing with him, said—

" Do you know, Monsieur, that you are very likely to be a king some day ? "

" Et Achille ? " said Murat, who stood by.

" Achille?   Ah! Achille will be a good soldier," replied Napoleon ; then, turning to the little Napoleon, he added—

" But, my poor child, if you wish to live, I advise you never to accept a meal from your cousins."

Achille Murat was a spoilt, passionate, conceited boy, whom Napoleon did not like.   One day the Emperor, who was always rough with children, pinched his ear till the boy, who was only three years old, cried, and in a passion called Napolean " *méchant* " and " *vilain*," whereupon the Emperor gave him a violent box on the ear.   Caroline began to cry, but said they must not tell Murat.   The only one who was not afraid to defend his children was Lucien, who said he was not going to allow them to be ill-treated.

CHAPTER XVIII

1808

Disastrous effect of Peninsula War—A duel—Quarrel of Lannes and Bessières — Essling — Death of Lannes — Rapacity of Napoleon's generals—Battle of Wagram—The mystery of Mr. Bathurst.

THE Empire was at the height of its power and grandeur; for several years yet its gigantic fabric was to stand unshaken by the attacks of its enemies; but there began to be a difference in the public feeling, beginning with the ill-advised war with Spain and the divorce of Joséphine.[1]

The armies of France were, after all, not invincible; the Emperor was not always victorious; while the sacrifices he exacted were fearful. People began to ask whether even glory and conquest were not too dearly purchased by all the sufferings and horrors of this new and terrible war; and when it appeared that the price had to be paid not for success but for disaster, when the bones of thousands of Frenchmen lay on the plains of Spain and Portugal, when fresh

[1] During the calamities of the Russian campaign many of the soldiers attributed their misfortunes to this divorce, which they declared had brought Napoleon bad luck. " He should not have separated from 'la vieille,'" they said, "and then this would not have happened."

levies were raised in haste to be sent to fill the places
of those that had perished, when horrible stories
reached France of the frightful revenge of the
Spaniards, a cruel people cruelly provoked by the
iniquitous invasion of their country, the destruction,
plunder, and massacre perpetrated by the French;
then, in Paris and throughout France murmurs and
discontent grew more vehement and persistent, and
for the first time the popularity of the Emperor
diminished.

The defeat of Junot by the English at Vimiero and
the capitulation of Cintra were a blow to Napoleon,
and although he went to Spain himself, and by his
presence brought a transient success to the French
arms, he had not been there more than two months
when he heard from a clerk, a paid spy in the War
Office of Vienna, that Austria was preparing for
war.　He left at once for Paris, and after his departure
the tide of misfortune rose again over the armies of
France.　The quarrels and jealousies amongst his
marshals and generals were not only a scandal but
a public danger, and excited the indignation of
Napoleon, who forbade his officers to fight duels with
each other.

Two young officers, disregarding this order, fought
a duel in the front of their battalion, amidst a shower
of the enemy's bullets.　Their colonel sent them
under arrest to the citadel of Burgos.　Shortly afterwards the regiment was reviewed at Madrid by the
Emperor, who ordered the colonel to present to him
the officers recommended for promotion in the place
of those killed.　Amongst those presented was one
of the young *sous-lieutenants*, who had received a

sword-cut on the cheek in the unlucky duel. The Emperor, on seeing him, remembered the story, and asked in a stern voice—

" Where did you receive that wound ? "

" Sire," replied the young man, laying his finger on his cheek, " I got it here."

Pleased with the quickness and presence of mind shown in his answer, the Emperor smiled and said—

" Your colonel proposes you for the rank of lieutenant ; I grant it you, but be more discreet in future, or I shall cashier you." [1]

Much more important were the frequent quarrels among the superior officers. In the Peninsula War the disputes and disagreements of Masséna, Ney, Soult, Junot, and others, were a serious disadvantage to the French arms, and in other of the armies of France the same dissensions prevailed. General de Marbot, in his memoirs, relates the following adventure which he experienced when he was *aide-de-camp* to Lannes at the time of the battle of Essling.

Lannes could not bear either Murat or Bessières. Murat was in the first place his successful rival with Caroline Buonaparte, whom he wanted to marry, and Lannes having spent 300,000 francs too much in the equipment of his soldiers, Bessières, who was on the *conseil d'administration*, told Murat, who told the Emperor.

Napoleon deprived Lannes of the command of the Guard, and gave him two months to restore the money. At his wits' end to find it, Lannes appealed to Augereau, who lent it to him; but he did not forget either the assistance or the offence.

On the battlefield of Essling, Bessières was under his command, and Lannes, seeing that the Austrians were making a retrograde movement, wished all the cavalry to charge, and said to one of his *aides-de-camp*—

"Go and tell Marshal Bessières that I order him to charge *à fond*"; which meant to go on till their sabres touched the enemy, and implied that his charge had not been vigorous enough; harshly expressed from one marshal to another.

"What did you say to Marshal Bessières?" inquired Lannes, when the *aide-de-camp* came back.

"I informed him that your Excellency requested him to order all the cavalry to charge."

"*Vous êtes un enfant!*" exclaimed Lannes, shrugging his shoulders; "send me another officer."

He gave the same message with the same result, when, as he turned angrily away, Marbot rode up.

"Marbot," he said, "Marshal Augereau assured me that you were a man one could rely upon, and the way you have served me confirms me in that opinion. I want a further proof of it. Go and tell Marshal Bessières that I order him to charge *à fond :* you understand thoroughly, Monsieur—*à fond.*"

Marbot understood perfectly, and disliked his errand, but having no choice, he obeyed orders, and amid a hail of bullets galloped up to Bessières, who was surrounded by his staff and several generals and other officers, and respectfully asked if he might speak to him alone.

"Speak out loud, Sir," was the answer.

"M. le Maréchal Lannes desires me to tell your Excellency that he orders you to charge *à fond.*"

"Is that the way to speak to a marshal, Sir?" cried Bessières, in a fury. "What expressions! 'I order you!' and '*charger à fond!*' You shall be severely punished for this impertinence."

"M. le Maréchal, the more disrespectful my words seem to your Excellency, the more you should be convinced that I am only executing the orders I received."

And he turned and rode back to Lannes, who asked—

"Well! what did you say to Marshal Bessières?"

"That your Excellency ordered him to charge *à fond.*"

"That's it; at any rate here is one *aide-de-camp* who knows what he is about."

The charge took place, a general was killed, but the result was successful.

"You see," said Lannes, "that my strict command has produced an excellent effect; without it Marshal Bessières would have dawdled about all day."

Night came on, the battle ceased at the centre and the right wing; Lannes resolved to go to the Emperor, whose bivouac was near the bridge, but had scarcely begun his march when, hearing a brisk fusillade at Aspern, where Masséna commanded, and wishing to see what was going on there, he ordered his staff to proceed to the Emperor's bivouac, and desired Marbot to lead a party to Aspern, where he had been several times that day.

Marbot dismounted, as the path wound amongst

fields of tall, standing corn; Lannes did the same,
and walked by his side, talking of the battle which
had raged all that day and was to continue on the
morrow; their way being lighted by the moon and by
the flames which were devouring Essling and shining
with a lurid light over the dark plain. All around
Aspern were the camp-fires of Masséna's troops, and
Lannes, wishing to speak to him, sent Marbot forward
to find out where he was. Presently he saw him
walking up and down with Bessières, who, recognising
him but not seeing Lannes, came forward and
exclaimed—

"Ah! it's you, sir! If what you said just now
was upon your own authority, I will teach you to
choose your expressions better when you speak to
your superiors; and if you only obeyed your marshal
he shall give me satisfaction for this affront, and I
charge you to tell him so."

At that moment Lannes rushed forward and seized
Marbot by the arm, exclaiming—

"Marbot, I owe you an apology, for though I felt
certain of your fidelity I had some doubt as to the
manner in which you transmitted my orders to this
officer, but I see that I did you injustice." Then,
turning to Bessières: "I consider it most audacious
of you to reprimand one of my *aides-de-camp*. He
was the first to lead the assault on Ratisbon, he
crossed the Danube, braving almost certain death,
and has just been twice wounded in Spain; while
there are mock soldiers who never received a scratch
in their lives, and only gained their promotion by
spying upon and denouncing their comrades. What
is your complaint against this officer?"

" Monsieur, your *aide-de-camp* came and told me that you *ordered* me to *charger à fond*. It seems to me that such expressions are improper."

" They are correct, Monsieur, and I dictated them. Did not the Emperor tell you that you are under my orders ? "

" The Emperor told me to be guided by you," replied Bessières with hesitation.

" Understand, Sir," cried Lannes, " that in the army men are not guided by advice, they obey orders. If the Emperor had wished to place me under your command I should have offered him my resignation ; as long as you are under mine I shall give you orders and you will obey them ; if not, I shall deprive you of your command. As to *charger à fond*, I desired you to do so because you were not doing it, but ever since this morning you have done nothing but parade before the enemy without approaching him properly."

" This is an insult ! " exclaimed Bessières angrily ; " and you shall give me satisfaction for it."

" At once, if you like ! " retorted Lannes, laying his hand upon his sword.

During this altercation old Masséna had been trying to interpose and calm them, but finding it useless he now assumed a tone of authority.

" Messieurs," he said, " I am your senior, you are in my camp, and I am not going to allow you to give my troops the scandalous spectacle of two marshals drawing their swords upon each other in the face of the enemy. I therefore call upon you in the name of the Emperor to separate immediately." Then taking the arm of Lannes, he led him in a more persuasive manner to the limit of the bivouac, while Bessières returned to his own.

Lannes mounted, rode straight to the Emperor's bivouac, asked to see him alone, and related what had happened.

The Emperor sent at once for Bessières, whom he received very badly.   He walked away with him, and could be seen with crossed arms pacing rapidly up and down, apparently addressing him in a torrent of wrath, before which Bessières appeared confounded. The Emperor then went to dinner, taking Lannes with him, but giving no invitation to Bessières, who was so cowed by the wrath of Napoleon that he sent the next morning to ask Lannes how he wished the troops to be placed, to which Lannes replied—

" I order you, Monsieur, to place them . . . and then await my commands." [1]

But before the end of the battle which raged through that day Lannes had received his death-wound.

The Emperor was delighted with the victory of Essling, to which he considered Rapp had greatly contributed.   After complimenting him highly he added—

" If ever you did well in not executing my orders, you have done so to-day ; for the safety of the army depended upon the taking of Esslingen." [2]

Lannes was a great loss to Napoleon, who went to take leave of him when he was carried out of the battle mortally wounded, having had both legs carried off by a cannon-ball.   He was one of the

[1] " Mémoires de Marbot "
[2] " Mémoires de Rapp."

bravest officers in the army. He was the son of a
groom at Lectoure, in Guyenne, had been a dyer,
then enlisted, rose rapidly, and had been made Duc
de Montebello and Marshal of France by Napoleon.
Like many of Napoleon's generals, he was a strange
mixture of qualities, defects, and characteristics, a
product of the chaos in which he had been born.

Men whose early years had been passed in poverty,
destitute of either education, religion, or refinement,
who had grown up amidst the most deplorable
surroundings, accustomed to scenes of violence and
bloodshed, were suddenly placed in powerful posi-
tions, with wealth and luxury at their command, able
to gratify every passion, absolutely devoid of self-
control, scruples, or principles. The consequences
were what might be expected, and the sufferings of
the unfortunate countries overrun by them were
terrible indeed.

In these days, when we read in the papers of a
soldier being severely punished by his commanding
officer because, in time of war in an enemy's country,
he took a chicken without paying for it, one can
hardly realise the awful scourge such troops and
generals must have been, and what a change a
century of progress in civilisation has wrought
amongst all nations in the conduct of their wars.

The memoirs of General Thiébault relate many
abominable deeds of this kind : how the French
officers would order extravagant dinners and costly
wines, of course with no intention of paying for
them, and then having dined, would destroy all the
china, plate, and everything in the hotel or restaurant,
even cutting down the great chandelier that hung in

the middle of the ceiling; how a friend of his, having been given shelter and refuge by a Swiss *pasteur*, repaid his hospitality by seducing and carrying away his young daughter, whom he soon abandoned. Of all these proceedings, besides cruelties, plunder, and assassinations, General Thiébault speaks as a matter of course, and yet he himself was rather a good specimen of an officer of that day; he was a well-educated gentleman, the son of a secretary of Frederick the Great, and a man of numerous good qualities, liked by the conquered Spaniards and Germans, whom he governed without oppression, and kind-hearted rather than otherwise, good to his parents, and infatuated with his wife, a silly, selfish, cruel, vain woman he called Zozotte, whose foolish conduct, spiteful sayings, and ill-tempers he recounts with enthusiastic admiration in his volumes.

But all this was a matter of course; Soult, Masséna, and the others cut pictures out of their frames, stole the treasures of palaces and convents, allowed their soldiers to make targets of splendid old pictures they could not carry away, and their officers sacked the houses of everything they could lay their hands upon.

Lannes was as greedy as most of them, but he had many virtues; besides being brave, which they all were, he was, Madame d'Abrantès and others declare, a good friend and a kind-hearted man, and he did not forget a benefit.

He was travelling once with General de Marbot, who was then his *aide-de-camp*, and they stopped to change horses and have supper. Lannes went up to the house of the *maître-de-postes*, from which the family rushed out in delight, receiving him with transports of affection, and placing before him and his companion every delicacy they could get. Lannes showed great affection for the whole family. When they left he gave a large sum of money to the wife, and a splendid gold watch and chain with diamond clasp to the husband. He told Marbot that the man had served with him and saved his life in Syria. During the assault upon Saint-Jean d'Acre, Lannes fell insensible from a shot ; his men, supposing him to be dead, retreated. The Turks were cutting off the heads of the fallen and sticking them on pikes This man, then captain, called to the soldiers to save the body of their general, and, seizing him by the leg, dragged him along ; the shaking revived him. The captain was severely wounded later on, retired, and married, ever since which Lannes had been the providence of the whole family. He bought the man a house, fields, and relays of post-horses, educated his eldest son, and promised to do the same for the others, but soon after this visit he was killed at Essling.[1]

The battle of Wagram, one of the most sanguinary ever fought by Napoleon, took place in July, and the French troops entered Vienna, where peace was signed. In the same month, Napoleon, who had seized the papal states, caused the Pope to be removed from Rome by General Radet, and Pius VII. wandered for some time from town to town, uncertain where to take refuge. Another violent disagreement between Napoleon and Bernadotte happened at the battle of Wagram. The Emperor

[1] "Mémoires de Marbot."

complained of the lukewarmness displayed by the Saxon troops. Bernadotte not only declared this censure to be unjust, but drew up a bulletin praising and congratulating them for their conduct, which he sent to the newspapers. This enraged Napoleon, who sent an order of the day contradicting it to all the marshals, and deprived Bernadotte of his command.

A mysterious and tragic occurrence took place after the peace of Vienna. The English minister in the capital, a young man named Bathurst, was travelling *incognito*, accompanied only by one official, carrying important State papers. They were about to embark for England by way of the Baltic, and stopped to rest and dine at a post-house outside a small town on the frontier of Mecklenburgh. As they were about to start again, Bathurst, who had already his hand on the carriage door, seemed to remember something, turned back towards the house, disappeared round the corner, and was never seen again. He had all the way feared to be attacked, had expressed his uneasiness to the governor of the town, and had then burnt several papers; but the idea that he committed suicide was supposed to be unfounded, especially as a fortnight afterwards his trousers were found lying by the roadside, with an unfinished letter to his wife in the pocket, and although the weather had been very wet, they and the letter were dry and uninjured. He was supposed to have been murdered for the sake of some despatches he carried.

CHAPTER XIX

1809—1810

Divorce of Joséphine—Her court and establishment- Failure of the system of Napoleon—His dreams and projects—Joseph—Louis—Jérôme—Three princesses—My uncle, Louis XVI.—Adventure at a masked ball.

THE long-talked-of divorce of Joséphine took place, the blow she had been dreading for years had fallen at last. Napoleon, in mingled compunction, satisfaction, and regret, did all he could to soften it. Joséphine had a large allowance, a *hôtel* in Paris, La Malmaison, and a château and estate in Normandy called Navarre, she had her ladies-in-waiting and her little court, and it was made known that not to pay respects there was to incur the displeasure of the Emperor.

She had many friends who faithfully stood by her and whom she loved, and the affection of her children and grandchildren was her greatest consolation. She could now frequently see Hortense, who had succeeded in separating herself from Louis Buonaparte, and lived at Paris and her country place, Saint-Leu. All the grandchildren adored Joséphine; one of the little sons of Hortense was heard to say on hearing that his cousin Stéphanie was going to rejoin her husband—

" She must love him very much indeed if she will leave grandmamma to go to him."

Eugène, his wife and children, were also a great source of happiness to her ; from them she was always certain of sympathy and love.

Napoleon, who kept assuring her of his continued friendship and affection, paid her occasional visits, and paid the debts she always kept making. Affairs were not going smoothly with him just then, and it was perfectly evident to him that his " system " was not answering at all, and never would answer with the material he had with which to carry it out. Therefore his only hope of ever being able to realise this gigantic conception was by means of sons of his own ; inheriting, as he fondly hoped, his own talents and characteristics, brought up by himself, imbued with his own opinions and tastes, ready and able to carry out his plans and do his bidding. And is there, amongst all the fallacies and disappointments people prepare for themselves in this life, any greater than this? Looking around one, amongst one's friends, or amongst the men of genius one reads of in history, where does one find the great intellect or great qualities of the parent transmitted to the child? There have, no doubt, been, and still may be, instances of a brilliant son of a brilliant parent, but they are so few as to justify the opinion that they are accidental. What one does see every day is the man who in any profession has risen above the average around him, the great soldier or lawyer, the statesman, the scholar, succeeded by a son who is one of Rudyard Kipling's "flannelled fools," who sells his father's pictures and books which he is incapable of understanding, and wastes his fortune upon idiotic dissipation, or spends his life in hunting foxes and playing games. In spite of the marvellous intellect which raised Napoleon so far above ordinary mortals, one cannot but feel that he must in any case have been doomed to disappointment, even if his plans had not been cut short as they were. At any rate, what one hears of the King of Rome, the only son he did have, gives no impression of any remarkable capacity or strength of character.

But at this time the Emperor's head was filled with his new prospects and the glorious dynasty he was to found. His eldest son was to succeed him as Emperor of France, his second was to be King of Italy—crowns and kingdoms were to be found for the others who might be born to him. Europe seemed too small and too narrow for his soaring ambition. Already he repented of the lands and sovereignties he had bestowed upon his relations, and began to think of taking them back.

The one brother who possessed any capacity set him at defiance ; the four, including Murat, whom he had made kings gave him nothing but trouble.

Joseph could not maintain himself upon the throne of Spain, the Spanish nation was against him ; he could not conduct a campaign or command the French troops Napoleon sent to his assistance, and he was jealous of Bessières and the other French generals who could. He wrote to ask the Emperor to tell him once for all whether the Duke de Rorigo was to command in Spain, or himself—as it must be one or the other. And he asked Napoleon to let

him give up Spain and give him back Naples, which
he much preferred,[1] but the Emperor refused to put
such an affront upon Murat and Caroline.

Joseph then became more and more resolved to
identify himself with the Spaniards, to gain their
affections, to free himself from the control of France,
and to admit no authority in Spain but his own;
a determination natural and praiseworthy enough if
he could have carried it out; but, as it was only by
the help of the French troops that he could stay in
Spain at all, and he was, as the Emperor told him,
" not a soldier in the least," and knew nothing about
commanding an army, the result of his attempts was
deplorable. The Emperor was perplexed and angry
at the reports he got, and exclaimed—

" The army seems to be commanded not by
generals but by postmasters!"

And the only thing that saved Joseph from the
full consequences of his plans and orders was that
nobody obeyed them. Bessières gave respectful as-
surances of obedience and then took his own way;
and Ney replied—

" This order comes from a man who knows nothing
about our profession. The Emperor has given me an
army corps to conquer, not capitulate. Tell the King
I have not come here to play the part of Dupont."

Napoleon grew more and more irritated, compar-
ing Joseph with those of whose interference he kept
complaining.

" Murat is an ass," he said; " but he has go and
daring, he has made war all his life. Murat is a
fool, but he is a hero."

---

[1] " Napoléon et sa famille," t. iv. p. 270 (Masson).

As affairs got worse Napoleon had an idea of making the south of Spain and Portugal into a kingdom and restoring it to the Bourbons, while he annexed the northern provinces to France ; but this idea he abandoned, and Joseph remained on the throne till the reverses of 1813 ; but always steadily tried to resist being a French prefect.

For Louis, Napoleon had no such deference, but, finding that he would not thoroughly adopt the continental blockade, and so sacrifice the interests of Holland to France, nor yet carry out the " system " in other ways, he deposed him and took possession of the country.

Even Jérôme ventured to object to the French *douanes* being introduced into Westphalia, tried to Germanise his government and army after the fashion of his brothers in Spain and Holland and his brother-in-law at Naples, complained bitterly of appointments being made in his kingdom by Napoleon without his knowledge, and said, as Joseph did, that there could be only one person to govern a kingdom, and that if he could not do it he would rather give it up, which sounds reasonable.   But it was nevertheless true that Jérôme did not intend to resign, and yet could not govern.   All he cared for was the splendour of his court ; he led a scandalous life, and was overwhelmed with debts ; he was, as Napoleon had remarked in former years, a continual expense and no use in any way [1] either in a government or in the army.   The Emperor wrote to Dresden to him, as follows :—

" I can only repeat to you that the troops you

[1] " Le Roi Jérôme " (Joseph Turquan).

22

command must be assembled at Dresden. In the army there is neither brother of the Emperor nor King of Westphalia, but a general commanding a corps. . . . I have seen an *ordre du jour* of yours which makes you the laughing-stock of Germany, Austria, and France. Have you no friend near you who can tell you a few truths? You are a King and brother of an Emperor: ridiculous qualities in war. You must be a soldier, *et puis soldat et encore soldat:* you want neither ministers, *corps diplomatique*, nor pomp. You must bivouac with your advanced guard, be in the saddle night and day, march with the advanced guard, or else stay in your seraglio. You make war like a satrap! Good God! is it from me that you have learnt that? From me, who with an army of 200,000 men am at the head of my troops. . . . Cease to be ridiculous, send the *corps diplomatique* to Cassel, have no luggage, no encumbrances, no table but your own. Make war like a young soldier who desires glory and reputation, and try to deserve the rank you have attained, the esteem of France and Europe, who are watching you, and, *pardieu!* have sense enough to write and speak properly." [1]

The important question now was who should replace Joséphine, and be the mother of the emperors and kings to come? Three princesses were in the mind of Napoleon, who was determined this time to have a royal alliance: a Russian grand-duchess, an Austrian archduchess, and a Saxon princess. The Beauharnais were in favour of the Austrian alliance, to which the Buonaparte family were strongly opposed.

[1] "Napoléon et sa famille," t. iv. p. 319 (Masson).

An Austrian, related to the Bourbons, would favour
the *faubourg Saint-German*, and would prefer the
Beauharnais to themselves. A Russian would be
more a stranger to these divisions and recollections, besides being cousin to Jérôme's wife, with
whom they all got on very well. But of the three
they preferred the Saxon princess, who had not the
difference in religion of the Russian, and not belonging to so powerful a family, would not be so likely
to treat them with *hauteur*. Murat was especially
violent against the Austrian marriage, as he was not
only King of Naples but was casting envious eyes
upon Sicily, where Marie Caroline, Archduchess of
Austria, formerly Queen of Naples and Sicily, sister
of Marie Antoinette and maternal grandmother of the
proposed Austrian bride, still reigned at Palermo.

But the Buonaparte family, after their first spiteful
triumph in getting rid of Joséphine, could not but
feel serious misgivings about her successor. What
they would have liked and actually proposed was
that Napoleon should marry Charlotte, eldest daughter
of Lucien by his first wife, then about fourteen years
old ; and Madame Mère had written repeatedly to
Lucien to send her to Paris, there having been at
one time an idea of marrying her to the Prince of the
Asturias. This plan, however, had come to nothing,
and the Buonaparte family were now considering
how, not having been able to live in peace with the
good-natured, gentle-tempered, easy-going Joséphine,
they would get on with a haughty princess of a
powerful royal house, who would be much less likely
to conciliate them than to treat them with ridicule
and contempt. For the Saxon princess turned out

to be unsuitable, and the Russian answer was delayed ; but it transpired that the Empress Catherine had declared that she would rather throw her grand-daughter into the Neva than give her to Napoleon. Not wishing for a rebuff, he hastened to ask for the eldest daughter of the Empress of Austria, who consented to sacrifice the Archduchess Marie Louise, as the King of Wurtemberg had the Princess Catherine.

Already the Emperor's mind was filled with the thought of the children who were to spring from this illustrious alliance, which was not only to bring him sons and daughters, who should be the grandchildren, nephews, nieces, and cousins of all the royalty of Europe, but to admit him also into the family circle of royalty to which he was eager to belong, to hasten the day when, after his marriage with the arch-duchess, he would speak, as he delighted to do, of " my poor uncle, Louis XVI.," and "my aunt, the Queen Marie Antoinette." Already he decreed that " the Prince Imperial" should have the title and honours of King of Rome ; already were discussed the dowries of the princesses his daughters — the appanages of his younger sons and of his grandsons, the sons of the King of Rome ; he had before decreed that all the Emperors, his successors, should be crowned at St. Peter's as well as in Paris.

In all these arrangements no mention was made of any of his brothers and sisters ; no obligation was attached by him to any gift or service of former days, no promise was binding, no rights were valid against the claims of the mighty race so soon to appear and possess the earth.

A CORNER OF OLD PARIS.

The kingdom of Italy with its succession to his children had been the condition of the marriage of Eugène de Beauharnais to the Princess Auguste of Bavaria; the solemn engagement to maintain it had been made to the Italian people in the face of Europe. Napoleon had repeatedly assured Auguste that he loved her as a daughter, and always declared that for Euègne, his adopted son, he had all the affection of a father, and that he could invariably rely upon his loyalty and devotion. He did not pretend to have the slightest fault to find with either of them. But he wanted Italy for his second son, and what were oaths or gratitude or affection if they stood in the way of his desires?

Eugène was to govern Italy, he was useful there; but his children were disinherited, and "the Grand Duchy of Frankfort," or "some state with a fine town for capital," was promised them instead.

The regrets and misgivings prevalent at the divorce of Joséphine were drowned in the excitement and *éclat* of the Austrian alliance. Paris was gay and brilliant, entertainments of all kinds were lavishly given and honoured by the presence of the Emperor, who delighted especially in masked balls, one of the most splendid of which was that of Count Marescalchi, "Ambassador of Napoleon, King of Italy to Napoleon, Emperor of France."

These balls were very much the fashion; the Emperor in black domino and mask usually walked about with Duroc, who was disguised in the same way, talking to the ladies who were mostly unmasked.

The strictest surveillance was always exercised; every one was obliged to unmask and show their

tickets to the *adjutant de place ;* the list of invitations
was submitted to the police, several of whose agents
in disguise were always at the ball, and the hotel
was guarded outside by a battalion of soldiers.

There was a certain Madame X., widow of a
highly-placed official, who, owing to his misconduct
and her own bad reputation, found herself with a
much smaller pension than she would otherwise
have received, and had come to Paris to complain.
She tried to carry her grievance to the ministers, and
to the different members of the Imperial family, all
of whom refused to see her ; she persistently followed
the Emperor, trying in vain to speak to him, and,
knowing that he would be at this ball, she managed
to get a ticket.

Madame X. was an extremely eccentric woman
in appearance as well as in character. Very tall,
rather loud and masculine, with a haughty air and
the voice of a man. She had been handsome, and
though she was over fifty and had no remains of
beauty except magnificent hair, thought she was so
still.

The dancing was on the ground floor, the rooms
for cards and conversation on the first floor. The
ballroom was crowded, while a quadrille was going
on composed of the most magnificent costumes,
when suddenly, amongst the mass of silks, velvets,
plumes, brocades, and jewels, appeared an enormously
tall figure dressed in white calico with a red bodice,
and hung all over with many coloured ribbons, with a
little straw hat and two great plaits of hair down to her
heels. It was Madame X. dressed as a shepherdess.
Every one's eyes were upon her, and, knowing

scarcely anybody present, she looked round till she
saw M. de Marbot, whom she had only met once at
the house of his cousin, and who had unluckily just
taken off his mask. Going up to him she took his
arm, exclaiming in a loud voice—

"At last I have a *chevalier*."

M. de Marbot relates this adventure in his memoirs.
His feelings may be imagined, for besides the annoyance of being seen with so absurd a figure, he was
afraid that her frantic way of behaving would lead
him into some difficulty. It was customary at these
balls for women to unmask whenever they liked, and
any one who has ever worn a mask and knows how
hot it is will understand that most of them availed
themselves of the permission. But although some of
the men occasionally did the same, it was not allowed
to any great extent, because if nearly every man had
been unmasked, Duroc and the Emperor, who desired
to be *incognito*, would of course have been recognised. Just then there happened to be many unmasked, and the secretaries of the embassy, travers-
ing the rooms, called upon all to mask. In order to
escape from his persecutor, Marbot pretended to
have left his mask, which was really in his pocket, in
another room, and saying he would fetch it and return,
got away from Madame X. and went up to the first
floor. Passing through quiet *salons de jeu* he saw at
the end an empty room, dimly lighted by alabaster
lamps. He got a *sorbet*, took off his mask, and sat
down to rest, when two men in masks and dominos
entered.

"We shall be out of the tumult here," said one,
and then he called Marbot by his name in a tone of

authority which, addressed to an officer of his rank (*chef d'escadron*), proclaimed a great personage.

"I am Duroc," he whispered as Marbot approached. "The Emperor is with me; his Majesty is very tired and overcome by the heat, and wishes to rest here out of the way. Stay with us to divert the suspicions of any one who may come in."

Napoleon sat in an armchair partly turned to the wall; Duroc and Marbot took others placed so as partly to conceal him; and Duroc directed Marbot to converse as if with friends; he kept on his mask, but Napoleon, taking off his, asked Marbot to fetch him a glass of water. As he came back with it he was accosted by two tall police agents dressed as Highlanders.

"Does M. de Marbot answer for the salubrity of that water?"

Having taken it from a decanter on the buffet, Marbot assented, and Napoleon, having drunk some, dipped his handkerchief in it, laid it on his face, and said, as Duroc went on talking of the Austrian campaign—

"You behaved very well, especially at the assault on Ratisbon and the passage of the Danube. I shall never forget it, and I shall shortly give you a distinguished proof of my satisfaction."

At that moment the horrible shepherdess appeared in the doorway.

"Ah! there you are!" she cried. "I shall complain to your cousin of your want of gallantry; since you left me I have been nearly suffocated. I have left the ball, for the heat is stifling. I shall come and rest here." And she sat down by him.

There was a dead silence. Duroc still wore his mask ; Napoleon had turned away, and his handkerchief over his face prevented his being recognised. He remained immovable, and Madame X., not thinking Marbot knew them, began to talk with her usual vehemence and absence of restraint, saying she was certain she had seen the personage she was looking for several times in the crowd, but it was impossible to get near him.

"However, I must speak to him," she said, "and he must absolutely double my pension. I know that people have tried to injure me by saying that when I was young I had lovers. Eh! *parbleu !* it's easy enough to see what's going on here to-night if you just listen by the windows. Besides, haven't *his* sisters lovers? Hasn't *he* mistresses? What does he come here for but to talk more freely with pretty women? They say my husband robbed, but the poor devil took to it very late and did it very unskilfully ; and as to those who accuse him, have not they robbed too? Did they inherit their fine estates and *hôtels ?* And *he !* hasn't he plundered in Italy, in Egypt—everywhere?"

"Madame," said Marbot, "allow me to point out that what you say is very improper, and that I am the more surprised that you should talk to me in this way, seeing that I met you for the first time this morning."

"Bah! bah! I say the truth before every one, and if *he* does not give me a good pension I will tell or write to him very plainly. Ah! ah! I'm not afraid of anybody."

Presently Duroc leaned towards Marbot, who sat in consternation, and whispered—

" Prevent this woman from following us."

He then rose ; the Emperor, who had put on his mask, rose also, and, as he passed before Madame X., said, " Marbot, those who are interested in you are glad to know that it is only to-day you have become acquainted with this charming shepherdess, whom you had better send to look after her sheep." Then, taking Duroc's arm, he walked out of the room.

Madame X. was thunderstruck ; then, guessing who it was, wanted to rush after the two masks. Marbot caught hold of her skirt, which tore with a great crack. Madame X. dared not pull lest it should come off, but called out "*C'est lui! c'est lui!*" vehemently reproaching Marbot, who held her till they were out of sight, and then left her in a furious rage with her skirt coming down, and crying out for pins ; but thinking she deserved to be punished for her intolerable conduct, he paid no attention. A few days later she received an order to leave Paris.[1]

The strict surveillance of the police and the precautions observed for the safety of the Emperor were occasionally disregarded by him, greatly to the anxiety of his friends, whose remonstrances were perfectly useless if he had set his fancy upon any intrigue or adventure. One night between eleven and twelve he called Constant, asked for a black coat and round hat, got into his carriage accompanied by Murat and Constant, with no other attendants than the coachman and one footman. After a short drive he stopped the carriage, got out, walked a few steps down the street, knocked at a great door, and disappeared into the house. Hours passed. Murat

" Mémoires de Marbot."

and Constant waited in the greatest anxiety, fearing that he had been led into some snare—Murat cursing and swearing at the Emperor's rashness, at the lady who was the cause of it, at everything and everybody, until daylight dawned, when, declaring that he could bear it no longer, he sprang out, hurried to the door, and seized the knocker. Just as he did so it opened, and Napoleon came out and laughed at their fears, saying—

"What nonsense! What are you afraid of? Am I not at home wherever I go?"

CHAPTER XX

1809—1810

THE misgivings of the Buonaparte family had been amply justified on the arrival of the Austrian Archduchess. Marie Louise was scarcely more than a child, and had been educated with more than conventual seclusion, upon a system so preposterously absurd that she and her sisters, besides never being, night or day, out of the presence of their governess, and having what books they were allowed to read so cut about and mutilated for fear they should read or hear or think of anything improper that it was impossible they could learn history at all, were not allowed to have any male among their pet animals. Dogs, cats, and birds were all to be of the female sex, and so of course were all their friends and acquaintances, while the pleasures they were permitted were the pleasures of children.

But if Marie Louise knew nothing of the world, of history, literature, or society, nothing even of the commonest facts of human life, there was one thing she knew very well, which was that she was Archduchess of Austria, Princess Royal of Hungary and Bohemia, eldest daughter of his Most Sacred and Imperial Majesty the Emperor Francis, and that her marriage was a terrible *mésalliance* by which she was sacrificed for the welfare of her country. She did not dislike the Emperor Napoleon, whose magnificent surroundings and powerful position impressed and satisfied her, but between herself and his relations was an abyss which widened every day. Their manners, habits, and ideas were alike shocking to her; and although at first she wrote home all the conventional civilities about them, she soon let them see her real feelings.[1]

Madame Mère might be, as she described her to her father, amiable and respectable, but she was ignorant, narrow-minded, could not pronounce a single language properly, but spoke a Corsican dialect which mortified Napoleon himself. Julie held as much aloof from the court of Marie Louise as she had done from that of Joséphine, and looked entirely out of place when she was obliged to be there. Pauline was an impossible person, entirely absorbed in her own beauty, dress, and lovers. Elisa was disagreeable and dictatorial, her only attraction being her little daughter whom Marie Louise petted. Hortense was the daughter of Joséphine.

Auguste of Bavaria, and Catherine of Wurtemberg were of her own *monde;* but besides the old hatred

[1] "Napoleon et sa famille," t. v. p. 31 (Masson).

MARIE LOUISE, ARCHDUCHESS OF AUSTRIA, EMPRESS OF FRANCE

between the houses of Wittelsbach and Hapsburg, she was the woman for whose sake the mother-in-law of Auguste had been divorced, her children disinherited, and possibly her husband deprived of his kingdom. Catherine was irritated because the Emperor, who, when he was flattered and pleased at her marriage with Jérôme, had thought no attention or politeness too great for her, now treated her with indifference and neglect, seeming to think nothing of any one but Caroline, who had been flattering and trying to please him lately, and whom he had sent to meet the Empress, and distinguished above the rest of his family. But Caroline was of all others the one the new Empress most disliked—she found her more presumptuous and disagreeable than the rest, was indignant at the audacity with which she had told her what to do, and offered her advice and opinion ; and when, soon after the wedding, the Empress was to accompany the Emperor to Belgium, she utterly declined to have Caroline with her. Napoleon, therefore, turned to Catherine, who was appeased by his renewed attentions and the friendly advances of the Empress, with whom in future she was on excellent terms.

As to Elisa, Pauline, and Caroline, they had every cause to regret the days when Joséphine ruled the court. Marie Louise kept them at a distance ; forbade them ever to come to her uninvited or unannounced, treated them with a distant *hauteur* which enraged them, and openly showed her dislike of them all.

"Thank God!" said Hortense, "we are indeed avenged, my mother and I, of the malice of our sisters-in-law. They find out now who they have to deal with in this archduchess who detests them, and does not take the trouble to hide it."

Far from all these petty quarrels, meanwhile, Lucien lived in peace in Italy. The discontent of Jérôme in Westphalia, the exile and difficulties of Joseph in Spain, the misery of Louis in Holland were not for him. Settled in his old villa in Canino, twenty-five leagues from Rome and six from Viterbo, he was perfectly happy with his wife, children, and pursuits. The villa itself had to be repaired and added to, the large estate had been entirely neglected. Lucien built barns and forges, looked after the farms, and in ploughing and digging discovered marvellous treasures of art, for beneath that soil lay the relics of three vanished periods of civilisation ; ruins, statues, vases, hundreds of curious and beautiful objects were the fruit of these excavations. In the day he walked over his farms, looked after his workmen, superintended the excavations ; in the evening he read, wrote, and arranged his affairs. Alexandrine also read and studied. "We are very quiet here," he wrote to his mother. "In this little village I look after the estate. In two months my wife will increase my family by a seventh child, and I hope sooner or later my brother will do me justice." [1]

Napoleon meanwhile had not relinquished his attempts ; the ill-success of Joseph, Louis, and Jérôme in their kingdoms had not induced him to change his mind about Lucien, whose happiness was a continual annoyance to him. In 1808, Joseph, when he stopped at Bologna on his way from Naples

---

[1] "Napoléon et sa famille," t. v. p. 50 (Masson).

to Spain, had, of course with the knowledge of the
Emperor, offered Lucien the vice-royalty of Spain or
the crown of Portugal or the Two Sicilies; always on
the same condition. He declined, and amused himself with his books at Canino, with village *feste*, with
picnics and the collections he was making of pictures
and curiosities.

Failing with him, Napoleon tried Alexandrine; he
charged Campi, a friend of the family, especially
of Lucien, to offer her the Duchy of Parma in
exchange for the divorce, two of her children to live
with her. She replied by a letter which Lucien
declared to be admirable, and of which no scoffs of
those whose adoration of Napoleon makes them see
a fool or a criminal in any one who opposed him,
can prevent impartial people from appreciating the
propriety, common sense, and good feeling. She
said that if she could believe it to be her duty to give
up her husband, and so sacrifice all the happiness of
her life, she certainly would not degrade herself by
accepting payment for it: that neither the Duchy of
Parma nor any other sovereignty on earth would be
the least compensation to her for such a loss; that
not the Emperor, but only God Himself in heaven,
could give her consolation. But that, as she knew
Lucien's love for her was so great that to separate
from him would ruin his happiness, she would consider it the deepest ingratitude and treachery to do
any such thing; that she and Lucien would have no
separation either private or public, that nothing but
death should divide them from each other, and that
all they asked of the Emperor was permission to live
in peace in some corner of his Empire.

It is difficult to see what fault there is to be found with this decision ; but it is perhaps an additional proof of the extraordinary personality of Napoleon that he should even now retain such a fascination over the minds of his devotees as to induce the belief in some French writers of our own day that Lucien ought to have divorced the wife he loved devotedly, who loved him and was the mother of his children, simply to please his brother. When we read their books we begin to understand that the catechism mentioned in a former chapter, which to us appears so preposterous and so blasphemous in its assertions that to oppose Napoleon was to oppose God Himself, and to be worthy of eternal damnation, &c., really expressed the opinions of a number of educated people in France.

The iniquitous letters of Madame Mère, in which she urges and tempts her son to forsake his wife for the worldly advantage of himself and his family, may appear "admirable," and "lofty," and "Socratic," to people who think in this way ; but such certainly is not, and never will be, the general opinion of the civilised world. Madame Mère might rail against Lucien, declare that there was neither honour, religion, nor love in the defence of his wife, but only obstinacy, and prophesy that the wife who refused to be divorced from her husband to please his relations would be "the victim of her ambition" ; [1]

---

[1] "If you do it (divorce) you will make the happiness of your husband and children. . . . Do not hesitate between a life full of bitterness and grief, which will be yours if you persist, and the prospect of a happy future. . . . Your children will be recognised by the Emperor, and perhaps succeed to crowns. . . ." (Madame Mère to Madame Lucien.)

but events did not justify her prognostications. Five years thence what had become of the thrones and riches and power for which love, honour, duty, and happiness were to be sacrificed?

Those of her children who had acted in the way she approved of were driven from the thrones they had usurped, deprived of the property they had plundered, expelled from France to wander aimlessly scattered about Europe and America. Napoleon, no longer to be obeyed like God upon earth, his short-lived Empire crumbled away, his crown and sceptre vanished, deprived of his longed-for son, deserted by his Imperial wife, finding in his royal connections only enemies and gaolers, a lonely captive on a distant island, saying as he remembered Joséphine, "I ought never to have left her"; while Lucien and Alexandrine, surrounded by their children and friends, lived in peace and prosperity in their Italian home, enjoying the sympathy and respect of everybody.

The anger of Napoleon at Lucien's resistance broke out in violent threats and abuse, and in various steps taken with a view to injure him. Charlotte and Christine, however, being the daughters of his first wife, whom Napoleon had recognised, did not come under his ban. By the desire of Madame Mère and with his approval, Charlotte, the elder one, now fourteen or fifteen years old, was sent to Paris to be in the care of her grandmother. "Lucien may stay where he is," said Napoleon, "but he may expect to be arrested at any time. I don't say it will be in a month or a year, it will be when I think necessary. As to Lolotte, Campi should have brought her. . . .

Lucien has chosen a bad time. but it does not signify. From Lucien's letter, Lolotte must have started, it will not do for her to go back or to stop. Go with Madame Gasson," he said to Campi, "fetch Lolotte, bring her back with you, and take her to Madame, she will present her to me. . . ."

Madame Mère suggested that if Lolotte came to her she should require more money, which annoyed Napoleon.

"Mamma said that to you?" he exclaimed. "Mamma will do her duty. She will take care of her granddaughter. Always her avarice!"

Charlotte arrived, escorted by Madame Gasson, a cousin of her mother's, whom Lucien had established in Italy.

The Emperor inquired with much interest what she was like—whether she was well educated, had a good disposition, and whether she knew anything about the family quarrels. "I will see her this evening," he concluded. "Mamma must present her to me. I have not yet determined what I shall do for her."

"She is your Majesty's niece," observed Campi; "the first marriage was recognised."

"Yes," replied Napoleon; "but when I recognised that marriage I was not Emperor. Lolotte will not be a princess until I declare her one. If Lucien does not come to terms I cannot give a king to Lolotte. Her father probably imagined that when his daughter arrived I should change my tone; he is mistaken— Lucien's branch will be cut off for ever. It will not be without precedent in history."

Lolotte was presented to the Emperor, on whom

she made a favourable impression. She was respectful but not at all shy with her formidable uncle, who
was pleased with her good looks and resemblance to
the Buonaparte family ; but he did not yet call her
" princess," neither did her grandmother. Louis, however, ordered all his household to give her that title,
all the foreigners did the same, and Lucien, hearing
this, addressed his letters in future to the " Princess
Lolotte."

Accustomed to the submission of all the rest of his
family, always enraged by the slightest opposition to
his will, no matter from whom, the failure of every
fresh attempt to coerce Lucien angered Napoleon
more and more. He uttered furious threats not only
against the liberty but the life of his brother ; actually
declaring that he had the power of life and death
over his family, and that he would use it if it were
necessary to his policy.[1]   Another threat was that
he would arrest his brother, with his wife and
children, throw them into prison, and leave him to
die there.

With the fate of the Duc d'Enghien before him,
Lucien began to be uneasy and to turn his
thoughts towards America, where at least he and
his family would be safe from the persecution of
his brother.

Meanwhile the position of Lolotte at her uncle's
court was a painful one. She was well received by
the family ; her grandmother was kind though
unsympathetic, but neither presents, honours, nor
pleasures could make her happy amongst people who
abused and ill-treated those she loved. For Lolotte

[1] " Napoléon et sa famille," t. v. p. 64 (Masson).

knew very well all about the family quarrels, and passionately took the side of the father she adored and the step-mother whom she looked upon as her second mother, against the relations who were strangers to her, whom she did not like, and whose injustice and tyranny towards her parents filled her with indignation. Her heart was in her Italian home; she cried and wanted to go back, and she wrote long letters to " Papa " and " Mamma," full of complaints of her grandmother's avarice and sarcastic descriptions and anecdotes of her uncles and aunts, and of everything she saw and heard. These letters before reaching their destination were opened in the post and copies of them sent to Napoleon.[1]

One Sunday at Saint-Cloud, after one of those wearisome dinners at which all the family was assembled, the Emperor took from his pocket about twenty of these letters, which he proceeded to read aloud. Everybody was furious except Pauline, who only went into fits of laughter, and the Emperor at first joined in her amusement. The satires against them were so unmistakably true that they were all the more angry, and Charlotte the more confused, as the reading went on. When it was finished the Emperor, assuming a serious air, reproached his niece for her ingratitude, and said that she should at once be sent back to her parents. Accordingly she left Paris the next day, June 4th, under the care of Madame Gasson, to her great joy, and when she arrived at Canino she threw herself into the arms of her father exclaiming—

" Ah! *mon petit papa*, how right you were not to

[1] " Mémoires " (Baron de Méneval).

go there! I am sure America would be much better "[1]

Lucien had never liked the plan of marrying her to the Prince of the Asturias. He had himself been ambassador at Madrid, and knew too much about Don Ferdinand, besides which it was generally believed that the Princess of the Asturias, his first wife, to whom he had been devoted, had been poisoned by his enemies at the court. There was latterly an idea of marrying her to the Grand-Duke of Wurzburg, who was much too old for her, and Lucien had already written desiring that his daughter might be sent back to him : " Send me my dear child," he wrote to his mother ; " I will not leave her at the court of my brother who threatens his brother with a dungeon and drives him out of Europe."

Lucien was now preparing to escape to America. He arranged his affairs, mortgaged his pictures (which also preserved them for him), and, as Napoleon refused to let him have a ship, thinking thus to prevent his departure, he sent a messenger to Murat, who was just then very angry because the Emperor would not allow him to meddle with Sicily. For, exactly as he feared, the new Empress had asked the Emperor that her grandmother's kingdom might be protected, and Napoleon had promised that it should not be interfered with.

Murat, therefore, sent a very friendly letter to Lucien, giving ten thousand scudi, to arm and get ready at once a large American ship, with three

---

[1] " Ah ! mon petit papa, que tu as raison de ne pas vouloir aller là-bas ! L'Amérique vaudra bien mieux, j'en suis sûre !" " Napoléon et sa famille," t. v. p. 97 (Masson).

masts, called the *Hercules*, now sequestrated in the harbour of Naples, which he promised to send as quickly as possible to Civita Vecchia. At half-past four in the morning, August 7th, Lucien embarked with his wife, Lolotte, and Christine, or Lili as she was called; Anna, daughter of Alexandrine by her first husband, her four children by Lucien, and a numerous suite.

The first night the weather was lovely, and they were all in high spirits at their freedom; but after that the wind rose, the children and servants were terrified, Anna and Lili, who were about twelve years old, lighted the little consecrated tapers they had been given to keep away shipwreck, and Lolotte, very seasick and angry, cursed the tyrant uncle who was the cause of their exile. Before many days, however, they were made prisoners by the English and taken to Malta, where, of course, they were very well treated. Lucien managed to send a message to Queen Maria Carolina, at Palermo, grandmother of the French Empress, begging her to let his mother know what had become of them, to which she sent a friendly reply, concluding that she would always take an interest in one whose firmness and decision of character inspired her with esteem which extended to his wife and children, to all of whom she wished happiness and prosperity. They spent the winter at Malta, in a charming house, surrounded by orange gardens, and then were taken to England.

On landing at Plymouth, they were met by a gentleman, sent by the King to receive them, and, much to their astonishment, were greeted with acclamations by the people, who crowded round them as they drove from the quay to the hotel, with cheers and shouts of welcome. For months the English papers had been publishing the history of Napoleon's ill-treatment of his brother, whom he had now tried to drive out of Europe, but who had, they declared, taken refuge with the English, and they were delighted to receive him. Paragraph after paragraph appeared, all of which were seen by the Emperor, and served to increase his annoyance and wrath.

" Lucien Buonaparte," said one, " may now consider himself safe, and as long as he exists will be a living reproach to Buonaparte. He will be a new example to add to so many others . . . which will prove the cruelty of his brother. . . . If he prophesies our ruin, it will be answered, ' Your brother Lucien trusted us . . . he thinks we shall last long enough for him, and he will probably live just as long as you.' " Each of these numerous paragraphs was a dagger-thrust for Napoleon ; the escape of Lucien was a severe blow.

" If Lucien fled," people said, " it was because the Empire was uninhabitable." The tyranny of Napoleon was such that his own brother could not live in his dominions, but was safer and freer in a hostile country, where he was not subject to his persecution.

There was nothing to be done—Napoleon had been beaten by the one member of his family who had always had courage to resist him, and who now settled quietly with his wife and children at a country place in England which he had bought, where they were soon surrounded by friends, amongst whom they lived contentedly until, in 1814, events permitted their return to France and Italy.

CHAPTER XXI

1810

THE mutual distrust and dislike between Napoleon and Bernadotte continued to increase, and
was only modified by the connection of the latter
with Joseph, and the friendly feelings with which the
former always regarded Désirée, which were shown
in many ways, trifling as well as important. In the
letter of approval he wrote to Bernadotte after he
was wounded, the Emperor, sending an affectionate
message to Désirée, complains that she has never
written to him, as she might just as well have done ;
and when the Emperor of Russia gave him three
magnificent fur pelisses, he kept one, gave one to
Pauline, and the other to Désirée—a special attention on his part all the more marked considering the
strained terms upon which he so frequently found
himself with her husband.

Wherever Bernadotte was governor he was popular, owing to the justice and mildness of his rule, which contrasted with the extortions and oppressions of most of the other generals, whose proceedings he regarded with contemptuous indignation. "It is such scoundrels as these," he observed, speaking of Davoust, "that injure the cause of the Emperor."

Napoleon had given Bernadotte the command of what was called the Army of Antwerp, and at the same time placed near him his *aide-de-camp*, Reille, with orders to act as a spy upon Bernadotte and make a daily report to the Emperor of everything he did and said. An officer named Jullian, attached to the staff of Bernadotte, and, in fact, one of the agents of Fouché, came secretly to the Marshal, telling him that the Emperor's health was seriously affected, and hinting that, should anything befall him, Bernadotte would be his most capable successor. Not knowing whether this might be a conspiracy or an affair of police spies of Fouché, Bernadotte merely protested his fidelity to the government sanctioned by the nation, but did not report the matter. Not long afterwards Napoleon, whose mind had been filled with suspicions by the reports of his spies, took away from Bernadotte the command of the Army of Antwerp and offered him one in Catalonia, which he declined, refusing also to retire to his little principality of Ponte Corvo, which he had never seen. He was then ordered to the Army in Germany, and met Napoleon a few days before the peace of Vienna ; another reconciliation was patched up, and Bernadotte reluctantly accepted the appointment of representative of the Emperor at Rome—a post of honour, but an exile in disguise—

A SWEDISH CASTLE.

when a new and extraordinary career was suddenly opened before him.[1]

In March, 1809, a revolution had taken place in Sweden, by which Gustavus IV. had been driven from the throne, and on signing his abdication, his uncle, the Duke of Sudermania, was chosen to take his place under the name of Charles XIII. But being an old man, without legitimate children, it was decided that he should adopt an heir to the throne, and a prince of Augustenburg was selected as Prince Royal, who, however, died in May, 1810, so that it became necessary to make another choice. The Swedes, in awe of their two formidable neighbours, Russia and France, tried to find out the ideas of the Emperor Napoleon on the subject. For Russia was so detested, especially just now, when Finland had been torn from Sweden and given to her, that the fact that the Emperor Alexander favoured the brother of the late Prince Royal was quite enough to prevent the possibility of his election. Napoleon secretly wished the King of Denmark to be also King of Sweden, but a number of Swedish officers who remembered the prowess of Bernadotte, his generous treatment of his vanquished enemies, his imposing appearance and statesman-like qualities, proposed to offer to make him heir to the crown, and the idea being universally approved, Count Wrede, son of the Duke of Sudermania, was sent to Paris to communicate with Bernadotte, who, after the first surprise at so unexpected a proposal, and after being with some difficulty convinced that it was serious and reliable, went to Saint-Cloud to

[1] " Bernadotte," pp. 90-92 (Pingaud).

see the Emperor. He said that Bernadotte might accept or refuse the offer as he chose, and that he himself would neither assist nor oppose him; notwithstanding which he made secret overtures to Stockholm proposing that the crowns of Sweden and Denmark should be united, and also offered the kingdom to Eugène. Both he and the Princess Augusta, however, declined either to live in Sweden or to change their religion.[1]

At first Bernadotte hesitated; but soon the advantages of the splendid destiny before him overcame any doubts or reluctance he might feel. For he had ambition enough; he saw crowns and sceptres lavished upon the mediocre brothers of Napoleon, upon Murat, his inferior in everything but courage, and he knew that Soult was aiming at the crown of Portugal, and Davoust wanted to be King of Poland. And this kingdom that fell to his lot did not come from Napoleon, but was the gift of its people, won by his own glory and great qualities. Sweden might not have the grandeur of Spain or the attractions of Naples, but there he would be king in reality, not a puppet to be dictated to and moved about Europe, or deposed at the pleasure of Napoleon. He would govern his dominions according to his own ideas and those of his people, and leave them to his son after him; he would be the father of a long line of kings —— And as he discussed all this with Désirée, walking up and down in the gardens of La Grange, a childish voice said—

" But, papa, why should not we go and make the happiness of this good people ? "

[1] " Méneval," t. ii. pp. 376 7.

Why, indeed? Why should not the boy be King of Sweden and sit on one of the most ancient thrones in Europe? They looked at Oscar and accepted for him and themselves the splendid future offered them; and if anything were needed to confirm their resolution, it was completed by a remark of the Emperor's, repeated to Bernadotte, that " he dared not accept it."

The prospect of the accession of Bernadotte to the Swedish throne was exceedingly distasteful to Napoleon. He told Duroc that he had seen in a dream two boats upon a stormy sea, one steered by himself the other by Bernadotte, who guided his boat safely through the tempest until he appeared to be enshrouded in mist and passed slowly out of sight, while he himself was left at the mercy of the hurricane.

This dream seemed to make a great impression upon the Emperor.

Bernadotte and Désirée, now Prince and Princess Royal of Sweden, spent part of the summer at the baths of Plombières, then exceedingly fashionable. The Queens of Spain and Holland were there also, the latter then in bad health. Louis had insisted on the elder of their two remaining boys being sent to him at Amsterdam (for this was before his abdication). The younger one, afterwards the Emperor Louis Napoleon, was always with her or her mother.

Julie, Queen of Spain, and Catherine, Queen of Westphalia, had never behaved to Joséphine with the malice and ingratitude of the three Buonaparte sisters and their mother, and after the divorce they continued their visits to her at La Malmaison. Julie was almost the only person Hortense would receive during the first part of her stay at Plombières, but she soon made an exception in favour of Madame de Souza and her son by her first husband, M. Charles de Flahault ; in fact, it was sometimes said that the society of M. de Flahault was a greater attraction to her than even that of Joséphine herself, who was also at Plombières. For Hortense, miserable in her married life, outraged by the tyranny and intolerable treatment of the husband whom she had been forced to marry and had always detested, never happy except in his absence, never with him if she could possibly help it, had now fallen in love with M. de Flahault, a friend of her brother, a man as attractive as Louis Buonaparte was the contrary. His father, the Comte de Flahault, had been imprisoned during the Terror, and had managed to escape, and remained in hiding until he was told by a friend who visited him that his lawyer had been accused of concealing him, and arrested in consequence. Knowing this to be a death-warrant, he went at once to the Commune, and gave himself up, saying—

"I am the Comte de Flahault. I hear that you have arrested the *citoyen* —— for having hidden me. It was not he who gave me shelter. Let him at liberty. I am here."

He was guillotined in a few days. His widow fled to England, then to Switzerland, and devoted herself to her son, whom she idolised. She was the original of " Madame d'Arligny " in " Corinne." She wrote a novel called " Adèle de Sénange," and other books. M. de Flahault was handsome, well educated, a brave soldier, a man who seemed to her a " hero of romance,"[1] in every way a contrast to Louis Buonaparte. The *liaison* between them was certainly known to Joséphine, and to many others. The Emperor could not have been ignorant of it, but his anger with Louis and his compassion for what Hortense had suffered with him must have made him look with indulgence upon the affair. Hortense was definitely separated from Louis ; Napoleon showed great favour to Flahault, whom he made his *aide-de-camp* and Count of the Empire ; he gave Hortense a large income, and she was second godmother to the King of Rome. The Empress liked her as much almost as she disliked Caroline, Pauline, and Elisa. The Duc de Morny, the result of this *liaison*, was brought up under the name of an old friend of Hortense by his grandmother, Madame de Souza.

On his return from the baths of Plombières, where they had spent part of the summer, Bernadotte, Prince Royal of Sweden, went to the Emperor to receive letters patent absolving him from his oath of fidelity to him. Napoleon said, with some hesitation, that there was a condition to be observed—that Bernadotte must take an oath never to fight against France. The Prince declined to give any such promise, saying that he would in future be bound only by the wishes and interests of Sweden ; whereupon Napoleon erased the clause.

Désirée was in despair when she found that she was expected to go and live in Sweden. She afterwards confessed that she scarcely knew where it was, and thought it was merely a question of taking the title, as they did of Ponte Corvo !

[1] The Comte de Flahault died 1870.

But she soon discovered that there was all the difference in the world between being Princess of Ponte Corvo and Princess Royal of Sweden. It was necessary that they should prepare at once for their migration to their new country, and although she managed to postpone her own journey, her husband set off in October, taking Prince Oscar with him to be shown to and brought up amongst his future subjects.

They hurried across Germany for fear of being detained, stopping at Cassel to see Jérôme, and spending a few days at Hamburg,[1] which Bernadotte passed in the society of Bourrienne, an old friend of his, whom he reminded of the prediction of the fortune-teller, saying, "Would you believe, my dear friend, that it was predicted at Paris that I should be a king, but that I must cross the sea to reach my throne?"

Bourrienne remarked that he owed his throne to no occult influence, but to his own good qualities and the justice and wisdom he had always shown in his governments.

He told Bourrienne that, on his refusing to sign the engagement never to fight against France, Napoleon said—

"Well, go then! Our destinies will soon be accomplished."

The day of his departure the Emperor said to Duroc :—

"Well! the Prince Royal of Sweden is gone?"

"To-day, Sire."

"Does he not regret France?"

---

[1] "Bernadotte," p. 106 (Pingaud).

" Yes, certainly, Sire."

" And I should have been charmed if he had not accepted, but, *que voulez-vous ? Au reste, il ne m'aime pas.* . . . We did not understand each other, and now it is too late. He has his political interests, and I have mine."

Bernadotte sold his principality of Ponte Corvo to the Emperor for two million francs ; only one, however, was ever paid to him. During the three days he spent at Hamburg he spoke much with Bourrienne of his future plans, and amongst others of the continental blockade. Bourrienne entirely agreed in his intention to reject this intolerable system. It could not possibly be fully carried out, and the attempts to do so led to nothing but ruin and disaster, besides the cruelty and tyranny it enabled the French governors to commit.

At Hamburg, in 1811, under Davoust's government, a poor man was nearly being shot for having bought a small loaf of sugar, and Davoust revenged himself upon the officer who had spared him by sending him eighty leagues away. A sandpit was discovered full of brown sugar, the oppressive decree was eluded whenever possible, but trade was being destroyed and many people ruined. In Oldenburg and other places there were regular battles between the French custom-house officers and the inhabitants, who took away by force the goods that had been seized. Hatred of the French, and especially of Napoleon, was spreading all over the Continent, and Bernadotte resolved that no such short-sighted tyranny should be perpetrated in his dominions.

OLD STOCKHOLM.

Although a Minister of France, Bourrienne spoke strongly on this matter.

"I advise you," he said, "to reject the system without hesitation. . . . It will in the end give the trade of the world to England. . . . It would be out of all reason to close your ports against a nation who rules the seas. It is your navy that would be blockaded, not hers. What can France do against you? . . . You have nothing to fear but from Russia and England, and it will be easy to keep up friendly relations with those two Powers. Take my advice, sell your iron, timber, leather, and pitch; take in return salt, wines, brandy, and colonial produce. . . . If you follow the continental system . . . you will draw upon you the aversion of the people."

Bernadotte took this sensible advice, and never repented having done so.

From Hamburg he went to Copenhagen, which he found illuminated in his honour. He travelled slowly towards Stockholm, where he arrived November 2nd amidst the acclamations of his new people.

"Surrounded by the Swedes, I regret nothing!" he exclaimed, looking round at the welcoming crowds as he entered his future capital.

To the old King, Charles XIII., it was a time of anxiety and misgiving. All his principles, feelings, and antecedents could not but make the prospect of adopting a General of the French Republic, a soldier of fortune of a different rank, language, and race to enter his family, and after him to sit on the ancient throne of the Wasa, repugnant to him. He dreaded the moment of his arrival, but at the first interview his heart was won by the handsome, courteous, kindly

soldier and the pretty boy he had brought to be heir
to Sweden.

"*J'ai joué gros jeu !*" he exclaimed ; "*mais je crois
que j'ai gagné.*"

The Queen and her sister, the Abbess Sophie-
Albertine, were equally pleased, and from this time
the greatest harmony reigned in this royal family, so
strangely composed.

The old King, thankful not to be troubled with
business, put everything into the hands of the new
Prince Royal, "Charles Jean," consenting to and signing whatever he wished. The Swedes congratulated
themselves upon his excellent government, the King
and Queen declared he was like a son to them, and a
really strong affection soon sprang up between them.

Désirée all this time was putting off her journey as
long as she could. She disliked the idea of Sweden
as much as Julie did that of Spain. She was perfectly
happy and comfortable in the *rue d'Anjou*, with her
three sisters and her tribe of relations living in Paris.
She was like Julie, accustomed to the absence of her
husband, and even though now her son must also
leave her, she could not at first make up her mind to
go away from Paris, especially to a cold northern
country, the very thought of which filled her with
dread. Every one remonstrated in vain, till the
Emperor himself interposed. He pointed out that
for the Princess Royal of Sweden to live in France
while her husband and son lived in what was now
their own country was most improper, and gave rise
to scandal ; that she must live where they did, and
where her duty and interests should lie. He regulated
all the most trifling details of her presentation before

her departure, as Princess of Sweden, and invited her to those family dinners on Sundays which Julie and the Queen of Westphalia so disliked, but to which it was supposed to be a great honour to be asked.

Désirée saw that she could not help herself; the Emperor spoke with authority; everybody laughed at her lamentations, and thought she ought to be thankful that so brilliant and prosperous a future was offered her; and events very soon proved that they were right.

The only people who agreed and sympathised with her were those selected to form her suite; these wept and lamented as if they were going to be sent as prisoners to the depths of Siberia, and when the carriages came to the door they started on their journey dissolved in tears and wondering how soon they could come back again. It was an unfortunate time to have chosen for such a journey to such a climate, for it was the middle of the winter, and in those days travelling was very slow. They passed leisurely through Germany and Denmark, and it was in January that Désirée at length entered the northern capital which was to be her future home and took up her abode with her discontented followers, who were made still worse by the rough sea passage which had ended their journey, in the apartments prepared for them in the great palace of Charles XIII. at Stockholm. By the old King, Queen, and Princess Sophie she was welcomed with all the kindness and consideration they could have shown had she been really a princess of their own rank. She found them already attached to her husband, whose courtesy and respect, the attentions he showed them, and the trouble he took to amuse and please them, had won their hearts. Oscar was the darling of the whole nation, who were delighted with his northern name and his extreme youth, declaring that he should grow up altogether a Swede. It was fortunate indeed for them that the choice of the nation had not fallen upon one of the rough, uneducated, unmannerly soldiers of the Empire, who would have made the court ridiculous, but just upon him who united to great military prestige and the capacity of a statesman the distinguished appearance and manners which were suitable to his present position. Bernadotte, through all the vicissitudes of his life, had ever had the greatest horror of the manners, language, and habits prevailing amongst his comrades, and the greatest anxiety and determination that his own should in no way resemble them ; and that so far as possible his wife, "Bonnette," as he called Désirée, should choose her friends amongst refined, well-bred, well-educated people ; all of which ideas did not suit nearly so well with his old republican notions as with the royalist principles he now adopted.

Désirée was sincerely grateful to the Swedish royal family and got on very well with them ; in fact, it is possible that if it had not been for her French suite she would have in time become reconciled to what was certainly a great and trying change and settled contentedly in Sweden. But being a woman absolutely without ambition, the high rank and powerful position she had attained had no charm for her, the affection she undoubtedly had for her husband and child was not strong and exclusive enough to compensate for the loss of all her other friends and relations, especially of Julie ; the court of Stockholm, with its simple life and old-world customs, was ineffably dull after the glitter and luxury and excitement of the court and society in Paris, and the climate was horrible. To one born and brought up in the south of France, to whom even Paris was cold and grey after the blue skies and sunny shores of the Mediterranean, this snowy northern land, in the midst of its long winter, was terrible and most trying to her health. The cold air gave her a rash upon her face, the French ladies and gentlemen of her household bewailed and lamented, assuring her that neither she nor they would live in such a climate, and at the end of three months Désirée, declaring that she was ill and could not stay there, set off on her return to France to recover her health.

CHAPTER XXII

1811—1812

In the *rue d'Anjou*—Talleyrand—The Prince of Wales and the French Ambassador—Remarks of Napoleon—Intrigues against him—Attempt to assassinate him—Escape of a German soldier —Bernadotte in Sweden—Napoleon's orders to Désirée Aix-les-Bains—Bad news at a ball—Paris during the Russian campaign—Return of Napoleon.

IT was with feelings of relief and delight that Désirée found herself once more in her comfortable *hôtel* in the *rue d'Anjou ;* and she poured into the sympathising ears of the friends who hastened to see her, the history of all she had seen and suffered since she left France.

" *Ah ! quel ennui, cher prince !* " she said to Talleyrand, who was one of her first visitors. " What a court! So cold, so dark! No excitement but to shoot at the King at a masked ball! And *such* balls—*grand Dieu !* " For the history of the assassination of Gustavus III. had profoundly impressed and seemed to haunt her.

" Madame," replied he, " it is all very well to begin with."

It has been said that for many years Bernadotte

cherished a secret hope of filling the place of Napoleon ; and that Talleyrand, who was disaffected towards the Empire, was desirous to attract by any hopes or ambitions the most important and influential persons to his own party.

He himself was one of the most remarkable figures of the time. His family, the Talleyrand-Périgord, was one of the most illustrious in France, a younger branch of the sovereign Counts of Périgord.

Charles Maurice was the eldest son, born in 1754, and would in the natural course of things have been brought up to be a soldier ; but, unfortunately, he was lame from his birth, which made that profession impossible. He was therefore destined to the ecclesiastical life.

The misfortune of his lameness, which would have been serious enough in any case, was increased tenfold by the heartless conduct of his family ; their disappointment made them take a dislike to the child who could never, they thought, be a credit to them ; his father and mother had never a kind word for him. He was sent to the care of an old aunt in the country, and afterwards placed at Saint-Sulpice to prepare for the calling, the prospect of which was intolerable to him. Even at the seminary he was solitary ; he could not stand for any length of time, the active games of the other lads were impossible for him, he grew melancholy and cynical ; such a life, he used to say in later years, must either harden one or one must die of grief.

As he grew up his disgust with the world, with his own profession and life, and with mankind in general, increased until his indifference and gloom were disturbed by a passion for the Princess Charlotte de Montmorency, which was returned by her, and which directed all his energies and endeavours to get himself freed from the vows which had always been odious to him. He seemed on the point of succeeding, and the Pope might very possibly have been induced to grant his request, when the breaking out of the Revolution put an end to the negotiations. Then he threw himself into the great movement which was to sweep away the customs, principles, and prejudices of which he had been the victim. As he said, he liked the Revolution, and his great talents, learning, and knowledge of the world raised him immeasurably above his companions—the elegant, dissipated young abbés so popular in society—whose tastes and manners he also shared. He was sent to London by Louis XVI. in 1792, but ordered to leave by the English Government as a Jacobin in 1793. He passed the next three years in America, returned to France in 1796, and by the influence of Madame de Stael with some of the *Directoire* was made Foreign Minister. He was welcomed by Napoleon, who always delighted in receiving any one belonging to the old order of things; but he was detested by those who looked upon him as a renegade, such as his father's friend, the old General de Lautrec, who said, as he passed before him to go to the left, where he now sat, " *Monsieur, si M. votre père vivait, il vous mettrait les bras comme nous avons les jambes,*" M. de Lautrec had a wooden leg.

Talleyrand was a great personage both politically and socially during the Empire. He negotiated the treaties of Lunéville, Amiens, Presburg, and Tilsit, he

CHARLES MAURICE DE TALLEYRAND-PÉRIGORD, PRINCE DE BENEVENTO.
(Gerard.)

was accused of being one of the active agents who
took part in the murder of the Duc d'Enghien, he
was universally regarded as politically powerful and
far-seeing, socially brilliant and charming, devoid of
religion, scruples or principles of any kind. In spite
of his lameness his strength was remarkable; he
would sit up for two or three nights at suppers and
various dissipations with his friends, and on the fourth
day, after an hour's sleep and a bath, would be ready
for any serious study or occupation in perfect condition of body and mind. When, in the days of the
Directory, he was introduced by M. La Motte at the
Luxembourg, an attendant in the ante-room insisted
on taking away, much to his inconvenience, the stick
with which he walked, he remarked to his companion
as he gave it up, "*Mon cher, il me parait que votre
nouveau gouvernement a terriblement peur des coups de
bâton.*"

Napoleon made him Grand Chamberlain and
Prince of Benevento, but his disapproval of the
Peninsula War threw him out of favour, and from
this time he intrigued against the Emperor. He was
Foreign Minister under Louis XVIII., and was mixed
up in all the political events that took place until his
death in 1838. Having been released from his vows by
Pius VII., he married his mistress, Madame Grandt,
which caused much disapprobation amongst his
friends who saw no reason for the marriage, Madame
Grandt having long lost all her attractions, and
besides, found his house much less amusing than
when she used to preside there without the legitimate
title to do so.

Talleyrand mocked at the choice made by Napoleon

at one time of Andréossi as ambassador to England,
where he caused nothing but ridicule, being a
common, awkward man without an idea of good
manners. He addressed the Prince of Wales as
" *mon prince*," until that royal personage said to
some one with irritation, " Tell General Andréossi
not to be always calling me ' *mon prince*,' it will end
in my being taken for a Russian prince." Talleyrand
differed from Napoleon in this respect : that whatever
his own practice might be, he was capable of admiring
excellence in others, he always respected good priests
in spite of his own shortcomings. Cynical as he was,
he declared that it was better to feel, even if it brought
suffering.

Napoleon, however, made a remark of the same
kind to M. Maret, who brought him the excuses of
the Marquis de Sémonville for not keeping an appointment, saying that he was overwhelmed with
grief at having just heard of the death of his adopted
daughter, Madame Macdonald.

" It is singular," said the Emperor, looking very
grave. " I thought Sémonville was *un homme d'esprit ;*
I thought he was a superior man. He is in despair.
I am just thinking about it : if any one came to me
and told me Hortense was dead—well ! I should go
on working. How often I have seen men go, how
often I have sent men to battle, when they never
could return. I was not at all affected. Well ! this
Sémonville, he is in despair ! Perhaps I envy him,
perhaps he is happier. Let us work, let us work," he
added brusquely, " and say no more about it." [1]

When Bessières was wounded at Wagram the

---

[1] Chastenay Mémoires, t. ii. p. 166.

Emperor saw him fall from his horse and asked, "Who is it?"

"Bessières, sire." Napoleon turned his horse, saying—

"Let us go. I have no time to weep." He sent to inquire if Bessières were still alive, and found he was only wounded and stunned. [1]

The Emperor was not at all pleased at Désirée's return to Paris, but it did not really affect the terms of friendship on which they were.

She arranged her household and life in a manner to attract as little attention as possible; she had no court, only one *dame de compagnie* and a *majordome*, both French; nothing marked her as Princess Royal of Sweden except that in her *salon* were to be met all the Swedes of distinction who came to Paris, and very often the Swedish Ambassador, M. de Hochschild, and his young son, who afterwards wrote her life. But the *salon* of Désirée was not merely a rendezvous for her own family and friends, literary people and distinguished Swedes, it became to some extent a centre of political intrigues. Through her Napoleon carried on from time to time secret negotiations with Bernadotte, with whom he maintained a constant correspondence, relating to him everything that she could discover of the political events and ideas around her. And if the Emperor's slave, Savary, was at once a guest and a spy in her house, Fouché and Talleyrand were also its *habitués*, and made her their means of communication with the Prince of Sweden. There was spreading in

[1] Bourrienne. Bessières was killed in the fight before Lutzen, 1813.

France and throughout Europe a feeling of hated
and vengeance against Napoleon.

Some time before, during the war with Prussia,
Blücher said to Bourrienne, " I rely confidently on the
future, because I foresee that fortune will not always
favour your Emperor. It is impossible but the time will
come when all Europe, humbled by his exactions and
impatient of his depredations, will rise against him.
The more he enslaves the nations the more terrible
will be the reaction when they break their chains.[1]

And Bernadotte, recently admitted into the family
of sovereigns, now began to realise the strength and
extent of the league which was being organised
against him who was looked upon as the enemy of
peace and the scourge of Europe.

A young man named Staps, son of a Lutheran
Minister at Narrenbergh, was arrested with a long
knife with which he declared he was going to kill
Napoleon, saying that he considered it a duty to do
so because he ruined Germany. He persisted to the
last in his resolution and in his indifference to death,
only regretting that he had failed in his attempt to
deliver his country from her oppressor.

A more amusing incident happened a little later
near Freistadt, on the Oder, where the French troops
were quartered in the strongly-fortified Castle of
Herzogwalden, while the Germans lay encamped at
some distance across the river.

In the army of Napoleon were, of course, numbers
of Italians, Germans, &c., belonging to the countries
conquered by him, and forced to serve under his
banner. Amongst these was a German chasseur

[1] Bourrienne.

named Tanz, who had got drunk, threatened the officer who was conducting him to the guard-room, and was condemned to be shot. When the guard came to fetch him out for that purpose they found him naked, and he explained that he had taken off his clothes because he was too hot. The adjutant did not insist on his dressing again, but allowed him merely to wrap himself in a cloak. As they passed over the *pont léris*, crossing the great moat of the castle, Tanz suddenly threw off the cloak, sprang over into the water, swam across, and running for his life, gained the open country, crossed the Oder, and joined the enemy, his countrymen, on the other side.

Bernadotte had steadily refused to apply to Sweden the odious continental blockade, which of course exasperated Napoleon. A stormy interview had taken place at the palace of Drottningholm in August, 1811, between the Prince Royal and the French Minister, two French *corsaires* having been ill-received and insulted in the Pomeranian ports; the feeling between France and Sweden was becoming more and more strained.

" I shall do nothing for France," said the Prince, "until I know what the Emperor will do for me. I find my own consolation in the feeling professed for me by the Swedish people. I have seen them trying to unharness my horses and draw my carriage; such a proof of their affection almost overcame me. I have seen invincible troops executing their manœuvres with much more quickness and precision than the French troops, to whom I have only to say, ' Forward ! March !': giants, who will overthrow everything before them. . . . I will make of the

Swedes what I did of the Saxons, who, when I commanded them, were the best soldiers in the last war. . . . They had better not try to insult me; I am not going to be degraded. I had rather die at the head of my grenadiers, or plunge a dagger into my breast, or throw myself into the sea, or sit on a barrel of gunpowder and be blown up! . . . Here is my son," as the young prince came into the room ; " he will follow my example. Will you, Oscar?"

" Yes, papa."

" Come here, that I may embrace you ; you are my true son." [1]

The attitude of France towards Sweden had now become so threatening that it was considered better to seek an ally in their old enemy Russia than to continue to follow in the wake of France, whose Emperor expected from his ally not friendship but subservience. The Princess, on the other hand, wrote conciliatory letters to her husband. " Do not declare against the French," she said, " lest you should lose the popularity you possess amongst them. If Napoleon falls you may play a great part in your old country and dispose of the regency."

But it was of no avail. The French troops entered Pomerania, the following year (1813) Sweden joined the coalition against France, and the Prince Royal, chosen *generalissimo* of the forces, landed with 30,000 Swedes at Stralsund.

Meanwhile the position of the Princess of Sweden at Paris was unsuitable, not to say dangerous ; and that she did escape the fates of Mesdames de Stael, de Chevreuse, Récamier, and others, can only be

[1] " Bernadotte." p. 141 (Pingaud).

attributed to her relationship to Joseph Buonaparte
and the friendship or affection of the Emperor. He
perpetually complained to the Duchesse d'Abrantès
that she and her husband received his enemies,
whereas he had no more loyal and devoted servants.
They would never have dreamed of permitting any
plots against him to be discussed in their house ;
while the *salon* of Désirée was filled with those who
were disaffected and ready to conspire against him.
She was living in Paris against his express desire, and
yet she had no sentence of exile, but only while
peace or war with Sweden seemed still trembling in
the balance, received a hint through the Swedish
Minister that the Emperor saw with regret the
prolonged sojourn in France of the Princess Royal of
Sweden, whose presence there at such a moment was
contrary to all custom, and who ought to be with
her husband ; followed by a message brought by
Cambacérès to the Queen of Spain, to the effect that
the Emperor desired the Princess of Gothland to
return to Sweden, as it was not proper that she
should now live in France.   There was an idea that
the *hôtel* in the *rue d'Anjou* might be attacked by a
mob if the people became excited against Bernadotte.

Not liking openly to disregard the injunctions of
the Emperor, Désirée gave orders that all preparations should be made to leave Paris.   It was a very
hot summer, every one was going away as fast as they
could, and a general depression prevailed.   Husbands,
fathers, brothers, and sons were at the war, the women
of their families were setting off for their country
places, Italy, Switzerland, or the baths.   All the
fashionable milliners and dressmakers were working

PRINCE OSCAR BERNADOTTE

(Afterwards Oscar I , King of Sweden and Norway.)

night and day, for, as Madame d'Armaillé observes,
their grief and anxiety did not seem to have
diminished the number and richness of the toilettes
most of them, Désirée among the number, had
ordered for the summer. It was generally understood
that at last the Princess of Gothland, as she was also
called, was about to proceed to Stockholm to join
her husband and son. But as the time for departure
drew near Désirée's courage failed her. She could
not make up her mind to leave France for Sweden.
She sent most of her servants to her country house
at Auteuil, and started for Aix-les-Bains, where her
sister Julie had already gone.

Aix was so crowded that summer that it was
almost impossible to get rooms, and some complained
that the fashionable throng spoilt the enjoyment of
the lakes and mountains of that enchanting country.
The Empress Joséphine was there, Madame Mère,
the Princess Borghese, the Queen of Spain ; Désirée
found plenty of friends and plenty of amusement.
Balls, dinners, picnics, water-parties on the lake, *fêtes*
of every description went on perpetually, whilst the
air was full of sinister rumours both from north and
south. From first to last the Peninsula War had been
a series of disasters, and now still greater calamities
appeared to be gathering round the Emperor and the
mighty host he had led over the desolate plains of
Russia.

Not satisfied with the festivities of Aix and the
brilliant society with which that lovely watering-place
now overflowed, Désirée was attracted to Geneva by
the "*fête du lac*" and other entertainments there.

It was at a great ball given by M. Saladin at his

house, the delightful gardens of which went down to the lake, that the intelligence of the battle of Salamanca was first announced to the careless, light-hearted throng who were dancing in the ball-room or sauntering on the terraces enjoying the loveliness of the night as they looked through the tall, shadowy trees upon the calm beauty of the lake below and the solemn grandeur of the mountains around them.

Suddenly the music stopped, the news spread amongst the assembled crowd, who, with faces of consternation, were eagerly discussing it, asking anxious questions, and preparing to depart. Marmont had lost a great battle ; Wellington had taken the whole of the French artillery and 5,000 prisoners ; 8,000 had been killed and wounded. Marmont himself was wounded, and his wife, who was at the ball, started at once for Spain. There was an end of the kingdom of Joseph Buonaparte, and Julie and Désirée stopped their entertainments at Aix and returned to Paris. Désirée took up her abode again at her house at Auteuil with renewed confidence, for the Emperor had certainly enough upon his hands to prevent him troubling himself about her ; and after spending the autumn peacefully there she returned for the winter to her beloved *hôtel* in the *rue d'Anjou.*

Not, however, to the usual pleasures and gaieties of the winter in Paris, for never since the days of the Terror had that brilliant capital[1] been plunged in such gloom and despondency as now. The Parisians were long accustomed to read nothing but victories in their bulletins, for if by chance they suffered a

[1] "Mémoires de Joséphine," t. ii. p. 317 (Avrillon).

reverse—such as Trafalgar, for instance—it was carefully suppressed. But now, in spite of the continued attempts at concealment, it became impossible; the disasters were too numerous. Private letters told the tale of loss and suffering; every courier that came from the army in Russia brought fresh tales of defeat and misfortune, and long lists of dead and wounded. Hundreds of families were in mourning; scarcely one was not devoured by anxiety for some of its members. The cold, which was destroying the armies of France on the snowy steppes of Russia, also prevailed at Paris, where severe frost and snow increased the sufferings of the poor.

Some people muttered that this was the Emperor's first expedition since he divorced Joséphine, and that it had always been said that his luck would desert him; as for Joséphine herself, she remained at La Malmaison in the deepest grief and anxiety,[1] for her thoughts and good wishes were still with Napoleon; besides, her son was with the army, and constantly sent her letters which contained nothing but evil tidings.

According to his custom of giving lavishly and then repenting of his generosity and taking away his gift, Napoleon had, in the full tide of his anxiety to persuade Joséphine to consent to the divorce, given her the Élysée Palace, promising that it should be hers for life. Just before the Russian campaign he had taken it away again, so that on her return from Milan, where she had been to visit her son and daughter-in-law, she had to remove all her possessions there to La Malmaison in haste.[2]

---

[1] "Mémoires de Joséphine," t. ii. p. 338 (Avrillon).
[2] "Mémoires de Joséphine," t. ii. p. 318 (Avrillon).

Although Désirée's husband and son were safe in Sweden, she had many other relations and friends with the army ; she suffered, as a patriotic Frenchwoman naturally would, for the calamities of her country ; and the position in which her husband now stood towards France filled her with regret and uneasiness, for which the only consolation she found was in the affection of her family and friends. Amongst them, as she used to say in after life, one whose kindness and sympathy did much to sustain her courage and cheer her spirits was the Princess Catherine, Queen of Westphalia, who appears to have been very fond of her, and the fact of their husbands being on different sides never interfered with their friendship for each other.

One morning, a few days before Christmas, the news spread through Paris that the Emperor had returned. Far different was this from his other arrivals, when he had entered his capital in triumph and driven through its streets through shouting, welcoming crowds. Now, after a fortnight's hurried flight day and night in a sledge over the frostbound plains of Russia, narrowly escaping the Cossacks, by whom he was nearly captured before he gained the frontier of Germany ; changing his sledge for a carriage, and journeying on across Germany and France, he drove up in the middle of the night to the gate of the Tuileries.

Behind him were the terrible, snowy plains, strewn with the many thousands of dead and dying whom he had sacrificed to his remorseless ambition ; the devastation and ruin that marked his path, the remnant of the gallant army that he had deserted and left to its fate ; but as he stood by a blazing fire in his palace of the Tuileries, he warmed his hands, exclaiming joyfully, "This is better than Russia!" and the next morning issued a bulletin announcing his safe return, and saying that "his health had never been better."

CHAPTER XXIII

1813

Gathering storms—Hortense—Madame Mère and her daughter-in-law—The portrait of Joséphine—The coalition—The German campaign—Joseph Buonaparte—Refuge at Mortefontaine—Renown of Bernadotte—The Comte de Rochechouart—Battle of Leipzig—A romance of the Revolution.

"WHAT," exclaimed many people of a superstitious turn, "can we expect a year to bring forth, that is the thirteenth of a century and begins on a Friday?" [1]

They might have consoled themselves by reflecting that the whole of Western Christendom was in the same case, and that, except Russia and Greece, any European nation with whom they might be at war would have equal reason for alarm. There was, however, nothing to reassure them in the state of affairs at Paris as the New Year began.

Murat, following the example of his imperial brother-in-law, had made his escape, and gone home to Naples, leaving his soldiers to their fate. Eugène de Beauharnais had succeeded to the command and had done his best, assisted by the gallant Ney, to

[1] "Mémoires sur la reine Hortense," t. i. p. 18 (Cochelet).

lead the shattered remnant of the Grand Army back to France; but of the 400,000 who had left their country, scarcely more than 50,000 survived the slaughter of the campaign and the horrors of the retreat.

Every day marshals, generals, and other officers kept returning to Paris, all relating their fearful losses; the women who were plunged into mourning did not appear in public, but those whose relations had returned in safety were ready to hope and rejoice; the Emperor ordered balls and parties to be given as usual, and so far as possible suppressed all signs of mourning.

Hortense, amongst others, was obliged to entertain, though she was in great anxiety about her brother, who had not yet arrived.

Sadly she looked over her old lists of invitations, erasing many names of those who had fallen. Her chamberlain, with whom she consulted, pointed out that her list contained many who had lost an arm or a leg or who still wore bandages, and suggested that they had better be left out, observing—

"Your Majesty's ball will look like a hospital; at least, the Emperor will perhaps say so; he wishes people to dance in order to distract the capital from melancholy thoughts; but, on the contrary, it will be the very way to arouse unhappy recollections to place before people the unfortunate results of our disasters."[1]

Hortense, however, would not hear of excluding any one on such grounds, and the ball was *triste*, as her chamberlain had predicted; but it was scarcely

[1] "Mémoires sur la reine Hortense." t. i. p. 33 (Cochelet).

likely to have been very lively at such a time, even if she had complied with his rather heartless recommendations.

The life of Hortense seems to have been always full of misfortunes, beginning with the murder of her father in the Terror, the imprisonment of her mother, the dangers and poverty which surrounded her mother, her brother, and herself in her childhood, and the natural grief of a girl at the re-marriage of her mother with an officer of the republican army, who must have been repugnant to the daughter of the Vicomte de Beauharnais. Perhaps her happiest time was spent at school, for she always through life seemed to cling to Madame Campan and her school-fellows. The days of luxury and pleasure which followed her introduction into society as the adopted daughter of Napoleon were soon cut short by the miserable marriage into which she was so cruelly forced with the most disagreeable of the Buona-parte brothers—cold, unsympathetic, hypochondriac, gloomy, suspicious, fidgety, always influenced against his wife by the spite of his mother and sisters, whose state of health was revolting to her and added to the iniquity of the sacrifice. Then banishment to a dull, ungenial climate, the loss of her idolised eldest son, the shameful abuse she was obliged to listen to of her mother by her husband, who raked up all the past of Joséphine to torment her daughter at the very time that he was being influenced and egged on by his sisters, whose dissi-pated lives and disgraceful *liaisons* were the scandal of France. And when she had succeeded in freeing herself from her tyrant, the divorce of her mother, the persecution and exile that followed the fall of the Empire, the death of her second son and the imprisonment of the third; surely such a tissue of misfortunes was enough to overwhelm the not very strong-minded woman whose gentle, kindly nature is attested by the devoted affection of her friends and household, and for whose faults and weaknesses the circumstances of her life furnished so many excuses.

Hortense loved to surround herself with a literary, artistic society, which was frequented by Mesdames d'Abrantès, de Rémusat, and many of her old school friends. They met in the evenings at her house to play, sing, draw at a large table round which they sat, play games, &c. One wonders what sort of things could be the production of their pencils or brushes—done at a table by candle-light by a number of amateurs; however, it was a harmless amusement, and their music was much better than their drawing; some of them played and sang well. Hortense composed, amongst other songs, " *Partant pour la Syrie*," "*Le bon chevalier*," " *En soupirant j'ai vu naître l'Aurore*," &c.

It was in vain that the Emperor commanded the Parisians to amuse themselves and be happy, or tried to force them to conceal their grief at the loss of those dear to them. Entertainments were given because such were his orders, but nobody enjoyed them; if people were not mourning the loss of a near relation, they were in desperate anxiety for some one with the army in Spain or elsewhere; the people both in Paris and the provinces were becoming more and more terrified and discontented; the frightful slaughter was draining the country of its men. The Russian campaign had cost France 350,000 soldiers, enormous numbers had perished in Spain, Portugal, Germany, everywhere. Fresh levies were made of mere boys of eighteen, and as the people saw their young sons torn from them to fill the places of their husbands, fathers, and brothers who had fallen, they began to curse the ambition of the Emperor and cry out for peace and rest.

Nothing, however, was further from the mind of Napoleon. He spent the rest of the winter in Paris, for the last time, encompassed with cares and anxieties, both from abroad and at home. The conspiracy of Malet had been promptly suppressed and punished, but the growing dissatisfaction of the country was evident ; gloom, depression, and mourning had taken the place of the triumphant delight with which he had formerly been received.

The discontent in his own family was greater than ever, but for that he cared little ; his marriage with Marie Louise had made them much less important to him. He had decreed that his brothers and Murat were no longer to be treated as kings in France, but only as French princes, which much offended them.

Their countenances at the christening of the King of Rome were more like those to be expected at a funeral than at an occasion of rejoicing. Madame Mère found her new daughter-in-law did not trouble herself to conciliate her like Joséphine, and was now rightly punished for the ingratitude and unkindness with which she had treated that good-natured, easy-going person.

The success of her designs and wishes gave
satisfaction, and she showed neither pleasi
interest at the birth of her grandson, the lor
King of Rome.[1] The Emperor ordered her
a visit of congratulation to the Empress
lady-in-waiting [2] took the precaution to
all the armchairs from the room of the E
who allowed no "*fauteuils*" to the Buo
in her presence. When Madame Mère ¿
daughters appeared they found only plair
placed round the sofa of the Empress.]
declined to sit down at all, and left afte
minutes.

Madame Mère was just then much afflicte
death of Jérôme, only son of Elisa, and ¡
Mortefontaine to her favourite daughter-in-la
who always tried to console every one. Bei
mother she was obliged to appear at the chri
where the godfather was the Emperor of
represented by the Grand Duke of Wurzbu
the second godmother was Hortense.

There were plenty of people ready to try t
the jealousy of Marie Louise against Joséphir

One day the Emperor suddenly coming i
Marie Louise in tears, and on his eagerly
what was the matter she showed him a
miniature of Joséphine as a young woman
nothing of the scornful dislike of tears anc
which he had always displayed to Joséph
the different women who had loved him, he
her in the most affectionate manner, asking

[1] "Napoléon et sa famille," t. vi. p. 350.
[2] Madame Lannes, Duchesse de Montebello.

THE KING OF ROME
(Gérard.)

who had given her the portrait, to which she replied
that she had found it upon the sofa.

Although he did love Joséphine, and repeatedly
declared that she was the woman he had loved better
than any other, and though his marriage with Marie
Louise was entirely one of ambition, yet there was
all the difference in the world between his treatment of the ex-Vicomtesse de Beauharnais and the
Emperor of Austria's daughter. After the first few
months he had been, in spite of the affection he professed, constantly and openly unfaithful to Joséphine,
and angry if she objected, though furious if she gave
him the slightest ground for jealousy. But he was
most careful to give no such cause for complaint
to the Austrian Archduchess, from whom any *liaisons*
he might have were carefully concealed, while she
herself was treated with nearly as oriental a restraint
as in her childhood at Vienna, though at the same
time she was loaded with every luxury and indulgence. She had jewels, money, everything she
wished for, at her disposal ; she had only to ask
for the removal of a person or the change of a
plan she disliked, but she was not allowed to
receive any man except an old professor. Even
the man who came to wind up the clock excited
the displeasure of Napoleon, whose ideas about
women were more oriental than western, and
whose love, or what he called love, was really
more an insult than a compliment. It had no
equality, no justice, no refinement, and no constancy ; it was entirely selfish, absolutely and only
material ; the love of a master for his slave, or of
a Mahommedan for a favourite in his harem :

anything and everything but the feeling of an educated gentleman of Christendom for a woman he respects.

Marie Louise obeyed his orders with an apathetic submission which charmed him, as long as it was her interest to do so; when he lost his power and riches she deserted him at once, transferred the same submission to her father, and even before her intrigue and tardy marriage with the Count de Neippberg allowed Napoleon to be spoken of in her presence as "*le Monsieur d'Elbe.*"

In March, 1813, the Prince of Sweden joined the coalition against Buonaparte, and that he did so is, perhaps naturally, resented by French writers; but when they go on to call it "treason" one may naturally ask, "Treason to whom?"

For Sweden was not a province of France, and its prince was in no way whatever the vassal of Napoleon, nor was the crown of Sweden given by him. It was not his to give; he had never conquered that country, and Bernadotte was the free choice of a free people, who elected him for his military renown and personal qualities. Having accepted their trust it was not for him to betray it for the advantage of any other country. The case seems simple enough: he could not be both Swede and Frenchman; if he had intended to act as a Frenchman he could not in honour have accepted the crown of Sweden.

Even Madame d'Abrantès in her "Mémoires" remarks—

"Perhaps we have not sufficiently followed the royal career of Bernadotte from the moment he

left France to belong to another country. The
interests of his new country became duties to him;
perhaps we are too apt to forget that. . . . Then
came the invasion of Pomerania, and then were made
the proposals of Russia and Prussia. . . . Perhaps a
positive wrong was that Napoleon tried to treat
Bernadotte like Murat, and the case was entirely
different. Murat was the creation of the Emperor,
to which his magician's wand alone had given the
appearance of royalty, while the Prince Royal of
Sweden was sovereign by the election of a free,
generous nation, and to that nation he owed his
loyalty and gratitude." [1]

A definite convention with the Cortès of Cadiz
stipulated the restoration of Ferdinand VII. to the
throne of Spain, and, in spite of his affection for
his brother-in-law, Joseph Buonaparte, the Prince
of Sweden could not but agree to it, and prepare to
drive the French out of Swedish Pomerania, which
they had invaded.

In April the Emperor left Paris for a new
campaign in Germany; he was now opposed by
England, Russia, Prussia, and Sweden. On the
2nd of May he won the battle of Lutzen, and on
the 19th that of Bautzen, in which he beat the
Russians after three days' fighting. It was a great
victory, but it cost him another, and perhaps the

---

[1] Madame d'Abrantès is here exceptionally impartial. Usually she
allowed her patriotic feelings to overpower her reasoning powers
to a rather ludicrous degree. She thought it perfectly right and
fair that the French should rob Italy, Germany, and Spain of all
their greatest works of art and carry them off to Paris. When the
fortune of war was reversed she was indignant and horror-
stricken that those nations should take back their own property!

most beloved, of his remaining marshals, for Duroc was killed.

An armistice was arranged, Austria offered to mediate between Napoleon and the Allies, and a congress assembled at Prague. If Napoleon had closed with the proposals at first set forth it is interesting to think what a powerful and extensive country France would have been. The Hanse towns and Holland were to be set free, but France was to retain the Rhine, Belgium, Piedmont, Nice, and Savoy. But Napoleon, who again thought himself invincible, refused, and went to Dresden, where the Empress spent a few days with him, after which the armistice expired, and Austria joined the Allies.

The battle of Vittoria placed Spain at the disposal of England, Suchet was driven back over the Ebro, Moreau returned from America and entered the Russian service.

Désirée, Princess Royal of Sweden, was in a painful position ; her husband in arms against France, her brother-in-law driven from Spain and ordered by the Emperor to remain at Mortefontaine, where he had returned after years of absence. At times, when Joseph had found matters going badly in Spain, he had asked to be allowed to give it up and return to Mortefontaine, which he had left so unwillingly for Naples, and still more for Spain, but this request always irritated the Emperor.

"The King writes to me that he wants to go back to Mortefontaine," he said on one of these occasions.

"He thinks to put me into a difficulty; he takes advantage of a time when I certainly have other

occupations, which is mean. He threatens me when I
leave him my best troops and go to Vienna alone with
my little conscripts, my name, and my great boots.
. . . And what is Mortefontaine ?   It is the price of
the blood I shed in Italy.   Did he get it from his
father ?   Did he get it by his own works ?   He got
it from me. . . . When the King says he will come
to Mortefontaine does he think I shall allow him
to come ? . . . He is not fit to live in retirement ;
he thinks he is capable of living at Mortefontaine,
but he flatters himself extremely." [1]

However, Joseph's rule in Spain was now over, and
he was back at his beloved Mortefontaine, where he
and Julie and Désirée, in the greatest anxiety, watched
the course of events.   Suchet was the husband of their
niece, and his defeat filled them with consternation.   Désirée, on the other hand, with all her
sympathy for France and for her tribe of relations,
could not wish for the defeat of her husband and
the ruin of his kingdom and Oscar's inheritance.

For the last time it might have been possible for
France to make peace on good terms in August,
after the battle of Dresden had been won by the
Emperor, in which battle Moreau was killed.   But
almost directly afterwards Macdonald was beaten
in Silesia, Vandamme at Kulm, and Ney sustained
a crushing defeat from Bernadotte on the 6th of
September near Berlin.   That the Empire was falling
became more and more evident ; the gigantic fabric
which the extraordinary genius of Napoleon had
raised so rapidly was as short-lived as it was brilliant.
As one reads of the many astonishing changes and

[1] " Napoléon et sa famille," t. iv. p.   (Masson).

marvellous events that were crowded into the time
it is difficult to realise that all this happened within
twenty years. Désirée could not but see that hers
was nearly the only safe and prosperous position
amongst the family circle. The fame of the Prince
of Sweden was rising every day. After the battle
of Dresden the Emperor of Russia sent him the
Order of St. George, the Emperor of Austria that
of Maria Theresa, the King of Prussia the Iron Cross.
The Comte de Rochechouart, a Frenchman naturalised in Russia, arrived first with his decoration, and
had a long interview with the Prince of Sweden,
whom he regarded with enthusiastic admiration.
As they talked together the thoughts of the great
commander, heir to a throne, upon whom were now
the eyes of all Europe, went back to the old days
when he fled from his father's house and enlisted as
a common soldier.

" *Entendez-vous, mon ami*," he said ; "who could
have told the poor Sergeant Bernadotte twenty years
ago that he would be treated as a friend and brother
by the Emperors of Russia and Austria and the
King of Prussia ? "

The next morning, as the Comte de Rochechouart
was mounting to depart, the Prince detached from
his buttonhole the cross of the Sword of Sweden,
and presented it to him, saying—

" M. de la Rochechouart, here is what the Prince
of Sweden gives you "; then drawing him into the
embrasure of a window he gave him a gold snuff-box
set with diamonds, adding, " Here is what your
countryman, Bernadotte, begs you to accept."

Whatever might be the result of the campaign, or

the fate of her family and friends, Désirée could reflect, at any rate, that a safe and splendid home was always waiting for her. It was she, not Julie, who was now the most important and powerful of the family, and she was equally ready to help and protect the others to the best of her ability. Her love of France and of her family kept her with them through the evil days that were coming on so fast.

They spent the summer and autumn at Mortefontaine, where they had been joined by the Princess Catherine, wife of Jérôme, whose kingdom of Westphalia was so soon to melt away like the royalty of his brothers and sisters.

The Comte de Mélito observes that it was a singular assembly : a King and Queen of Spain, who did not possess an inch of land in that country; a Princess of Sweden, whose husband, the Prince, had been a French general, and now led a hostile army against France ; a Princess of Wurtemberg, whose husband was a brother of Napoleon, and her father in the ranks of the enemy; from time to time mass was said by the Patriarch of the Indies, Grand Inquisitor of Spain ; while they were surrounded by a crowd of courtiers, French, German, and Spanish, who no longer belonged to any courts. They spent their time in sport, picnics, playing cards, &c., waiting anxiously for news.

But it was then, as always, impossible to get the truth from the French bulletins, though what useful purpose can be served by denying or concealing a misfortune, which is certain to be disclosed after a few days, it is difficult to see.

However, this was the course pursued on the present occasion.   An *aide-de-camp* was sent by the Emperor to Paris with twenty banners taken by him in two or three of the battles, to be presented to the Empress, with expressions of satisfaction with her conduct as regent.

The banners were received in state by the Empress and the troops in Paris, but it was a melancholy pageant of the vanishing empire.   And even that was a mockery, for though the banners arrived at the beginning of November, the battle of Leipzig, dealing a fatal blow to the power of Buonaparte, had been fought on the 18th of October.   The troops of Saxony, Baden, and Wurtemberg had gone over to the enemy, the French were defeated and driven across the Elster, and, the bridge over it being blown up too soon, ten thousand French soldiers left on the other side were made prisoners.   The blame for this was by many persons attached to the Emperor, who was declared to have ordered the bridge to be blown up directly he had crossed to ensure his own safety ; but many attribute it to a mistake.

Prince Poniatowski was killed in this battle.   He plunged on horseback down the steep bank into the Elster, where both rider and horse were drowned. He was a great Polish patriot, nephew of Stanislas Augustus, King of Poland, and had fixed his hopes on Napoleon being the restorer of his country.   A romantic story is attached to one of his *aides-de-camp*, M. Berthot, or rather to his family, and is related by Madame d'Abrantès.[1]

The Polish Princess Lubormirska, *née* Rezewouska, was in Switzerland at the time of the Terror.   She

---

[1] " Salons de Paris," t. ii. p. 270 (Edition Garnier frères).

was a widow with one child, a daughter, and was at that time twenty-five years old, beautiful, charming, and attractive, like so many of her countrywomen. She could not, however, have been equally gifted with prudence and common sense, since, for some unknown reason, she actually left that haven of safety and went to Paris with her child, fancying that as a foreigner she would be unmolested, especially as she knew Barrère. She might as well have ventured into a den of tigers.

On one of the usual preposterous excuses she was arrested, thrown into prison, and condemned to death, but gained a short respite by declaring herself to be *enceinte*. She then wrote to Barrère, telling him that she had only said this to gain time, and begging him to take measures to save her, as in a month or two it would probably be found out that she had deceived the tribunal of murderers. Whether or not she was betrayed by the wretch to whom she trusted, her letter fell into the hands of the revolutionary tribunal, she was condemned again, and executed a few days before the death of Robespierre. If only she had waited, and not written, she would probably have been saved, as after the fall of that monster the appetite for slaughter seemed considerably to abate, the executions were much fewer, and many prisoners were set free.

She commended her child, who was only five years old, to the care of her fellow-prisoners, but they quickly met with the same fate, and the poor little one, whose name was Rosalie, was committed to the care of Madame Berthot, the laundress of the prison, an excellent woman, who, although she had five children of her own, said to her husband, "Well, God sends us a sixth. Let us adopt the orphan."

These worthy people accordingly took the child home with them, and brought her up with their own children. They did not know to what country she belonged, and if they had, Poland would have been all the same as Patagonia to them. Three years passed. Rosalie Lubormirska was good and beautiful as her mother, whom she strongly resembled. She attached herself strongly to the kind-hearted woman who had saved her, and with whom she lived as safely as any one could in France just then.

The unfortunate Princess Lubormirska had a brother who was devoted to her, the Count Rezewousky. Alarmed at the disappearance of his sister, especially, of course, when he learned that she had rashly gone to France, he made inquiries about her, but it was not until 1796 that he heard of her fate. Overwhelmed with grief, he then tried to find out what had become of his little niece, and came to Paris for that purpose. For six months he inquired and advertised, offering a large reward to whoever should bring Rosalie, Princess Lubormirska, to her uncle, Count Rezewousky, *hôtel et rue Grange-Batelière*, Paris.

But Madame Berthot did not read the newspapers, and knew nothing of the inquiries.

One day Count Rezewousky happened to be in his valet's room when the laundress brought the linen, accompanied by a little girl whose face attracted his attention.

"What a pretty child," he remarked in Polish to his valet.

The child looked at him and turned pale.

He fancied she was like his sister, and said so to the valet, again speaking Polish.

"Ah!" cried the child, "that is how my mother talked!"

The Count caught her in his arms and, amidst tears and caresses, he heard her history from the good laundress. When she had finished he said—

"You shall never be separated from her; you shall come with us to Poland, where you will be happy and beloved by us all, for you have saved my darling."

The next day Madame Berthot and her family were installed at the *hôtel*, and three days later they all started for Warsaw. The daughters were brought up in the house of the Count, and well married: the sons were sent to the University of Wilna, and became distinguished men. One of them was *aide-de-camp* to Prince Poniatowsky. Rosalie married her cousin, Count Gabriel Rezewousky, a man of high character and superior talent, with whom she was perfectly happy.

CHAPTER XXIV

1814

IT was not until the beginning of the new year
that Désirée and the Joseph Buonaparte household returned to Paris. Joseph was not in favour
with the Emperor, in whose opinion he had mis-
managed affairs in Spain, for Napoleon, like many
lesser people, always insisted on laying the blame
upon somebody else when matters took a turn he
did not like.

In November, 1813, Wellington drove Soult out of
Spain; that country was now completely cleared of
its invaders and restored to its own people. In the
same month the news was also received at Mortefontaine that the Emperor had arrived at Saint-Cloud,
which, under ordinary circumstances, would have
brought them all back to Paris, especially as the
winter had begun; but neither Napoleon nor his
brother were at all anxious to meet, and Désirée

thought it prudent to keep as quiet and attract as little attention as possible.

As an instance of the injustice with which some historians, worshippers of Napoleon, treat Bernadotte, it may here be mentioned that the Emperor had concluded a secret treaty with Ferdinand VII., depriving Joseph of the crown of Spain. And yet they are filled with indignation with the Prince of Sweden for consenting to a treaty necessary to the defence of his country, which the French were invading, because it dispossessed his brother-in-law of a crown to which he had no right whatever, while they have not a word of blame for Napoleon when he did exactly the same thing, and to his own brother.

Joseph, in spite of his complaints when made King of Spain, was very much injured when he discovered that he was deprived of that throne, but after a long correspondence between the brothers it was decided that Joseph should be simply a French prince, but that he should still be called king and should continue to inhabit the Luxembourg. Thither accordingly he returned with his family in January, and at the same time Désirée went back to her *hôtel* in the *rue d'Anjou*, where she lived in the strictest retirement.

The household of her sister at the Luxembourg resumed the habits of eight years ago ; senators and officials paid ceremonious court there, friends crowded the *salon*, all seemed to go on as usual. But Désirée, though she had no fears for her personal safety, considered that it would be neither prudent nor decent to show herself in public when her husband was in

JOSEPH FOUCHÉ, DUKE OF OTRANTO.

arms against France, therefore she only received quietly her old friends, amongst whom were Chiappe, of course, and also Talleyrand and Fouché, the latter of whom was a remarkable example of successful villany.

A native of Nantes, he was *préfet des études* of the Oratoriens when the Revolution broke out, embraced its cause with ardour, became deputy to the Convention, and was sent with Collot d'Herbois to Lyon, in 1793, charged to execute the decree of destroying that splendid city by the bloodthirsty monsters who were governing France. His crimes and cruelties there were conspicuous even amongst the ruffians with whom he was associated. Later on he was made Minister of Police by Barras, and continued in that office under Buonaparte, to whom his great talents and absolute unscrupulousness made him invaluable, though once or twice he fell out of favour with him. Napoleon made him Duke of Otranto, and after the Russian campaign, Governor of Illyria. During the Hundred Days he was again Minister of Police, and after Waterloo president of the *gouvernement provisoire*, and treated with the Allies. Even under Louis XVIII. he was Minister of Police and Ambassador at Dresden, to the scandal of many. The only sort of punishment he received was that, after the decree of 1816, he was banished for having voted the death of Louis XVI., and spent the last four years of his life at Trieste. This personage, whose hands were stained with murders [1] enough to

---

[1] From Lyons, Fouché wrote to Robespierre : "To celebrate the *fête* of the Republic suitably, I have ordered two hundred and fifty persons to be shot" (Bourrienne, &c.).

have hung or guillotined a score of men less guilty
than himself, was an agreeable person in society, and
on friendly terms with numbers of unexceptionable
people—Madame de Chastenay, for instance, Madame
de Rémusat, and the Princess of Sweden. It was
for political reasons, however, that Désirée was at
this time receiving him and Talleyrand so often and
so secretly in the *rue d'Anjou.*

There was undoubtedly in the minds of many of
his friends and supporters an idea that Bernadotte
might possibly succeed Napoleon, whose reign was
seen to be coming to an end ; and this hope was of
course a reason for Désirée's residence in France,
where she was in touch with the plots and intrigues
going on, and able to keep her husband constantly
well informed.

To reign in France instead of Sweden, which in
that case would have been restored to the heir of the
Wasa, the son of Gustavus IV., who was nephew of
the Emperor of Russia, was indeed a daydream to
Désirée, as well as to her husband ; but it was not
to be fulfilled, and the Prince and Princess of Sweden
might well be thankful for their splendid refuge from
the ruins of the Empire.

Before Joseph and Julie had settled themselves in
the Luxembourg, Blücher had crossed the Rhine
with the vanguard of the hosts that were gathering
to overwhelm the Empire which had spread slaughter
and devastation through their lands.

Wellington led the English, Spaniards, and Portu-
guese from the south ; over the frontiers in endless
succession came Russians, Dutch, Danes, Germans,
eager to revenge the last cruelties at the Hanse

towns;[1] the Army of the North, commanded by Bernadotte, was on the banks of the Rhine.

The Prince of Sweden, however, would not lead the invading army into France. He tried to persuade the Allies not to cross that boundary, and, finding his representations useless, he retired to his adopted country and employed six weeks before his return to France in a brilliant campaign in Norway, which he conquered and annexed to Sweden to take the place of Finland, which had been torn from her and given to Russia by Napoleon, whose memory the Finns must surely be cursing now, as they groan under the oppression and tyranny of that iron despotism.

The news of the defection of Murat was at first received with incredulity at Paris; the Emperor declared it to be impossible.

"No!" he exclaimed, "it cannot be! Murat, to whom I have given my sister! to whom I have given a throne! Eugène must be misinformed; it is impossible that Murat has declared himself against me!"

The desertion of Murat may well be called treachery. It was an entirely different case from

---

[1] Davoust, having fortified Hamburg and finding provisions running short, turned thousands of men, women, and children out of the town in December. They were dragged from their beds on a bitterly cold night, and several old people died from exposure. If any tried to remain, they were cruelly beaten. The property of the inhabitants, even the money of foreigners in the banks, was all seized. The town was nearly ruined. At Lubeck the departure of the French troops was marked with blood. Before they went they shot a butcher because he said, "The devil take them!" They also condemned an old man, but he escaped (Bourrienne).

Bernadotte. He was, as before observed, the creature of Napoleon, to whom he owed everything ; he reigned at Naples only by the will of Napoleon, who had conquered that country, given it to Murat, and maintained him there by the force of his own troops and money without the consent of its people.

It was a blow to Napoleon, who had thought of ordering the troops of Murat and Eugène to attack the Allies in the rear while he defended the soil of France.

The Parisians, accustomed for the last twenty years to constant success and victory, were overwhelmed with consternation as the hostile armies drew nearer and nearer to their capital. The Emperor was gone, after a pathetic farewell to his little son, leaving the Empress regent ; it was his last farewell, for he never saw them again.

On the 11th of February the announcement of a victory filled Paris with rejoicing. The streets were thronged with joyful crowds, congratulating and embracing each other, and saying that, after all, success had not deserted them. The weather was fine ; Joseph Buonaparte ordered a review ; again shouts of enthusiasm and cries of " *Vive l'Empereur !* " rent the air ; the boulevards were a scene of gaiety and cheerfulness, thronged with people in the highest spirits ; and a few days later, with still greater excitement, they gathered to see the Russian and Prussian prisoners pass. But these were not like those of former days, ragged, travel-stained, and worn with fatigue ; no, their dress and appearance reminded the lookers-on that they had been taken not so very far from Paris, and that their countrymen in immense numbers were pressing on behind them at no great distance.

Elegantly-dressed women of the *faubourg Saint-Germain* were seen mingling with the crowd, encouraging the prisoners with friendly signs, giving them money and parcels with words and looks of sympathy which irritated the crowd, who put a hostile interpretation upon their conduct, to which, to do them justice, they would not under other circumstances have objected. A murmuring arose, and if the *garde nationale* had not come up and protected them from the tender mercies of a Paris mob, these ladies would certainly have been attacked.

Eugène de Beauharnais had sent Count Tascher to his sister with news of the victory; and after his return from Paris he was sent with orders to Augereau, who commanded at Lyon, and whom he found in bed. Having with great difficulty gained admission, he delivered the Emperor's message.

" The Emperor says, M. le Maréchal, that you have 10,000 or 12,000 men of the old troops, two cavalry regiments, the 15th Cuirassiers and the 4th Hussards, and a *gendarmerie* of old soldiers; that with these forces and the new levies you are to march at once upon Macon, where is the Prince of Homburg's corps composed of new troops of all the little German princes, which you will easily crush——"

" Have you written orders?" interrupted Augereau.

" No, but as *aide-de-camp* to Prince Eugène, I can bring verbal ones, and I repeat to you the Emperor's words."

" I am not a corporal to be made to march in that

way!" replied Augereau, angrily. "I know what I have to do."

Tascher went to the *Préfet* of Lyon, who said sorrowfully on hearing his story—

"That is the way everything is going on here now."

Augereau was one of the roughest of Napoleon's marshals. He also had made a great fortune, and had bought the *hôtel de Rochechouart*, where he maintained a rowdy, hospitable household. His wife being delicate, part of the house was kept quiet for her. She had two *dames de compagnie*, one of whom was the famous Mademoiselle Sans Gêne, daughter of one of the officers who defended Lyon against the Convention, 1793. She fought by her father's side, escaped with him, joined the 9th Dragoons, was wounded several times. Napoleon when First Consul often witnessed her daring courage, gave her a pension, and placed her with Joséphine, but she hated court life, and became secretary to Madame Augereau, where the free and easy life was much more to her taste.

The exultations in Paris were short-lived.

"On the morning of the 28th of March," writes Mademoiselle Cochelet,[1] "I had been to the Tivoli baths when I met a woman of my acquaintance who told me that the enemy's army was not more than five leagues from us, and the *barrières* were closed. This news, already circulating in Paris, was spreading terror and dismay; on all sides were to be seen preparations for departure; the streets were blocked with carts loaded with people's property; the poorest fled, carrying upon their shoulders whatever they

---

[1] Lectrice to Hortense, Queen of Holland.

could. . . . Directly I got back I went to the Queen and told her of the reports going about.

"'Is it possible?' she said, 'that the enemy's army is nearer than ours? No doubt these are manœuvres of the Emperor which we don't understand; he will not let us be surprised; he will come when we least expect him and save the capital.' . . . During the morning she went to the Tuileries; on her return I eagerly asked for news.

"'The Empress knows no more about it than I do,' replied she. 'There is to be a council this evening which will decide what we are all to do. I entreated the Empress not to leave Paris; it would be a great mistake. I think I convinced her, but she is very young to take a determined part, and without energy all is lost. Anyhow, my dear Louise, get all my things ready and my diamonds packed, so that I may be able to start at a moment's notice or to remain as I think best.' . . .

"After dinner the Queen went to the Tuileries; the time she stayed there seemed to me enormous. M. de Lavalette came to wait for the Queen in my apartment, he was very uneasy. . . . At eleven we went up to the Queen's rooms, where we found the Maréchale Ney waiting too; we stayed there till one o'clock in the morning, when the folding doors were thrown open, and the Queen entered with an expression I had never seen. I felt that all was over."

Then began a regular stampede. All the Buonaparte fled—Joseph, Louis, and Jérôme accompanied the Empress and the King of Rome, who was very angry at being taken from the Tuileries, cried, and clung to the balustrade of the staircase, saying that he would not go. Louis sent to Hortense to leave also with their children. Hortense sent a messenger to the Empress Joséphine at La Malmaison, begging her to go to her château of Navarre, which she did. Hortense with her two boys slept at Versailles and Rambouillet, and joined her mother at Navarre. The hostile armies could be seen before they left Paris, the road to Rambouillet was one procession of fugitives; all night long it went on, and as at daybreak the inhabitants of Versailles looked out of their windows on to the confused stream below they realised that it was the Empire departing with all its pomp and splendour. Ministers carrying away their *portefeuilles* in carriages with six horses, with their wives, children. and jewels, the *Conseil d'État*, the crown diamonds, the archives, private carriages and carts loaded with luggage, men on horseback, poor people on foot carrying what they could from their deserted homes, left, as they supposed, to be pillaged; all mingling together and forming the most astounding spectacle. It was the passing of the Empire.

The Princess of Sweden had, of course, only to await in her *hôtel* the appearance of her husband's troops with the Allies. Neither had the Princess Catherine any occasion to fly before the army of her father and her countrymen. Her cousin, the Emperor of Russia, came to see her directly he arrived.

There was, of course, no pillage or violence; Queen Hortense sent Mademoiselle Cochelet back to bring some things from her *hôtel*, which she found occupied by Swedish soldiers, who, although every-

thing was left open, had meddled with nothing, and
took away when they left nothing but a few books of
small value as souvenirs.

On the 23rd of April the Prince of Sweden arrived,
but only spent a fortnight in the *rue d'Anjou*.   It
was now evident that he would not reign in France ;
he was absorbed in the affairs of his adopted country.
Oscar was losing his French associations and growing
up to be a thorough Swede, to the delight of the
people, who called the boy *their* prince, and declared
he was all their own.

Under these circumstances Désirée might have
been expected to have been willing to leave Paris,
where her favourite sister could no longer be with
her, and go to Sweden.

But such was her aversion to that country and
affection for Paris that she insisted on remaining
there, and after only a fortnight's stay in the *rue
d'Anjou*, the Prince went back to Stockholm, which
he entered in triumph.

Madame d'Abrantès relates that one day while she
was out a man who said he came from the Prince of
Sweden presented himself at her *hôtel*, said that he
wanted rooms for a number of the officers of his staff,
and insisted on being shown all over the house,
marking the doors of different rooms in spite of the
remonstrance of the *majordomo* and behaving with
great insolence.

Madame d'Abrantès wrote to the Prince, who sent
his *aide-de-camp* at once to express his regret and
promised to call in a day or two, which he did, to
repeat his apologies.   He knew nothing, of course,
about the conduct of the fellow, who, upon inquiry,

FONTAINEBLEAU

proved to be an under official of his household and a Frenchman.

Fontainebleau, so often the scene of the pleasures and splendours of the Imperial Court, was to witness the close of that magnificent drama unparalleled in the world's history.

It was there that the Emperor Napoleon signed his abdication upon the day when the Comte d'Artois entered Paris.

There the Emperor took an affecting leave of the Old Guard, embracing the eagles which had so often led them to victory; there, before his departure, he took leave of Macdonald, one of the few remaining of his marshals who was faithful, when most of those who devotedly loved him had fallen, and many of the remaining ones had deserted him. When Macdonald returned alone, after trying to obtain more favourable terms for him, Napoleon said—

"I am not now rich enough to reward these last services."

"Sire, interest never guided my conduct."

"I know that, and I now see how I have been prejudiced against you. . . ."

"Sire, I have already told you that I am devoted to you in life and death."

"I know it. But since I cannot reward you as I should wish. . . . Vicenza," turning to Caulaincourt,[1] "ask for the sabre given me by Murad Bey in Egypt, which I wore at the battle of Thabor." It was brought, and he presented it to Macdonald, saying,

---

[1] Caulaincourt was unjustly accused of being concerned in the kidnapping of the Duc d'Enghien, in which he was not involved.

"Here, my faithful friend, is a reward which I believe will please you."

"If I ever have a son, Sire, this will be his most precious inheritance. I will never part with it as long as I live."

"Give me your hand and embrace me."

With tears in their eyes they parted. Caulaincourt also was faithful to the last.

The Emperor complained bitterly that his wife and son were not allowed to accompany him to Elba, which was the last thing Marie Louise desired or intended. She is said to have wished to take leave of him, but finding it was not considered expedient, she returned contentedly with her father to Vienna, where the Count von Neipberg soon banished from her mind any tender recollections she retained of Napoleon.

The only relations who accompanied him to Elba were the Princess Borghese, who had, after all, more affection for him than any of the others, and Madame Mère, who never forgave Caroline for the treachery and ingratitude shown by herself and Murat, who was influenced by her. She broke off all relations with her, refusing to see her until one day Caroline managed to force herself into the presence of her mother, and, approaching her with looks and words of affection, asked what she had done to be so treated.

"What you have done! *bon Dieu!*" exclaimed Madame Mère; "you have betrayed your brother, your benefactor!"

Vainly Caroline represented that she was not responsible for the politics of her husband, that he

had acted for the good of Naples, &c.—that in any
case she was not to blame.

"You have betrayed your benefactor," repeated
her mother. "You ought to have used your influence
over your husband to dissuade him from his disastrous
resolution; Murat ought to have passed over your
dead body before he arrived at such baseness. The
Emperor was his benefactor just as much as yours.
Retirez-vous, Caroline." And she turned her back
upon her.

That Napoleon expected Marie Louise to join him
at Elba is certain. He remarked: "The air is good
here, and the inhabitants excellent. I shall not do
badly, and I hope Marie Louise will not find it very
bad either.[1]

[1] "Mémoires de l'intérieur du palais impérial," t. ii. p. 242
(L. de Bausset).

CHAPTER XXV

1814—1815

ON the 30th of May Joseph wrote to Julie: "I think, if your health permits, you ought to go away with the children, and whoever you want to take with you. If not, you must send off the children ; your sister's house will be your best refuge."

Mortefontaine was now deserted, for Joseph and Julie fled to Switzerland, and took up their abode at a place called Trangins, which belonged to them.

But Désirée had still many relations in Paris, and plenty of friends. Madame Récamier came back from exile, so did Madame de Stael, who had lately been in Sweden, where she was heartily welcomed by her old friend Bernadotte. She brought with her a pretty daughter of seventeen besides her sons ; she was now re-married to M. della Rocca, a handsome Italian much younger than herself, but devotedly attached to her.

The pomp and splendour of the Empire had

departed, but Paris was gay, brilliant, and crowded with the most illustrious personages in Europe.

Joséphine remained at La Malmaison and Hortense in Paris and at Saint-Leu, where they were visited by all the most distinguished persons, especially by the Emperor Alexander, whose interest and powerful protection were of the highest importance to them. Eugène had had a narrow escape, for the Italians, eager to throw off the French yoke, had risen, murdered the Prime Minister, and threatened the Viceroy, who escaped in disguise to Bavaria, where his father-in-law gave him the title of Duke of Leuchtenberg, and he lived contentedly with his wife and children.

The little sons of Hortense, puzzled by the new state of things, having been accustomed to the Emperor and the kings his brothers, asked whether these sovereigns were also their uncles. Joséphine adored these children, especially the younger one, afterwards Emperor of the French.

She did not long survive the fall of Napoleon. On a cold day in May she gave a dinner at La Malmaison to the King of Prussia, before which she walked in the park with him, where she took a chill. During the day or two following she entertained the Emperor Alexander and the Grand Dukes Nicolas and Michael, with the assistance of Eugène and Hortense. But her cold got worse and worse, till it attacked the lungs, and she died on the 29th of May. Throughout her short illness she was surrounded by her children, her household, and friends, who were all devoted to her. The Emperor Alexander, who had contracted an affectionate friendship for her, was with

them the day before her death.   All the consolations
of religion and affection were hers.

Different indeed were her last hours from those of
Napoleon—forsaken by his imperial wife, divided
from all his family on a distant island with the
small group of faithful friends who alone remained
to him.

A night or two before his death he said to General
Montholon, " I have just seen my good Joséphine ;—
she sat there - -it seemed as if I had seen her yesterday—she was not changed—always the same—
always devoted to me.   She told me we were going
to see each other again, and be separated no
more."

Under all the apparent rejoicing the state of things
throughout France was very unsettled.   There was
undoubtedly a great deal of enthusiasm, loyalty, and
delight amongst certain classes whose sympathies
were entirely Royalist and Catholic, and to whom
the restoration of religion and the King fulfilled
their most ardent desires.

But there were always the Jacobins, diminished
and discredited but by no means extinguished, and
Napoleon had still his partisans, especially in the
army.   Many a soldier, when he drank the King's
health and shouted " *Vive le roi !*" added, in a lower
voice, " *de Rome et son petit papa.*"

And the satisfaction of many people had no
concern with either Bourbon or Buonaparte ; to them
it was merely a question of peace or war ; they had
just passed through twenty years of glory, but of
continual slaughter, the Emperor, at any rate latterly,
declaring that he only wished for peace ; just as some

persons will interfere with, annoy, and irritate their friends, and when their actions or speeches are resented say that the quarrel was not of their making. Napoleon's idea of peace was that nobody should venture to oppose him, which, after all, is the idea of many lesser people without the same excuse, and happily without such fatal consequences.

The French people did not believe that as long as Napoleon sat on the throne they would ever be safe from those sudden levies which they hated and dreaded, by which they or their children might be sent to die in Spain, or Egypt, or Russia, or come home mutilated cripples for no reason at all that they cared about.

What they wanted was peace, security, and a good government, and just then whoever gave them these would be welcome. Except their own followers and partisans, few people in France knew anything about any of the Bourbons but the Duchesse d'Angoulème, Madame Royale, of whom Napoleon once remarked that she was the only man of her family, and around whom there seemed to be a halo of saintliness and suffering. But of the rest people scarcely knew the names or relationships ; and they were not calculated to take the nation by storm, being neither young, handsome, nor particularly talented, but conspicuous only by their birth and misfortunes. If they had possessed the gallant grace and stately beauty of the Valois, or the distinguished appearance and fascinating charm of the Stuarts, if the people could have admired and been proud of them, their chance of re-establishing themselves firmly in the affections of the country would have been far greater.

But Louis XVIII., with all his capacity, common sense, and useful qualities, was an elderly invalid a martyr to gout; neither did any of the other three princes possess that superiority of intellect or force of character necessary in such a crisis.

They and their party, as has often been repeated, had forgotten nothing and learned nothing; while between the old and the new society there was bitter jealousy and hatred. To a certain extent it was only natural. Could those who had returned forget the murder of their parents, husband, wife, or children, the destruction of their homes, the desecration of their religion, the long years of poverty and exile in a foreign land, or see with indifference their estates and houses inhabited by strangers, their dearest possessions stolen and scattered? Though Louis XVIII. could receive and employ Fouché, the man who voted for his brother's death, what must have been the feelings of the Duchesse d'Angoulême when she saw the murderer of her parents?

On the other hand, there is no doubt that they endeavoured to carry out their principles and ideas in a manner and to an extent which they ought to have seen to be extravagant and impossible under the altered state of affairs; which proved fatal to themselves, and into which, of course, in a book of this kind, it is impossible to enter.

The other party adopted an equally hostile attitude, misrepresented and maligned their rivals, were aggrieved and indignant when they endeavoured to recover their own property, and lost no opportunity of ridiculing their old-fashioned ways and the manner of speaking and behaving which, in many cases, it would have been better to imitate than to mock at. Some of the returned *émigrés*, however, showed the most despicable ingratitude to those who had helped and saved them, and whom they chose to ignore now they no longer needed their services ; others took the opportunity to annoy, by various petty slights, the members of the new *noblesse*, which they called the *noblesse à plumes.* It was said that when presentations were made to the Duchesse d'Angoulême, the words "*à plumes*" were whispered by the *dame d'honneur*, Madame de Serrant, after the name and title of any one belonging to the Empire, in order to regulate the cordiality of their reception.

The school of Madame Campan was closed, as the château in which it was established was restored to the Prince de Condé, to whom it belonged.

Madame Cochelet, in her interesting memoirs, complained that the Prince should have claimed his own property ; but as Madame Campan had already made a large fortune out of it, she can scarcely be considered a victim.

Her three nieces were educated there with Queen Hortense, who was very fond of them. One married a M. Garnot, another M. de Broc, and the third Marshal Ney.

Hortense always liked to place her old schoolfellows in her household, and Madame de Broc was appointed to some post there. Her husband, to whom she was devoted, was killed in battle, and she never recovered from his loss. A year or two after it she was at Aix with the Queen ; they made an excursion to see a waterfall. Over the deep gorge of the torrent was only a plank, across which they had to go.

As Madame de Broc stepped on to it her foot slipped and she fell into the abyss below. In spite of all efforts, it was impossible to save her, and it was some time before her body could be recovered. This was a great shock and grief to Hortense.

The Maréchale Ney had been one of Joséphine's ladies, and wanted to go with her to La Malmaison, but was prevented by her husband. She was a quiet, gentle, not particularly clever person, whose sympathies and early connections were royalist, and who, when a child, used to play with the Duchesse d'Angoulême, by whom she was now very kindly received ; but as the wife of Ney she was looked down upon by the court, where her present friends thought she was too eager to push herself, and where more than one annoyance befel her.

One evening she was at the Tuileries, while it was still decorated all over with eagles and bees and Imperial crowns, when the Princesse de Léon (*née* Montmorency) made her first appearance there, and sitting down by her, exclaimed—

" Is it possible that they have left all these indignities here? They do well to trample these ridiculous emblems under foot ; why don't they feel the necessity of getting rid of them altogether?"

Another time Madame Ney was at the English embassy when a *grande dame* of the *faubourg Saint-Germain* came in, and, taking no notice of her, said to the wife of the Ambassador, or to some other English lady standing by—

" Ah, Madame! it is to England that we owe our happiness! It is she who has saved us by delivering us from those brigands and giving us back our kings."

Julie, ex-Queen of Spain, had gone with her husband and children to Switzerland, Mortefontaine was sequestrated, and Joseph Buonaparte could not, of course, return to France or take any measures to regain possession of it ; therefore they decided that Julie, who could claim the protection of her sister, the Princess of Sweden, should go to Paris and see what could be done.

Désirée was glad enough to see her sister again and to receive her in the *rue d'Anjou*, where she stayed all the time she was in Paris, and where many of her old friends came to see her, amongst others Hortense, ex-Queen of Holland ; for Julie had never joined in the malice and spite her husband's family had shown to the Beauharnais. But do what they might, Julie and Désirée could not succeed in getting the sequestration taken off Mortefontaine, and Julie again took leave of her sister and returned to Switzerland.

Summer and autumn had passed, winter was nearly over, for March had begun, when suddenly, like a thunderclap, came the news that Napoleon had landed and was marching towards Paris. He was said only to have five or six hundred men with him, but none could tell how many would have joined him before he had gone many leagues. The royalists and many others who viewed with dismay this new disturbance, declared that he would be hunted down like a wild beast, that he would get no support from any party in the country, that he would be assassinated by the peasants, and so on ; but in spite of all these boastful words Buonaparte advanced, his followers increased, and consternation spread through Paris.

Hortense was having tea with two or three friends when the Maréchale Ney appeared in great agitation.

"Ah, Madame!" she cried, "what a misfortune this landing is! We were so peaceful! My husband starts this evening for Besançon; he is collecting troops to march against the Emperor."

Hortense was silent, and the Maréchale went on—

"But what folly can have possessed the Emperor? He will soon be the victim of it. Who will join him? Nobody; every one is released from their oaths to him and has taken others."

Hortense, whose sympathies were naturally with Napoleon, replied coolly—

"No doubt there are many against the Emperor, but is it to be believed that not a Frenchman will take his side? . . . This return is a great calamity, and I deplore it as much as you do (using the familiar *tu*, as she always did with her early friends), but I don't agree with your conviction about the complete abandonment of the Emperor. My opinion is that we shall have a civil war, and it is a frightful idea."

"A civil war!" exclaimed the Maréchale. "Ah, Madame! you know France very little! Nobody wants the Emperor back, and my husband, who is a better judge of the state of things than we can be, deplores the sad position in which he has placed himself. He will have nobody on his side."

"Your husband judges by his own sentiments, but not by those of the whole army," replied Hortense. "He will not make me believe that not a single regiment will be found that remembers its old general and hesitates to fire upon him."

Madame Ney seemed overwhelmed.

"*Mon Dieu !*" she exclaimed, "do you remember our anguish during all those terrible wars? I have seen you as glad of peace as I was."

"I am not talking of my own opinions," replied Hortense . . . "I regret the Emperor's coming as much as you do; I would give anything in the world that it should not have happened, because any way I foresee nothing but misfortune for him in the first place, and for everybody else. But when you come and tell me that the Emperor will be tracked and seized by Frenchmen, as every one is saying, and that not a single man will embrace his cause or defend him, then I tell you that that is impossible; that you forget the man of whom you are speaking and the nation for whom he has done so much; but as plenty of officers will agree with your husband we shall have a civil war, and we may be permitted to lament about that, for there is nothing worse."

The Maréchale was in despair; it was as if she had a presentiment of the terrible calamity preparing for her. Two days after the departure of her husband she went to the Tuileries, where she was this time received with caresses and flatteries by those who had scorned her before.[1]

"Your husband will save us!" they cried; and they repeated the promises Ney had made to the King.

"My husband will do his duty," said the Maréchale; "but he never said that he would bring back the Emperor in an iron cage; it is a calumny; my husband never said that."

Very soon the news arrived that Labédoyère, who

[1] "Mémoires de Mademoiselle Cochelet," t. ii. pp. 276 279.

was in command at Chambéry, had been sent to
Grenoble against Napoleon, but had joined him with
all his troops. Grenoble had opened its gates to the
Emperor, who had entered the town in triumph.

Paris was in a frenzy of excitement as people
waited for what the next few days would bring
forth.

The following sarcastic verses represented the
state of mind of many persons :—

> " Bonaparte s'avance
> Je suis de son parti ;
> Mais s'il reçoit la danse
> Je ne suis plus pour lui.
>
> De crainte d'anicroche
> Je n'ai jamais d'avis ;
> Je porte dans ma poche
> L'aigle et la fleur-de-lis." [1]

The King and royal family fled ; so did some of
their most intimate friends and conspicuous supporters. The position was dangerous for many
persons in the event of the return of Napoleon,
who had acted with great cruelty after his victory
over the Allies at Montereau, upon taking possession
of Troyes. He had caused bombs to be thrown into
the wooden quarter of the town without waiting till
the expiration of the time accorded for its evacua-
tion ; had abused and insulted a M. Bourgeois
because the Emperor Alexander had lodged with
him, had taken away and sold for the benefit of the
poor a diamond clasp given by the Emperor Alexander to Madame Bourgeois ; and ordered to be

---

[1] " Mémoires de Madame de Chastenay," t. ii. p. 545.

arrested and shot two unfortunate *émigrés* for no
other crime than that of wearing their old decorations of Saint-Louis during the sojourn of the
Allies. One of them, M. de Widranges, fled after
the retreating column and managed to join it ;
but the escape of the other, M. Gonault, was frus-
trated by Napoleon, who, when he was arrested,
overwhelmed him with abuse.[1] He underwent his
sentence bravely, and in spite of all the sympathy
with which one regrets the fate of Ney and rejoices
over the escape of Lavalette, one cannot help asking
which was the most unjust—to shoot an officer who
had broken his oaths, deserted his flag and led his
troops against his king, or to kill a private citizen
because he had worn a cross and ribbon on his coat.

The Emperor was at hand, the Buonaparte were
coming back, and to the Princess of Sweden this was
a time full of conflicting emotions. Whichever way
things went she was safe enough ; although the success of the Emperor would be in opposition to the
wishes and interests of her husband, it brought her
the joy of her favourite sister's return. Such members of the family as had collected together went to
the Tuileries to greet the Emperor on his return, but
they were few in number. Joseph, his wife and
daughters, Hortense with her little sons, who were
brought from the place where they had been hidden
in Paris—for Hortense, with her usual bad luck, was
suspected by both parties ;[2] by the Royalists of

---

[1] " Mémoires de Madame de Chastenay," t. ii. p. 288.

[2] Cochelet, " Mémoires," t. ii. p. 321. After Waterloo, Hortense,
accused of intriguing with the Buonapartists, was banished like the
members of that family.

intriguing for the return of Buonaparte, and by him of being what he called the friend of his enemies.

It was about eight o'clock on a foggy March evening when Hortense and Julie arrived at the Tuileries—where scarcely any one noticed them, for the Emperor's carriage had just driven into the courtyard, and Napoleon, descending at his usual entrance, had been seized upon by the excited crowd and carried to his own apartments, where the ex-Queens of Spain and Holland had the greatest difficulty in following, half-stifled by the pressure of the throng.

He embraced them rather coldly, asked Hortense where her children were, and, on hearing where they had been hidden, said—

" You have placed my nephews in a bad position ; among my enemies."

The next morning, March 21st, Hortense brought the two boys to the Tuileries. The Emperor looked at them with emotion, evidently reminded of the son from whom he was separated ; but directly he was left alone with Hortense, he began angrily to reproach her that she and Joséphine had asked for and accepted the protection and assistance of the allied sovereigns ; especially that Joséphine had asked the permission of Louis XVIII. to retain her title of Empress. Considering that he had ruthlessly sacrificed Joséphine to his own ambition and that she was now dead, even Hortense, whose gentleness was apt to become too passive, was roused to answer with becoming spirit—

" My mother had nobody to support her but herself, Sire, in this struggle when she was involved

in the vengeance which you had provoked. Poor
victim! twice struck . . . was she, then, to remain
silent—not even to ask to secure a tomb in the place
where, after possessing two thrones, she was reduced
to fear not to have a refuge where she might die in
peace?"

"The Empress Joséphine," said Napoleon, "ought
to have waited until I was *incapable* of helping her,
until it was *certain!* *Eh quoi!* it was not a month
that I was exiled, and already she was treating with
my persecutors! . . . she, Joséphine! . . . the wife
of my choice . . . she whom, without the imperious
question of reasons of state I would never have
banished from my palace! . . . Joséphine! Oh! I
should never have expected it of her!"

"But, Sire," said Hortense, "your Majesty always
forgets in what position you left us. My mother had
no resources; as to me. . . ." Her voice failed and
she burst into sobs and tears.

"I know very well that you are excusable," said
Napoleon. "But Joséphine! . . . They accuse Marie
Louise of weakness, but at least she had not received
from the Pope an indelible character in being
crowned by him. Your mother ought to have
remembered that and been worthy of it. . . ."

"Sire," exclaimed Hortense, "I dare to conjure
your Majesty to be kind towards my mother. . . .
Alas! the last word she spoke was your name."

"The more reason to respect it. . . . Then, according to you, to love is enough to free one from ever
reproaching oneself."

As they walked up and down talking, they came
to an open window looking upon the Pont Royal.

Seeing the crowd below, who began to cheer as he
appeared, the Emperor drew Hortense on to the
balcony, and she was naturally obliged to salute and
smile through her tears.   Next day in the *Moniteur*
appeared a paragraph :—

"Yesterday, *S. M. l'Empéreur* was in his study
with Queen Hortense and the Princes his nephews ;
the acclamations of the people . . . drew them on to
the balcony ; Queen Hortense was so overcome by
the proofs of attachment of the people of Paris . . .
that she offered to the sympathising crowd the touching spectacle of her face bathed in tears, caused to
flow by the love of the people for her august
father ! ! " [1]

The Emperor showed less callousness when a little
later he sent word to Hortense that he wished her to
entertain him and a certain number of guests whose
names he mentioned, at a *déjeûner* at La Malmaison.

Hortense sent out the invitations, gave the
necessary orders to her *chef*, and then drove down to
La Malmaison, where she arrived shortly before midnight.   The place had, since the death of Joséphine,
been unoccupied except by servants, who were all in
bed and much astonished and affected at the sudden
appearance of the daughter of their beloved mistress,
who had not been there since she left, just after her
mother's death.

The empty rooms, the silent corridors, the deserted
melancholy look of the place formerly gay and
luxurious, the memories which, as so many of us
know by experience, cling to and haunt an old home,
oppressed Hortense and filled her with sadness.

[1] " Mémoires sur la Restauration," t. ii. p. 139.

She controlled herself, however, and prepared to meet the Emperor next day with all the cheerfulness she could summon.   But the recollections of the place proved too much for his equanimity also : the *déjeûner* was rather a silent one, as neither Napoleon nor Hortense spoke much, and when it was finished and they had driven round the park, visited the Swiss farm of Joséphine, and returned to the château, the Emperor said, in a voice which he did not entirely succeed in controlling—

"I should like to see the Empress Joséphine's room."

Hortense rose.

" No, Hortense, stay here, my daughter ; I will go alone—it would agitate you too much."

Hortense sat down again without speaking, her eyes full of tears, and the Emperor, with a look of emotion, left the room.

He remained absent for some time, and when he returned, although he was evidently forcing himself to be calm, he seemed oppressed and saddened : his eyes bore the traces of tears and his look was grave and reserved.

No one ventured to interrupt the silence which fell upon the *salon*, and presently the Emperor, looking round and seeing some newspapers upon a table, desired M. Molé to read him a letter in the *Moniteur* from himself to General Grouchy ordering all the royal family to be permitted to leave France in freedom, and that the Duc d'Angoulême should be escorted safely and with proper respect to Cette, where he would embark.

He then drove back with Hortense to Paris.

CHAPTER XXVI

1815—1817

THE Emperor was back at the Tuileries, his
party was triumphant, his followers were filled
with enthusiasm ; but the capital was plunged in
gloom and apprehension. In the *faubourg Saint-
Germain* was, of course, nothing but melancholy :
ladies went about in dark dresses looking like mourning, every one's face was sad. But all over Paris
during the Hundred Days the same depression prevailed. No one believed in the stability of the
Empire except its fanatical supporters. It was
evident enough that immense numbers were against
it, the Jacobins were again about the streets, which,
but for them, were silent and deserted, and which
their presence certainly did not enliven—for again
terrible figures and faces were to be met parading in
gangs the boulevards and faubourgs with yells and
shouts of "*Vive la République!* Death to the royalists!"
the bloodthirsty songs of the Terror resounded in the

streets, revolutionary airs were played at the theatres, there was general alarm and dissatisfaction. No responsible person believed Napoleon's assurance that Marie Louise and her son would shortly be restored to him : the Allies refused to treat with him, and their armies were again preparing to attack France. He seemed terribly alone, too, in spite of the admiring mob that followed him, the remnant of his veterans left from the years of slaughter and the few of his old generals and friends who had rallied to him—so many names were missing. Where was the brilliant group of heroes with whom he had gained his past victories? Davoust, Lefèbre, Bassano, Mortier, Suchet, and Ney had joined him ; Murat would do so if he could be accepted ; but Desaix, Kléber, Lannes, Junot, Bessières, Duroc, and many others were dead ; Macdonald would not break his oath to the King, Bernadotte was amongst his enemies, Soult, Augereau, Berthier, Marmont, and Masséna were against him ; even Rapp would not join him in disturbing the peace of Europe.

He made Cambacérès Minister of Justice, Carnot the regicide Minister of the Interior, and Fouché Minister of Police.

Most of the Buonaparte family returned. Madame Mère, Joseph, Julie, and their daughters, Louis, and Jérôme. And early in May, Lucien, whom the Pope had just made Prince of Canino, arrived in France, stopped at Charenton, and sent to know whether the Emperor wished him to enter Paris.

Napoleon could not but be touched by the generosity of the brother whom, when he was powerful and prosperous, he had oppressed, ill-treated, whose life he had threatened, and who, now that he was in danger and deserted by those who had flattered and bowed before him, came back to take his place at his side.

It was late at night when Lucien's letter was brought him, but Napoleon immediately sent a messenger to welcome his brother, begging him to pass that night at the palace of Cardinal Fesch, and sending one of his carriages, in which the Prince of Canino re-entered Paris after a banishment of so many years.

At the *barrière* he was met by a crowd of artists and literary men and women, young and old, whom he had formerly helped, who had heard with joy of his return, and had come to show their gratitude.

Next morning M. de Las Cases and M. de Villoutreys were sent by the Emperor as chamberlain and equerry to Prince Lucien. Immediately afterwards General Bertrand, Grand Marshal, brought him the orders of the Legion of Honour and the Iron Cross, at the same time informing him that the Palais Royal was at his disposal, and he could take possession of it at once, having done which, Lucien proceeded to the Tuileries.

The meeting of the brothers was cordial and affectionate, and presently Napoleon said—

"How are *my sister-in-law* and my nephews? I will send a frigate to Civita-Vecchia to fetch them."

Never till now had Napoleon so mentioned Lucien's wife, and this sign of reconciliation won Lucien's heart.

Madame d'Abrantès, who relates this incident, and who was a great friend of Lucien's, observes that she would have preferred that Napoleon should have done this whilst he was more prosperous.

Everybody was delighted to see Lucien, especially his brother Joseph; when he drove through the streets he was followed by cries of "*Vive, Lucien!*" The French, always appreciating a generous action, were pleased with his return to his brother at such a time.

Soon afterwards his second daughter, Christine, who was in England, arrived, and was received with royal honours at Paris, and with affectionate kindness by the Emperor, who was now anxious to show consideration for Lucien, would not allow his younger brothers to take precedence of him, but said—

"In the Imperial family there are only elder and younger brothers, therefore every one is to be placed according to his rank, Joseph on my right, Lucien on my left, Jérôme after. Louis was, of course, not then present. He talked much of the past to Lucien, of Marie Louise, of his regrets for Joséphine, of Madame Récamier, and many others, saying of Madame de Stael—

"I was wrong. Madame de Stael has done me more harm in exile than she would have done in France."

But Napoleon was no longer the same. His constitution was undermined; already fatigue, anxieties, and profligacy had incurably affected his health, he suffered from frequent and violent pain, and also from an overpowering tendency to sleep, and general inactivity, contrasting strangely with his former decision, vigour, and apparently exhaustless energy and strength.

Lucien saw this with alarm, and deplored the waste of time, as Napoleon lingered at Paris instead of marching to meet the enemy, occupying himself with preparations for a great *fête*, known as the Champ de Mai ; when, as Lucien and others declared, he ought to have been weeks ago at the head of his troops.

An idea was started that the Emperor might abdicate in favour of his son, receiving for himself the island of Martinique, where whoever chose to do so might accompany him.

Madame d'Abrantès relates a story which was hushed up and contradicted at Vienna, but which she declares to have been certified by many persons, of an attempt made to carry off the King of Rome from Schönbrunn, where he lived with his mother, his governess, and his household, some of whom were French. He had also as playfellow a child of his own age, who was very fond of him.

The plan was to carry off the King of Rome in a basket of linen ; Marie Louise, of course, knew nothing about it. On the evening fixed upon, the person charged with the execution of this plan brought one of the large baskets used to carry away soiled linen, and said to the child—

" Get into this basket, Sire. You are going to see the Emperor, but you must not speak."

" Oh ! I will say nothing if we are going to see papa !" he exclaimed, and he crouched down joyfully in the basket and was covered with handkerchiefs, when just as the basket was being carried away piercing shrieks came from a corner of the room and the other child screamed out—

" I want to go and see the Emperor too! I will go
with the little King! I will go in the basket."

They could not quiet the little nuisance, and at that
moment an official entered and saw what was going
on. The King of Rome got out of the basket and
said nothing, but the other child threw his arms
round his neck and with tears and sobs told the
whole story.

Before the Emperor left Paris, Lucien tried to persuade him to forgive Murat, who wanted to fight by
his side, but Napoleon would not hear of it, saying
that severity, if not hatred, were all Murat could
expect from him, and ordering that he should not
stay in France.

"Say no more about him," said Napoleon. " As
for us, Lucien, my brother, we are reunited, and now
it is for life. No more quarrels or discussions . . .
but you must not meddle with either peace, war, or
politics. . . . Let the Palais Royal be the centre of
the arts, let artists find in you a protector . . . my
brother, Prince Lucien, famed for his talents and
learning. War and politics belong to me. . . ."

" If I conquer," continued Napoleon, " I will really
rest—it is time. We will spend the summer at
Fontainebleau and Compiègne . . . we will act . . .
we will hunt. I will surround myself with men distinguished in art and literature. . . . It is time to
rest and enjoy ourselves and occupy ourselves with
beautiful France. . . . You will help me, Lucien, will
you not? "

Melancholy forebodings hung over the departure of
the Emperor.

There was a great dinner at which all the family

NAPOLEON.
(Meissonier.)

were present on Sunday evening, June 11th, and at
four in the morning he left the Tuileries for ever.

A week later the news of Waterloo shattered the
hopes of the Buonapartists, and spread consternation
over Paris.

The Emperor returned, shut himself up in the
Elysée, the Allies came back ; again he signed his
abdication, and his family were scattered. The last
to take leave of him was Madame Mère. Tears
fell slowly from her eyes as she stretched out her
hand, saying—

" *Adieu, mon fils.*"

" *Ma mère, adieu,*" was Napoleon's answer ; his
face was like marble ; they embraced in silence and
parted.

The Signora Letizia Buonaparte was from henceforth separated from her elder children. Napoleon
departed to the melancholy captivity which, however
necessary it might have been to the peace and safety
of Europe, one cannot help regretting, even when
remembering the fate of the Duc d'Enghien, Hofer,
Palm, and others, as the tragic conclusion of a
magnificent career.

Joseph, against whom there was an order of arrest,
fled to America ; Elisa could not obtain permission to live at Rome, but settled at Trieste, as did
Caroline.

But, with the last-named exception, the younger
children of the Signora Letizia, as well as her
brother, Cardinal Fesch, lived around her. Pauline
and Lucien returned to their Roman homes,
Louis also took up his abode there, as did later on
Jérôme and the Princess Catherine. Lucien's

daughter, Charlotte, was already the wife of Prince Gabrielli.

The King returned, the *faubourg Saint-Germain* was triumphant: at Avignon and some other southern towns there were deplorable reprisals and massacres, of the same kind which had disgraced the Revolution ; the generals who had broken their oaths and gone over to Napoleon were tried ; but the only ones executed were Ney and Labédoyère. Lavalette was saved by the heroism of his wife and friends, French and English.

Such officials as had held posts under the Government of the Hundred Days were placed under police surveillance.

Carnot, being obliged to make inquiries of Fouché, who, by betraying every one else, always managed to save himself, and was now Minister of Police, wrote to him—

" *Où faut-il que je me rende, traître ?* " [1] to which Fouché's reply was—

" *Où tu voudras, imbécile.*"

For three months only had Julie and Désirée enjoyed the society of each other, their visits to Mortefontaine, and the habits of their former life. They were now more definitely separated, for the regulations against the Buonaparte family were much stricter than before. They could not live in Switzerland ; some of them might not live in Italy or Belgium ; they must have passports and permissions to go here or there, and even then their movements were watched with suspicion.

---

[1] " Where am I to go, traitor ? ' " Wherever you like, fool." (Cochelet " Mémoires," t. iii. p. 276).

The absence of her favourite sister did not incline
Désirée to leave Paris and transport herself to
Sweden.   She had still her brother, two elder sisters,
and a number of nephews and nieces, against whom
there was no edict of banishment.   The Duc d'Albuféra, otherwise General Suchet, husband of her niece,
was not involved in any misfortunes after the
Hundred Days, but was high in the favour of
Louis XVIII.

The Princess of Sweden now entirely altered her
manner of living ; far from remaining in retirement
amongst her relations and intimate friends, she went
occasionally to court, where she was received with
great distinction, and entered eagerly into the
altered society around her.

The habits and conditions of it were very different
from any she had ever experienced before.   The
pomp and glitter and display of the Empire had
given place to a refined, well-bred, comparatively
simple state of things ; the enormous costliness of
entertainments was no longer the fashion, neither
was the extravagant expense of dress.   People of the
highest rank did not consider it necessary whenever
they appeared, even at a large party, to be always
covered with diamonds, and women who had been
accustomed to the Imperial Court looked amongst
their costly dresses, heavy with gold embroidery and
precious stones, and turned over their jewel-cases
full of rivières, tiaras, and clasps of diamonds,
emeralds, rubies, and pearls, to find a gown and
a *parure* simple enough for the court of Louis
XVIII.[1]

[1] Duchesse d'Abrantès.

Désirée soon became used to and pleased with this altered state of affairs; she liked the perfect freedom which, in spite of her exalted rank, she possessed. She kept up no state, but drove and walked about just as she chose. Her dear friend, Madame Récamier, established herself in a little house almost next door to her. Among the intimate friends with whom they were constantly associated were Madame de Stael, Madame Moreau, MM. de Laval, Ballanche, Matthieu de Montmorency, and Chateaubriand. They would meet without any ceremony in the evenings, and often sit under the lime-trees in the garden till far into the summer nights.

The authoress of a charmingly-written sketch of her life suggests that Désirée may have gone back to her lonely *hôtel* to shed bitter tears and evoke the memory of *le grand proscrit de Saint-Hélène ;* but to most people it will not seem at all likely that she did anything of the kind. There never was any tragic element in Désirée's character ; she had never had any great affection for Napoleon since she was a girl of sixteen; she had married the only man she thought might oppose him; she had engaged in plots with his enemies in the interests of her husband ; she had been on terms of friendship with him certainly, but without the slightest approach to love ; and if she lamented and shed bitter tears about any one, it was probably about Julie.

She appears, however, to have been as happy as possible, to have been generally liked for her pleasant, kindly, sunny disposition, and to have found her life too delightful to change it and go to Sweden, though she wrote constantly to her husband and son, and interested herself in what went on there.   It was certainly an extraordinary state of things.

The Duc de Laval, one of her most intimate friends, was, although extremely polite and agreeable, celebrated for his remarkable absence of mind.   On one occasion, when Ambassador at Vienna, he was dining with Prince Metternich and sitting next the Princess.   He did not like the cooking, and, unfortunately, fancying himself at home, suddenly exclaimed—

"Ah! how sorry I am to give you such a bad dinner!   My cook must have lost his senses! for he generally does very well, but to-day everything he has given us is detestable!"

Then, the stupefaction on the faces of everybody, and their evident endeavours to restrain their laughter, revealing to him what he had done, he continued with admirable presence of mind :—

"That is what I said to my cook the day after you had condescended to accept a bad dinner at my house, in return for which you now give me this exquisite banquet, in which everything is so excellent." [1]

A different and very prominent figure in the society of the Restoration was the Duc Mathieu de Montmorency.   In his youth he had yielded to the fascination of the specious doctrines set forth by the earlier revolutionists, and, like the Vicomte de Noailles and several other enthusiastic, generous, inexperienced young men, been drawn, to the despair of his family, into a movement of which the development was so different from his expectations, the

---

[1] Ancelot.

crimes and cruelties of which were abhorrent to him, and which he had long abjured.

"I was just entering life," he said of himself, "with all its illusions and passions. . . . Contrary to the principles and advice of my family, I adopted the revolutionary ideas then beginning openly to declare themselves. I did more than that; by a public act I declared my contempt for the titles which were the glory of my parents, and I wholly forgot the religion of my fathers. Then, since I had renounced my duty, all the calamities in the world burst upon me. This Revolution, which I had blessed as a good inspiration of the most generous hearts, changed into crimes inspired by the most violent hatred. My parents, my friends, my King perished before my eyes. I felt stained with their blood, frozen with horror. Almost out of my senses, I fled from France, and found myself in England proscribed, ruined, hated by all those who had survived of my family, and abandoned by every one. Then . . . a Catholic priest came to me, nursed me through my illness, consoled me in my despair, and showed me that there can be no happiness in this world but in the thought of God ever present to the soul, and of the eternal recompense for the passing sorrows of this life. . . . From that moment peace came back to my soul. . . . Heaven in its mercy will doubtless forgive me, for all the blessings I had lost are now lavished upon me. I have a charming wife who loves me . . . beautiful children; I have recovered a considerable fortune; my King is upon the throne and overwhelms me with honours."

Mathieu de Montmorency saw no more revolutions.

One Good Friday as he knelt in the church of St.
Sulpice at the hour of the death of Christ, those
near him observed that he was very still, and going
up to him, found that in the fervour of his devotion
his soul had departed.

CHAPTER XXVII

1817—1822

Coming of age of Prince Oscar -Death of Charles XIII. The Duchesse d'Albrantès - Madame de Genlis—Madame Récamier at the Abbaye-aux-Bois- Two stories of the Revolution- The Duc de Richelieu - The Queen of Sweden and her son- Meeting of Julie and Désirée Prince Oscar betrothed to Princess Joséphine de Leuchtenberg.

ON the 4th of June, 1817, Stockholm was the scene of rejoicing and festivities to celebrate the coming of age of Prince Oscar, Duke of Sudermania, now eighteen years old. That event was magnificently celebrated in the picturesque northern capital, and the people were transported with delight, for the young prince was adored in Sweden, and the popularity of Bernadotte increased as his justice, capacity, kindness of heart, and excellent government became more universally recognised.

The affection felt for him by the old King was expressed in the public address of Charles XIII. to Prince Oscar—

"My age and infirmities do not permit me to express in this solemn moment all that my affection for you and long experience inspire. I confine myself to reminding you that you will one

day govern two free nations. Prove to them by
respecting their rights how you desire them to
respect yours. And do not forget, my dear grandson, that I enjoin upon you to-day as a sacred duty,
to fulfil when I am gone the debt I owe your father
for the devotion and indefatigable tenderness he has
lavished upon me since the first moment he united
his lot to this country. Be always to him what he
has been to me ; be his support as he is mine ; render
to his latter days all the happiness and consolation
he has given my old age. May the Almighty protect you, my grandson, and guide you according to
His will."

The following February, 1818, Charles XIII. died,
and Bernadotte, under the name of Charles XIV.,
was crowned King of Sweden in due state at
Stockholm ; and three months later, with still
greater pomp, King of Norway, at Drontheim, where
he was, of course, accompanied by Oscar, now Crown
Prince.

After being for three hundred years an oppressed
province of Denmark, Norway became a free
country when united to Sweden, under the beneficent
rule of whose kings she has prospered until now.

Never was any person more indifferent ; it may
even be said, more averse to a crown than Désirée.

The news was brought to her while she and her
niece, the Duchesse d'Albuféra, were occupied with
their music ; they were practising the overture to
Grétry's " Caliph of Bagdad."

Désirée shut the piano with a melancholy sigh, put
on the cover, and began to arrange her piles of music,
saying mournfully—

CATHEDRAL OF LUND.

"Well, it will be no use for me to study now : they will say I play like a queen."

Nothing would induce her to play any more : she gave up her music from that day, and for some time she could not conceal the vexation and uneasiness caused her by the news of her husband's accession to the throne, which she feared might be the means of putting an end to the pleasant life amongst her friends and relations in Paris, and removing her to the northern kingdom over which she was so reluctant to reign.

In some measure she realised that this way of living could not go on, that sooner or later she *must* go to Sweden : but she kept putting off the evil day, month after month, even year after year went on, and still she lingered, living the same pleasant, unfettered, social life as she did before : going about by herself very simply dressed, and often unrecognised, for, owing to her being subject since her visit to Sweden to what we should now call erythema in the face, she frequently wore a veil which was more than a piece of transparent net. She had it on one day when she went to call upon Lady Elizabeth Stuart at the English Embassy, and the latter, who was expecting the visit of a governess she had made an appointment with for that hour, took her for that lady, and sitting down, proceeded to ask her a string of questions, which the Queen patiently answered, until presently, to her consternation, the supposed governess said—

"It is very cold, and the King, my husband, writes to me, . . ." which, before she could say more, revealed the situation.[1]

[1] "Mémoires de Madame Récamier."

A few days afterwards the well-known Miss Berry was calling on Madame Récamier, and talking with her of this story which was circulating about Paris, when the door opened, and the Queen of Sweden came in. Not knowing who it was, Miss Berry persisted in going on speaking about it, in spite of Madame Récamier's hurried whisper to be quiet, for it was the Queen again. She thought Madame Récamier was joking, and Désirée found out what was in question to her great amusement and Miss Berry's confusion. Lady Elizabeth Stuart became a great friend of Désirée, who was often to be seen at the English Embassy.

Some few of the early friends of Désirée had shared in the splendours of the Empire without being ruined by its fall, even surviving its destruction with almost undiminished prosperity. For their husbands had not only made immense fortunes, but had saved so much as to be still rich, had been able to preserve the estates they had gained, or had obtained good appointments under the government of the Restoration. But to numbers the disappearance of the Empire meant ruin, although to very few it meant exile.

The Duke and Duchess d'Abrantès, for instance, had begun life, he the son of a small country lawyer, she the penniless daughter of a ruined contractor, and an equally penniless daughter of the Comneni. But they were favourites and devoted followers of the Emperor, by whom in a few years their fortunes were so changed that in one year they received more than 1,500,000 francs, and yet were nearly 50,000 francs in debt.

The washing bill of the Duchess when in Spain
was 1,500 francs a month. She spent 10,000 in
needles and thread alone at one time, and their
cook made 300,000 francs out of their table in ten
months.[1]

Just before the break-up of the Empire the Duke
died, after having fallen out of favour with Napoleon,
and leaving nothing but enormous debts, a palace in
Paris, and estates in different foreign countries, which,
of course, could not be claimed when those countries
had shaken off the French yoke. The Duchess was
left with four young children and two old uncles
depending on her, and little or nothing but a pension
allowed her by the King and her own literary work
to support them. She lived in the country, at Versailles, and in the *Abbaye-aux-Bois;* but in spite of
her great talents and literary success, was so devoid
of common sense and incapable of managing her
affairs that even then she squandered her money as
fast as she got it, and ended her brilliant career many
years later in a miserable lodging.[2]

Madame de Genlis also had lost a good friend in
Napoleon, who had shown her great kindness. With
him departed her pension and lodging at the Arsenal.
She was looked upon coldly in legitimist circles, and
by her relations who belonged to them, owing to her
connections and association with the Orléans family
and the Empire. She had married both her daughters,
one of whom died early; the other was still living.
She had grandchildren, nephews, nieces, and even
great-grandchildren, who were attached to her. She

[1] " Baron de Méneval—Mémoires."
[2] " La Générale Junot," p. 449 (Joseph Turquan).

had a number of friends, and her literary work and superior capacity for managing her affairs kept her from poverty like that of the Duchesse d'Abrantès. She tried living at Écouen and Versailles, and then established herself in a small lodging in the *faubourg Saint-Honoré*, where she lived in a Bohemian sort of way, painting, writing for reviews, &c., and receiving in her leisure hours all sorts of distinguished people.

The Duchesse de Bourbon, Madame de Grollier, Madame Moreau, Madame Récamier, and the Queen of Sweden were amongst her favourite friends.

One evening, while Désirée was sitting with her, absorbed in the interest of their conversation, the only lamp in the room went out, and as Madame de Genlis rose to ring for another, the Queen stopped her, saying—

"We don't want a lamp to talk by; and besides, they will interrupt us. Do let us stay as we are."

And they continued their conversation in the dark for an hour and a half, until the Queen got up to take leave, and allowed herself to be lighted downstairs.

Madame Récamier was another of her friends who had to look back to a prosperous youth from the poverty of later years. A new reverse of fortune obliged her after some time to give up her house in the *rue d'Anjou*, and she finally decided to go and live at the *Abbaye-aux-Bois*, where she had succeeded in getting an apartment, much to the regret of Désirée and of the other intimate friends who lived near her. For the *Abbaye-aux-Bois, rue de Sèvres*,

was on the other side of the Seine, a quarter un-
frequented by them, almost unknown to them ; they
scarcely ever crossed the river, their homes, friends,
and pleasures, like those of all the modern society to
which they belonged, were then and afterwards in the
quarter of *Saint-Honoré.*

The vast *hôtels* and gardens of the *faubourg Saint-
Germain*, its narrow, winding, ill-paved worse-lighted
streets, were to them unfamiliar, oppressive, and at
that time even dangerous ; and the heavy, lumbering
carriages of that day toiled slowly through them.

Madame de Genlis declared she was afraid to go
there, that she had lived there two years ago, and had
been attacked in broad daylight at the corner of the
rue de Vaugirard by masked robbers.

Madame de Pastoret observed that her coachman
would probably refuse to go there, as the horses had
become unaccustomed to see lanterns, and would
most likely take fright at a torch.

"What shall you do, *ma chère ?*" asked Désirée,
turning anxiously to Madame Moreau.

" I shall dine at least an hour earlier, so as to drive
as long as possible by daylight, and I shall have my
servants fully armed."

However, they all found it quite possible to pass
safely through the terrors and dangers of the drive,
and soon became accustomed to visit Madame
Récamier, who found plenty of interesting people
to come and see her.

Humboldt, Bertin, Benjamin Constant, Ampère,
Gournet, Gerando, Auguste Périer, the Queen of
Sweden, the Duchess of Devonshire, the Duke of
Hamilton, Lord Bristol, Madame Gay and her cele-

HÔTEL DE SENS

brated daughter, the two Miss Berrys, Miss Edge-
worth, and many others distinguished in art, literature,
and society of different nationalities, came to the
simple room high up under the tiles of the *Abbaye-
aux-Bois*.

Chateaubriand, one of the most frequent guests,
thus describes it : "The bedroom served also for a
salon ; it contained a bookcase, a harp, a piano, a
portrait of Madame de Stael, and a view of Coppet
by moonlight. There were pots of flowers in the
windows which looked into the gardens of the
Abbey, the green bower of the *pensionnaires*. The
highest boughs of an acacia came up to the window,
pointed steeples appeared against the horizon, and
the hills of Sèvres far away in the distance. The
setting sun gilded the picture, and shone through
the open windows ; birds roosted upon the drawn-up
Venetian blinds. One seemed to pass above the
noise and tumult of a great city to the distant silence
and solitude." [1]

Madame Récamier lived for some time in this
picturesque, peaceful abode until she got a better
apartment in another part of the Abbey.

The circumstances of that time and of those preceding it gave rise to many strange episodes,
romantic stories, and extraordinary situations.
While the Terror reigned over the country, the son
of a noble family that had emigrated returned in
secret to the *château* of his father to find some paper
or document, or on some other important business.
His presence was betrayed, and he was only saved
by a young girl, daughter of one of the republican

[1] "Désirée Clary," p. 242 (Comtesse d'Armaillé).

authorities of the village, who, hearing her father and
his friends arranging to seize the young seigneur,
hurried to the *château* to warn him. She was surprised there, before he had time to escape, by a
furious party of "patriots," amongst whom was her
father. Attributing the only motives they were
capable of comprehending to her presence there,
and her attempt to preserve a victim from their
clutches, they consented, on the representations of
one or two less bloodthirsty than the rest, to spare
the life of the young seigneur if he would at once
marry, according to the civil rite, the young girl who
had risked so much for him. To save her reputation
and his own life he agreed. They then separated,
and it was not till some years afterwards that
political events allowed him to return to France,
when he at once inquired after the wife who had
been forced upon him, and found that she had no
intention of ever making any claim upon him, but
was willing to agree to a divorce, not considering
such a marriage as theirs binding. But he did not
wish to desert in prosperity a woman who had saved
his life, and who showed not only heroism, but a disinterested, noble character. He went to see her, fell
in love with her, and the marriage turned out very
happily.[1]

An equally romantic history began at Nantes at
the end of the eighteenth century, when the unheard-
of atrocities to which that miserable town had been
subjected had subsided, leaving the cowed and
horror-striken population with the life nearly crushed
out of them, fearing and distrusting their neighbours,

[1] *Foyers éteints-Ancelot.*

mourning for their murdered friends and relations, and hating with all the fervour one can well imagine, the cruel and bloodthirsty monsters. guilty of such abominations, some of whom had already expiated their crimes on the scaffold.

Amongst these was one, conspicuous for cruelty and wickedness, even among the friends by whom he was surrounded, whose death was greeted with transports of rejoicing. and whose name was execrated in the town where so many families had been decimated by him. No one would live in his house, which was shut up and empty for seven or eight years. It was offered for sale, but no one would buy it, until at last it was sold to an old lady, who took up her abode there with two maids and a little grandson, a child of ten years old.

The house stood apart, and the new occupants lived there in retirement, making no acquaintance, never mixing with any one in the town, paying no attention when told of the evil reputation of the house, breaking off all attempts at conversation, avoiding everybody.

The old lady was scarcely ever seen beyond the precincts of the house and garden, except when she went to mass, dressed in black with a long black veil concealing her face, followed by the pretty, interesting child, whom she at first kept in the same isolation. But after a year the Oratorien Fathers, seeing that there was neither convent nor college for the education of children, opened a school in a deserted, half-ruined *hôtel*, to which the chief families of the province gladly sent their sons.

The old lady, who had become known as " the

Italian," also sent her little grandson, who was named Louis, but whose surname was unknown. The fathers began to repair and restore the *hôtel*, and it was rumoured that the money was provided by the mysterious stranger, who had bought the *hôtel* and presented it to them.

Years passed, still she lived solitary and secluded in her old house. The boy grew up gentle, affectionate, and intelligent in these strange surroundings, knowing nothing of his family history; a favourite with all, and deeply loved by the grandmother who was his only relation.

When he was eighteen years old she became dangerously ill, and seeing that she was going to die, said to him—

" My child, whatever it costs me and whatever may happen, I must now reveal to you the secret of your birth. Take courage, my child; what you will have to suffer from the events of the past, I have suffered too; because of them I have no name and none ever see my face."

The boy trembled, and she whispered—

" Your father was my son, and the name you have always heard cursed was his."

The lad swooned away; when he recovered his senses his grandmother was dead.

A few days later he left the place; he was rich, and for five years he wandered about Europe haunted by the horror of his own name, unable to forget the curses attached to it, afraid to make friends lest it should be discovered. At the end of that time he was taken ill when staying in a village in a remote part of Germany. The only person there who could

speak French was an old *émigré*, who had lived there
for some time in desperate poverty, subsisting upon
what alms charitable people gave him, and what he
could earn by working on the land.

But he was a French nobleman who had lost all
in the Revolution. He nursed his young countryman till he recovered; a strong affection sprang up
between them, and they confided to each other their
terrible histories.

The old man, a marquis with a great name, had
passed through numberless vicissitudes, had lost his
whole fortune, been unable to hear of any of his
family being alive, and nearly died of starvation;
life was intolerable to him.

The young man, rich, well educated, and honourable, found his life equally miserable because of the
curse of his name.

Both were alone in the world; they had become
strongly attached to each other, and a plan suggested itself by which they might both find consolation.

The marquis adopted Louis, acknowledging him
legally as his son, giving him both name and title;
while Louis thankfully shared his fortune with his
adopted father.

They went to Paris together, and, as M. le Marquis
and his son, installed themselves in the family *hôtel*,
in the *faubourg Saint-Germain*. The Marquis found
many of his old friends and a few relations who had
escaped the Revolution. The arrangement answered
perfectly. Louis made an excellent marriage, and
his name was known as one of the most generous and
charitable men in Paris, his *hôtel* being the resort of

many unfortunate, distressed people, who found help there.

The old friendship between the Queen of Sweden and the faithful Chiappe continued as before. He was frequently to be met at her *hôtel* when the secret plots and conferences had long ago ceased with the situation which gave rise to them. But a foolish and unfortunate fancy she had taken for the Duc de Richelieu had made Désirée latterly the subject of much gossip and ridicule.

When Louis XVIII. was restored to the throne he had expressed the desire to do anything in his power that might be agreeable to the Princess of Sweden ; upon which Désirée had asked that her sister, the ex-Queen of Spain, might not be banished.

But as a decree had just been published by which no member of the Buonaparte family was permitted to remain in, or even to visit France, the King found himself unable to grant this request, and sent the Duc de Richelieu to explain it to the Princess. The Duke, who was a remarkably handsome man, with all the grace and distinction of the old French *noblesse*, made his mission as little disagreeable as he could, and Désirée conceived such an admiration for him that whenever she met him afterwards she was always looking after him ; if he came into a room she would break off her converstion to listen to what he might be saying, and she was even said to have gone to different places where she knew he was going to arrive, in order to see him, and to have commissioned an artist of her acquaintance to paint a portrait for her, which could only be obtained from rapid and chance glimpses of him, and which, consequently, when it was sent to her proved to be of the wrong man.

Regrettable as it was, however, all this folly was perfectly innocent and harmless, except from its absurdity, for it is certain that after the interview about the ex-Queen of Spain there was no further acquaintance between them ; they never even spoke to each other,[1] which makes the affair still more incomprehensible.

But the time was coming when more sensible and natural ideas and interests were to occupy the Queen.

Many years had now passed since she had seen her son, who, since their last parting, had grown from a child into a young man, of whom she knew nothing except from his letters and her husband's ; as, for various reasons, his father would not allow him to go to France.

The patience of the King had become nearly exhausted by his wife's persistent refusal to live in Sweden. In addition to the domestic reasons, the presence of the Queen was necessary to the proper regulation of the court, and her absence gave rise to unfavourable comment.

Finding that she always managed to put off her coming in spite of all his representations, the King decided to arrange a meeting between her and Prince Oscar, in the hope that her son might be able to persuade Désirée to hear reason and return to her family and kingdom. Accordingly, he arranged that Prince Oscar should meet her at Aix-la-Chapelle, and Désirée, delighted at the idea of meeting her son, had

[1] "Désirée, Reine de Suède et de Norvège." p. 60 (Baron Hochschild).

at the same time the prospect of seeing her sister after their seven years' separation, as Julie had obtained permission to go to Brussels with her eldest daughter, whose marriage had been arranged with Charles Napoleon, eldest son of Louis.

It had been agreed upon and enacted after the Hundred Days that no member of the Buonaparte family might travel, change his or her residence, or sojourn in any European State without the collective authorisation of the five great Powers. Joseph and Julie, taking the names of Comte and Comtesse de Survilliers, had settled in the United States ; and it was now decided that Julie, who had come over in the early summer of 1822 for her daughter's wedding, should try to get permission to remain in Europe until the following year, and then accompany her daughter and son-in-law to America. She was also anxious to keep them with her for a few weeks after the wedding, as she dreaded even the separation of a few months from her daughter.

But the health of the Comtesse de Survilliers, never robust, had become so bad that the doctors forbade her again undertaking the long voyage to America, at any rate at present ; and it was proposed that the plans should be changed, that the younger daughter, who had come to her sister's wedding, should return to her father in America without waiting for her mother, and that the elder one and her husband should remain with Julie, and go with her to Rome for the winter.

Meanwhile Désirée was obliged to go on to Aix-la-Chapelle, from whence she wrote to Madame Récamier :—

" I regretted very much to be obliged to leave Paris without seeing you. But I received a courier from my son telling me that he would shortly arrive at Aix-la-Chapelle, and I had only just time to get ready to start. . . . I am very sorry you do not happen to be coming here this year; what a pleasure it would have been to see you and introduce to you my son, who combines various good qualities of intellect and character; as for his face and appearance, he is his father again at three-and-twenty. He has nothing of me about him; and it is well for him, for he would not have gained much."

Désirée was, in fact, so delighted with her son when she saw him, that for the first time she began seriously to think that she could go to Sweden; and Prince Oscar, who was equally delighted with his mother, and overjoyed to see her at last, added his persuasions to his father's wishes and her own growing inclination.

Julie's health, at the same time, caused her sister much anxiety, and she wrote again from Aix-la-Chapelle:—

" I am now occupied with the troubles of others. . . . On the way here I stopped at Brussels for a few days, and found my sister in an alarming state of health, and so unhappy, that I am afraid for her life. The thought of being separated from her daughter is killing her. She is in such a weak state that she certainly could not get to Rome without danger. Judge of my despair at being obliged to leave here at this time and not even being able to be present at the marriage of her daughter."

At the request of the Comtesse de Survilliers, the

KRONPRINS OSCAR.
(Afterwards Oscar I., King of Sweden and Norway.)

Queen wrote to Madame Récamier begging her to obtain the permission of Louis XVIII., through the Duc Mathieu de Montmorency, for her to delay a little longer before going south :—

"In this anxiety I come to you. As all who suffer are sure to find consolation from you, I entreat you to manage that my sister may have the comfort of her children in peace until the time when they must go to Rome, which will be early in August, because of the snow in Tyrol, which they will have to cross. . . . It seems to me that M. de Montmorency could quite well take upon himself to shut his eyes to this, for it would not be worth while to assemble the *Grand Congrès* for such a short stay. The King of Holland will say nothing unless he is pressed, and I should like at least to be with my sister, and console her, if possible, at the moment of such a cruel separation, which would be impossible at this moment, as I am detained with my son. I trust entirely to your friendship and the kindness M. de Montmorency has been good enough to show me. I will also claim the interest M. de Laval had the kindness to offer me, and I beg you to say *mille choses aimable* to him. Adieu, Madame, give me news of yourself, keep your friendship for me! I expect a great proof of it now. I beg you to believe that I shall be delighted to prove mine for you upon every occasion.—DÉSIRÉE."

The Queen of Sweden then went to stay with the Comtesse de Survilliers at Prangius, where the required permission was sent her by M. de Montmorency.

While she was there she received the news of her

son's engagement to the Princess Joséphine de Leuchtenberg, eldest daughter of Eugène de Beauharnais. It was then January, 1823, the two sisters prolonged their stay together in Switzerland as long as they could, and when Désirée was obliged to go back to begin preparations for her journey to Sweden to be present at the wedding of her son, she succeeded in getting permission for Julie to pay her a short visit at Paris before their new and final separation.

On May 20, 1823, she wrote as follows to Madame Récamier :—

" Madame Joseph will avail herself of the permission kindly granted to come to Paris for a short time, if circumstances require it, under the name of her sister, Madame la Comtesse de Villeneuve, in order to preserve the strictest *incognito* during the time she stays there.

" Her present residence is Brussels, under the name of the Comtesse de Survilliers.

" A word from his Excellency to Baron de Fagel would remove all difficulty from her departure from Brussels. I thank *la belle dame*, and beg her to express to the most amiable and obliging of Ministers[1] all the gratitude with which I am penetrated.— DÉSIRÉE." [2]

---

[1] " Chateaubriand."
[2] " Désirée Clary" (Comtesse de Armaillé).

CHAPTER XXVIII

1823—1860

AFTER many years Julie and Désirée found themselves together again in Paris, but under what changed circumstances. The time they had just spent together must have re-awakened all the old affection and memories which, in the long years of absence, had perhaps slumbered, only to make the coming separation more painful. It was, in one sense, exile in prospect for them both : the remainder of their lives were to be spent far from each other, and from the brilliant city and the scenes they had long loved ; but Julie was ill and dispirited, with nothing but banishment and uncertainty before her ; while for Désirée waited a palace, a throne, a son who adored her, a husband who was eager for her arrival, and two nations who would be at her feet. Neither did she realise as she prepared for her journey that this was indeed the close of her life in France, that she was taking a final farewell of most of her friends and relations, and that she would never see Paris again. She thought she would come back to the *rue d'Anjou*, if only for a time, and far from making arrangements to sell her *hôtel*, she left directions that it should be always kept ready for her return.

To Julie, on the other hand, it must have seemed unlikely that she would ever see either Désirée, her other sisters and relations, or Paris again. Even if, after her winter in Rome, she regained her health, the best thing to which she could look forward was to go out to America and join her husband and younger daughter there. Meanwhile she stayed with Désirée in the *rue d'Anjou*, where, of course, brothers and sisters, nephews, nieces, cousins, and friends flocked to take leave of the two who were going from them to such distant lands and such widely different destinies.

One favourite niece, Marcelle, Comtesse Tascher de la Pagerie, a daughter of their eldest brother Etienne, agreed to accompany her aunt to Sweden. Etienne was their step-brother, and head of the family, for whose life Désirée had gone with her sister-in-law to intercede on the memorable evening when she first met Joseph Buonaparte, and Marcelle was only a few years younger than her aunt, the Queen of Sweden.

The journey in no way resembled that terrible experience of former years, when, through the ice and snow and darkness of January, Désirée travelled to her unknown home in the far north. It was June when she left Paris for Lübeck, where she was to meet the new daughter-in-law, who had already been married by proxy to her son.

It is said that Charles XIV. at first wished to find his son's wife among the more powerful and important of the royal houses, but could not succeed on account of his recent admission amongst them.

The Princess Joséphine, however, though her father was only the son of a lesser French noble, was also, through her mother, grand-daughter of the King of Bavaria. Prince Oscar had seen and fallen in love with her at Eichstadt, after he left Aix-la-Chapelle. The marriage was an excellent one for her, her Bavarian and French relations were delighted that she should be the future Queen of Sweden, and every one was contented, including Désirée.

She found the Crown Princess a pretty, gentle child scarcely sixteen; so young for her age that amongst her other possessions she had brought her favourite doll.

Joséphine Maximilienne Eugènie was the grand-daughter over whose birth the Empress Joséphine had rejoiced with such pride and delight, and whom she would have so triumphantly seen on the throne of Sweden. Eugène de Beauharnais, no longer Viceroy of Italy, but Prince of Eichstadt and Duke of Leuchtenberg, was an old friend of Bernadotte, and Maximilian of Bavaria remembered with gratitude that during the wars of the Empire he had restored to him his capital and part of his estates.

Two Swedish warships, splendidly appointed, were waiting at Lubeck for the Queen and Crown Princess, who embarked together; not, as upon Désirée's last northern voyage, through storm and darkness,

but sailing over a tranquil sea through the long
bright days of the summer which has no night, while
songs and sagas and legends were sung by the
musicians sent to meet them and enliven their
journey, till after a time the towers and steeples
of Stockholm rose out of the water where the sea is
joined by the great Lake Malar, with its hundreds of
wooded islands. The thunder of guns from the fleet
announced the approach of the Queen and Crown
Princess ; multitudes of boats put off from the
islands, and in state, amidst public rejoicings, with
her daughter-in-law, the Crown Princess by her side,
Désirée, Queen of Sweden and Norway, entered her
capital and took possession of the vast palace which
was now to be her home.[1]

Stockholm was filled with delight and festivity,
brilliant *fêtes* celebrated the arrival of the Queen and
the wedding of the Crown Prince and Princess, which
was celebrated on July 19th ; and then Désirée had
to begin to accustom herself to the changed existence
which was now to be hers.

It was peaceful and happy enough ; safe and sheltered from the calamities which had overwhelmed
so many of her friends, and the storms and revolutions which, though with less fury and violence,
did not cease to trouble France ; but it was very
unlike the unfettered variety of her life at Paris ; the
constant companionship of her numerous relations,
the daily association with those most distinguished in
literature, art, and politics, the familiar scenes, faces,
speech, and customs ; and she could not but miss
much that had given interest and brightness to her

[1] Touchard Lafosse.

former years. At first she proposed to return to Paris, but to this the King, her husband, would never consent. He was too well satisfied with her return, and had found too much difficulty in achieving it, to allow her to go away again, and as time went on the idea of doing so grew fainter and more vague as she became accustomed to the land of her adoption.

She loved to talk, especially with her niece, the Comtesse Marcelle, of France, and of those she had left there, to recall with regret her beloved Paris and her still earlier recollections of the great southern city, the burning sun and bright shores of the Mediterranean, the busy Cannebière, the Provençal *patois* of her childhood. Her niece, whom she made Grand Mistress of her household, remained with her for several years, and when at length she returned to France the Queen had become habituated to her life and surroundings.

Their long separation had not affected the good terms upon which the King and Queen of Sweden always remained. The King had held a military kind of court, which was, of course, altered by the arrival of the Queen and Crown Princess; but the habits of life there were simple, aristocratic, and if not quite so devoid of restraint as in the *rue d'Anjou*, still pleasant and free from the constant cere-mony and state, against which Désirée would cer-tainly have rebelled. It was a simple, patriarchal country which suited Bernadotte; and Prince Oscar had become a thorough Swede, scarcely remem-bering the France of his childhood, all his interest and affection being centred in the country of his adoption and the people who called him " our child."

ROYAL CASTLE OF GRIPSHOLM, LAKE MÄLAR.

He was, as Désirée had said, tall and handsome like his father, of a charming disposition, and adored the mother from whom he had so long been divided. Désirée, on her part, idolised her son, was also very fond of her daughter-in-law, and devoted to her grandchildren when they appeared upon the scene.

Bernadotte, formerly revolutionary general and desperate radical, now seated on one of the most ancient thrones of Europe, was intensely anxious for an heir to the next generation of his family, which, Oscar being his only child, could not as yet be considered firmly established. The whole nation shared this anxiety, and when, in the words of the English Ambassador, "At two o'clock in the morning the birth of a prince was announced there was not a dry eye. Twenty minutes later the King appeared, carrying the royal child upon a cushion. . . . He lifted the fragile creature in his arms to show him to his future subjects. It is certainly the greatest and most important event in his reign." [1]

The dynasty of Bernadotte had soon every appearance of being secure, as four sons and a daughter were born to Oscar and Joséphine, all of whom grew up and flourished.

The royal castles and palaces of Sweden were many in number, and delightfully situated, for the most part, upon some woody island, or by the shores of some lake with great, shady trees and gardens going down to the water. It is a country of lakes and forests, and in the long summer days when the twilight lingers till nearly midnight, and the dawn breaks so soon afterwards, picnics in the woods,

[1] "Bernadotte," p. 364 (Pingaud).

boating excursions, or bathing were the most favourite amusements. Even the great palace in Stockholm was very near the water, and there Désirée installed herself in her own suite of rooms, another part of the palace being appropriated to the Crown Prince and Princess and their family.

The daily routine was simple and domestic. The King, who was in the habit of getting up late, transacted a great deal of business before he was dressed, worked hard all the morning, and joined the Queen in the afternoon in her *salon*, when they proceeded to dinner together. They dined at five with their suite, and after coffee the King returned to his own apartment, where he worked until half-past nine, and then returned to the *salon* of the Queen, where there was always a circle of guests and where tea was going on. Supper followed, and at about eleven the King usually retired ; but not so Désirée, who hated going to bed early, and would sit up half the night talking with her ladies-of-honour, or wandering through the great, empty, silent *salons*. Sometimes she would order a carriage at one o'clock in the morning and drive through the deserted streets out into the woods with her lady-in-waiting, now and then both of them falling asleep before they arrived at home again.[1]

The Crown Princess was graceful and kind, like her grandmother, the Empress Joséphine,[2] and a strict Catholic. Désirée, in spite of her apparent thoughtlessness on these matters, refused to change her religion as her husband had done ; a private chapel and chaplain were therefore allotted to them.

[1] " Bernadotte, roi " (Christian Schefer).
[2] Touchard Lafosse.

The early surroundings, habits, and dispositions of the two women, however, still showed themselves; for Joséphine was exceedingly devout, and was often distressed and scandalised at the laxity of the Queen, who, in order to please her, would listen to her representations and show rather more assiduity in her religious duties, going, for instance, to confession, although remarking that she could not think of any particular confession to make, as she did not seem to have been doing any harm.

In the summer the court went to one of the country palaces, generally Rosersberg or Rosendal, or else the Queen's favourite, Drottningholm, on Lake Mälar, a large palace and gardens in the Renaissance style, which probably reminded her of France, and were much more to her taste than the more gloomy picturesqueness of the ancient Swedish castles.

That she was by no means indifferent to the grandeur of her position was apparent from the great desire she had to be crowned, which she was always expressing to the King, who saw no necessity for that ceremony ; and might have been only expected to think that as Désirée would not come to be crowned at the proper time with him, she had better dispense altogether with the coronation than let it take place when, as she had been years upon the throne, it would appear rather unmeaning. But after some time he yielded to her persuasions, and she was crowned in the church of St. Nicholas, at Stockholm, August 21, 1829.[1]

[1] "Désirée, Reine de Suède et de Norvège," p. 68 (Baron Hochschild).

PALACE OF DROTTNINGHOLM, LAKE MÄLAR

That imposing ceremony is said to have made a deep impression upon the mind of Désirée, who, as the ancient crown of the Queens of Sweden was placed upon her head, must surely have gone back in recollection to the strange vicissitudes of her life, to her exiled sister, to the Buonaparte, once so powerful, now scattered about the world, to the great Emperor whose mighty career had already tragically closed, and perhaps to the days when she herself was a girl in the old house of the *rue des Phocéens*, trembling in terror of the Revolution, and considering whether she would marry Joseph or Napoleon Buonaparte.

She had a numerous court, she still showed considerable interest and satisfaction in her *toilette*, and took great pleasure in the opera; in fact, the delight with which she regarded these indulgences was, in her opinion, the most serious fault she had to confess.

She was always to be seen in the royal box on opera nights, but never understood the Swedish language well enough to be able to enjoy plays in it.

For some time, indeed, the only Swedish word she could say was "*Komme*" (come); which she lost no opportunity of employing. Sometimes she would return to the palace followed by a troop of poor people, to whom she had addressed it, and who always left her loaded with presents, for, like her sister Julie, her purse was always being emptied for those in poverty and distress, whom she herself would visit and help.

Like Julie, too, she took the greatest interest in her old friends and relations and their families; was delighted when they came to Sweden, and still more when they were permanently settled there; and while the King would find posts for them and their sons, the Queen would pension their widows, arrange marriages for their daughters, and provide *dots* and *trousseaux*; conferring all these benefits with sympathetic kindness and grace, often saying she wished she could do more for those she was helping.

As a middle-aged and an old woman, Désirée remained what she had been in youth—lively, capricious, impatient, kind-hearted, easily amused.

She never concerned herself with political matters, in which she had only mixed when she was a medium in the intrigues of Fouché, Talleyrand, and their party with Bernadotte against Napoleon.

The King still treated her almost like a child, though with much affection and consideration, and her manner to him was of the same kind, no sort of state or ceremony existed between them. The Queen would come into the King's room where he was at work, in a morning *négligée*, and he would rise or look up, exclaiming with pleasure: "Eh! good morning! how are you, my dear Désirée?" Sometimes the Crown Prince or Princess also appeared with their children; and all other occupations were thrown aside to caress and play with the little ones, who were adored by their grand-parents and always welcome.

Oftentimes those in attendance upon the King and Queen could scarcely preserve the gravity consistent with the respect due to their sovereigns, at whose ludicrous remarks they could hardly restrain their laughter. Now and then some bad news or vexation threw the King into one of the fits of passion to which he occasionally gave way, when he would storm and rage, threatening to kill the person who was the object of his wrath, the Queen meanwhile sitting unconcernedly by, tranquilly fanning herself and saying—

"Why, he wouldn't kill a cat!"[1]

The Queen's sister, Madame de Villeneuve, whose marriage had been unhappy, who had separated from her husband, lost her son in Napoleon's wars, married her daughter, and spent a great part of her life in travelling about, came to Sweden, and was there a good deal with Désirée. She ended her days, however, at Florence with Julie, for the King of Sweden had obtained leave from the other powers for Joseph and Julie to leave America and settle in Italy, where they passed the remainder of their lives.

In 1813, Bernadotte had obtained the release of many of the French officers who were taken prisoners, and welcomed those who wished, as some of them did, to settle permanently in Sweden, giving appointments to the sons of many of his former comrades.

A son of Ney was made *aide-de-camp* to the Crown Prince, the children of Fouché, Duroc, Grouchy, and others were established and provided for in Sweden.

Every year the popularity of the family of Bernadotte increased among the Swedes; who declared that since Gustavus Wasa delivered them from the tyrant Christian of Denmark, no King had done so much for Sweden as Charles XIV. He had united her to Norway, raised her from the brink of ruin to prosperity and independence, made her the

---

[1] "Bernadotte, roi" (Christian Schefer).

fourth maritime power in Europe, and assisted the progress she had made in science, art, and literature.

On the 5th of May, 1821, he had told Count Braké, under the influence of a dream, that Napoleon had just died ; and some weeks afterwards, as he was entering the council-chamber, a letter was brought to him confirming the news.

The Béarnais, not sharing the bitterness of many of the followers of Napoleon for the only one of his marshals who gained a kingdom for himself and kept it by his own strength and wisdom and the love of his people, were immensely proud of their compatriot. They called a street in Pau after him, they spoke and wrote his praises ; and the legend of the fairy ancestress and the prophecy that a king should be among her descendants, became a favourite story for children to hear from their grandmothers on winter evenings.

The King, always glad to receive Frenchmen, preferred, above all, his countrymen of the south, and from time to time some of the learned and distinguished men Désirée had known in Paris came to enliven her northern home. The members of the scientific commission on their way to Spitzbergen ; the Vicomte d'Arlincourt, M. Ampère, and many others, came to Stockholm, and with them and the most famous *savants* of Sweden, Bernadotte loved to discuss the deepest and most intricate questions, scientific, legal, political, moral, and theological ; into which latter especially he concerned himself much more than in his earlier years.

It is difficult to say exactly what Bernadotte's religion was during his youth : an atheist he never was, neither does he seem to have been a good Catholic, nor yet to have been imbued with the Calvinistic tenets of his family, or at any rate of many of his relations ; but while nominally a Catholic, he was, in fact, indifferent to religious matters, and made no difficulty about joining the Swedish Church. This, though following Lutheran doctrines, yet with its bishops, clergy, the arrangements of its cathedrals and churches, and other matters which need not here be entered into, holds to ancient traditions and differs from the bald, unecclesiastical Lutheranism of Germany. "Religion is the safeguard of a nation," he would say. "A prince ought to be religious on principle. . . . If a prince is a Christian and a philosopher, his people will be religious and enlightened. . . . One must believe. Humility is that which is great and worthy of praise. God sent His Son upon earth, and has raised us to the throne." To the end of his life Bernadotte was tall, handsome, and stately ; his commanding figure was never bent with age ; at eighty he looked like a well-preserved man of sixty.

As the King advanced in years he became less and less inclined to leave Stockholm, which, from its situation close upon the sea and Lake Mälar, and its easy distance from the wooded country, was pleasant enough in summer, when he often remained there ; the Queen and the rest of the royal family going to Haga or to her favourite Drottningholm, which were close at hand.

He occupied himself as indefatigably as ever in the affairs of his kingdoms ; but, strange to say, in all the years of his residence there he never learned to speak

A SWEDISH CHURCH.

33

proper the language of his adopted country ; his speeches had to be translated into Swedish and read for him, and the interpretations of his ministers now and then gave rise to absurd mistakes.

There are some fanatical worshippers of Napoleon who cannot forgive Bernadotte for opposing him and for succeeding in spite of his dislike, and who try to make out that he must have regretted his former life, repented of the line of conduct he had pursued, and wearied of the lofty situation he had attained. All this is contrary to human nature, to reason, and to probability—in fact, to possibility. The only proofs brought forward are the impatient, hasty exclamations to which Bernadotte gave vent in his fits of irritation ; which those called upon to govern others will understand only too well, and to which they will certainly attach no serious meaning. One writer even goes so far as to say that Bernadotte grew old "without glory"!

Different persons have, of course, different ideas of what glory is. If it means a long career of slaughter, devastation, and plunder, then undoubtedly the word cannot be applied to the life of Bernadotte ; but in the opinion of most unprejudiced people, the man whose early heroism raised him from the ranks, who was a gallant soldier, a great general, a distinguished statesman, and an excellent King ; who was brave, upright, and merciful, who won his crown by his talents and virtues, raised his kingdom from ruin to prosperity, governed it wisely and well for thirty years,[1] and died beloved and mourned by his subjects,

[1] He practically reigned from the first time of his arrival in Sweden.

leaving an honoured name and a great inheritance to his descendants; has a record to which the word "glorious" can certainly not be denied. As to the "regrets," was it probable that the son of a small French lawyer should regret that he wore the crowns of Sweden and Norway?—that his son and grand-children had a secure and splendid future? Was he likely to regret that he was not still one of those former marshals and officers of the departed Empire who now came to him for assistance, whose families were thankful for his protection, and whose sons he could make *aides-de-camp* to his own?

On the 25th of January, 1844, the King went to bed perfectly well, though for some time he had been out of spirits and troubled with forebodings and pre-sentiments. His birthday was the next day, and was to have been celebrated as usual; but early in the morning he had a stroke of apoplexy, from which he partially recovered, and during his illness, which lasted till March, attended to business, ordered a dis-tribution of wood to the poor as the weather was very cold, and arranged his affairs with fortitude and resignation. His old friend and minister, the Count de Lowenhjelm, was constantly with him, and from the Bishop of Hedin he received the consolations of religion.

He had a great affection for his Grand Master of the palace, the young Count de Brahé, who scarcely ever left him. If he missed him from his side he would ask immediately, "*Où est Brahé?*"

He died on the 3rd of March, surrounded by his family. Raising himself in his bed, he stretched out his arms to bless them, murmured the word "Oscar," cast a farewell look to the Queen, and fell back dead.

He was eighty-two years old; the whole nation had watched his illness with anxiety; the churches were filled with crowds praying for his recovery, and showing the deepest grief at his death.

As to Count de Brahé, he would not be comforted, but died of a broken heart in a few weeks.

Wild, poetical, Scandinavian chants echoed through the ancient church of Riddarholm, the Saint-Denis of Sweden, as Bernadotte was laid in his splendid porphyry tomb amongst the kings—his predecessors.

"Oh! great Charles and Gustavus! noble shades! Here in your sanctuary sorrowing Sweden buries another Charles. Here the standards of your heroes, separated in life, meet among the banners falling into dust, never to be unfurled by mortal hand. In the tomb you are united, and he, the last one, comes to take his place with you! He will sleep on his bed of laurels, in the midst of trophies and tears. . . . None shall remain by the dead. . . . Night falls over the glorious standards. Silent *rendesvous* of kings. . . . In the calm silence sublime souls murmur words no mortal may hear. No sound disturbs their councils. But when the day of eternity breaks, death shall change to life, and life shall no more be broken by death."

The sorrow of the Queen was soothed by the devoted affection of her son, now Oscar I.

He would not hear of her giving up the apartments she had always occupied at Stockholm, now those of her grandchildren, King Oscar II. and Queen Sophie; he insisted also upon her retaining

DÉSIRÉE EUGÉNIE BERNARDINE CLARY, QUEEN OF SWEDEN.

those at Drottningholm, besides which he gave her the *château* of Rosersberg.

Never liking to be much away from her son, she often accompanied him on his journeys to different parts of Sweden and to Norway.

After his accession a French diplomatist, M. de Bacourt, who was sent by Louis Philippe to congratulate King Oscar, wrote that "the Queen-Mother must be a very good woman. She desired me to give her warmest thanks to the King and Queen for the marks of interest shown to the late King during his illness; in speaking of that sovereign she displayed such deep emotion that her feelings seemed to transform her. She gave me a letter for the Duchesse d'Albuféra, and charged me with messages for Madame de Tascher. When her thoughts go back to the past she shows a real regret at having taken a final farewell of France; and while she thoroughly appreciates the advantages of royalty, she takes pleasure in recalling the starting-point of that astonishing fortune for which she had seemed so far from being destined."

Seldom has an old age passed more peacefully and happily than that of Désirée, surrounded by her children and grandchildren, all of whom showed her the most tender affection.

Her favourite was her second grandson, Oscar, Duke of Ostrogothie, of whose beauty and many attractions M. de Bacourt spoke with great admiration.

During the thirty-seven years of her life in Sweden, Désirée always retained her *hôtel* in the *rue d'Anjou*. On one occasion, during the reign of Napoleon III., she heard it was going to be demolished, and the

JOSEPHINE VON LEUCHTENBERG, QUEEN OF SWEDEN AND NORWAY,
WIFE OF OSCAR I.

idea made her so unhappy that the Emperor, hearing
this, promised that it should be spared.

She did even once set off to go there on a visit,
and embarked for that purpose on a frigate commanded by her grandson, the Duke of Ostrogothie;
but whether she feared sea-sickness, or whether at the
last moment she remembered that the Paris she would
find would be a different Paris from the one she had
left, and shrank from the changes years and circumstances had wrought in the scenes once so dear to
her; whatever was her reason, she had not long left
Carlskrona before she desired her grandson to return
and take her back to Sweden, which she would never
leave again.

Désirée lived to see the third generation of the
Bernadottes, in the person of her grandson Charles
XV., upon the throne of Sweden and Norway; for
Oscar I., after having been for some years in bad
health, died in 1859, to the great grief of his people.

Queen Désirée survived her son scarcely more
than a year. On December 17, 1860, her daughter-
in-law, Queen Joséphine, was told that she had
fainted on returning from a drive; she hastened to
her, and just arrived before she passed peacefully
away.

Charles XV. was succeeded by his brother, the
present King, Oscar II., whose eldest grandson has
lately married the English Princess Margaret of Connaught, amidst the rejoicings of the two, it may be
said the three, nations. For although the Norwegians
are at this moment so unmindful of the freedom and
prosperity they have enjoyed since their union with
Sweden that they actually contemplate a separation

deprecated by the rest of Europe, yet they have sent an address, if not of loyalty, still of respectful congratulation, to the Prince and Princess, and have also petitioned the King that, although disuniting themselves from Sweden, they may still be ruled by a prince of the house of Bernadotte.[1]

[1] Prince Gustavus of Sweden, who has just married the daughter of the Duke of Connaught, inherits the blood of the ancient line of Wasa, besides that of Bernadotte. His mother is the great-granddaughter of Gustavus IV.

INDEX

with Désirée Clary, 61 ; Joséphine, 62 ; their marriage, 64 ; forbids Pauline to marry Fréron, 69 ; Duphot, 71 ; love-letters, 74-76 ; jealousy, 79 ; victories of the Italian campaign, 80 ; Pauline, 84, 85 ; return from Egypt, 90 ; dislike to Bernadotte, 91 ; 18th *Brumaire*, 92-94 ; First Consul, 101 ; the Tuileries, 102, 103 ; ignorant of his sisters' conduct, 108 ; the Tuileries, Saint-Cloud, and La Malmaison, 114 ; adventure of Junot, 117-120 ; Madame de Montesson, 124, 125, 128 ; undue familarity of old comrades, 129 ; of Lannes, 130 ; unfair bulletins, 131 ; Peace of Lunéville and loss of Egypt, 132 ; Madame Campan, 137 ; Jérôme, 139 ; the King and Queen of Etruria, 141 ; displeasure with Madame de Stael, 142, 146, 147 ; Rennes, 148, 149 ; The Concordat, 150 ; "I will do away with *Messidor*," 153 ; horror of the execution of Louis XVI., 158 ; pardons M. Bernard, 162 ; Lucien's *fête*, 165 ; Mesdames Récamier and de Stael, 166, 167 ; exile of Madame de Stael, 172 ; quarrel at Joseph's *fête*, 178 ; affection for Julie and Désirée, 180 ; Pauline and Prince Borghese, 182 ; Napoleon's system, 188 ; Joseph and Lucien, 189-199 ; the Army of England, 200 ; Madame de Rémusat and the camp at Boulogne, 201-205 ; *liaisons*, 205 ; a dangerous conspiracy, 206-210 ; the Empire, 219 ; the pretensions and praises of the Buonaparte family, 221 ; the Marshals of France, 221 ; the royalist conspiracy, 222-240 ; coronation of Napoleon, 244-246 ; letter to Pauline, 248 ; the new households, 249-251 ; Madame de Genlis, 261 ; Napoleon's catechism, 264 ; his *liaison* with Madame Duchâtel, 265-267 ; attempts to separate Lucien from his wife, 268 ; separates Jérôme from his American wife, 268 ; the King of Bavaria, 269 ; Joseph, King of Naples, 270 ; marriage of Eugène, 271 ; affection for the Beauharnais, 273 ; Stephanie, 274-276 ; Berthier, 278 ; Chiappe, 279 ; Bernadotte, 281, 282 ; Poland, Westphalia, Peace of Tilsit, 285, 286 ; dissatisfaction with Louis, 287 ; letter, 288 ; ball at Fontainebleau, 291 ; Julie, 292-295 ; Joseph, King of Spain, 295 ; Auguste de Stael, 296-300 ; the succession, 301-303 ; disasters in the Peninsula War, 306 ; duel, 307 ; Lannes and Bessières, 312 ; Wagram, 315 ; divorce of Joséphine, 317, 318 ; dreams, 319 ; failure of system, Joseph, 319 320 ; Louis, 321 ; Jérôme, 322 ; the future Empress, 323 ; "my uncle, Louis XVI.," 324 ; the Kingdom of Italy, 326 ; a masked ball, 327 331 ; a risk, 332 ; Marie Louise, 336 ; Lucien and his wife, 338-341 ; Lucien's daughter, 342 344 ; anger at remarks of the English, 346 ; Bernadotte and Désirée, 347, 348 ; the Swedish crown, 351 ; Napoleon's dream, 352 ; Comte de Flahault, 354 ; the Prince of Sweden, 355 ; Ponte Corvo, 356 ; "perhaps I envy him," 369 ; Bessières, 370 ; attempted assassination, 371 ; continental blockade, 372 ; invades Pomerania, 373 ; orders to Princess of Sweden, 374 ; reverses, 376 378 ; return from Russia, 379, 380 ; last winter in Paris, 382 386 ; christening of King of Rome, 386 ; Marie Louise, 387 9 ; Bautzen and Lutzen, German campaign—armistice -- Vittoria, Dresden, 390-393 ; Leipzig, 395 ; Murat, 404 ; Syracuse, 406, 407 ; abdication, 412 ; Elba, 413, 414 ; dream, 417 ; landed, 422,

CPSIA information can be obtained
at www.ICGtesting.com
Printed in the USA
BVHW06s1754121018
530020BV00002B/51/P